Westel Woodbury Willoughby

An Examination of the Nature of the State

A Study in political Philosophy

Westel Woodbury Willoughby

An Examination of the Nature of the State
A Study in political Philosophy

ISBN/EAN: 9783337080853

Printed in Europe, USA, Canada, Australia, Japan

Cover: Foto ©ninafisch / pixelio.de

More available books at **www.hansebooks.com**

AN EXAMINATION

OF

THE NATURE OF THE STATE

A Study in Political Philosophy

BY

WESTEL WOODBURY WILLOUGHBY, Ph.D.

LECTURER IN POLITICAL PHILOSOPHY IN THE
JOHNS HOPKINS UNIVERSITY

New York
MACMILLAN AND CO.
AND LONDON
1896

To My Wife

PREFACE

THE aim of this treatise has been the construction of a true system of political philosophy, the determination of the ultimate nature of the State and the grounds upon which its authority may be justified.

Philosophy has been defined as a criticism of categories, and thus, in the present work, the task has been to subject the principal terms and concepts of political science to as careful an examination, and as rigid a definition, as is possible. Beyond all previous periods, the present century has been prolific in the creation of new and complex political conditions. With the appearance of the modern constitutional State with its functions and organization reduced to definite written statement, with the formation of the greatest variety of federal unions between States formerly independent, with the rise of international relations into technical definiteness, with the clearer distinction between public and private rights, between moral and civic obligations, — with all these new phases of political life, problems in theory have arisen, which require for their solution the keenest of philosophical analysis, and the highest degree of accuracy in the application of the terms used. It is, therefore, with the greatest diffidence that the present work is offered as an attempt to afford some slight assistance in this direction. By no one better than by the author, is it appreciated that deficiencies may appear, and that his work will be subject to criticism from many sides. From the nature of the case, this must be so, where, as in the following pages, positions have been assumed that vary so widely from those held by other writers. It is Hobbes, we believe, who says, that the axioms of geometry would be disputed, were the interests of men concerned therewith, and if this be so, it cannot be a matter for surprise that the domain of political speculation should abound with varieties of opinions.

In judging the value of this work, it is only asked that it be remembered that that which has been attempted has been the distinction between essential nature and mere appearance, the discrimination between the legal and political character of institutions and forces, and their actual operation in the arena of civic life. Thus, sovereignty has been distinguished from public opinion, the legal omnipotence of the State separated from its actually limited coercive power, and the non-legal character of international principles shown to be independent of the recognition of their obligatory force by civilized peoples. In several instances, the strict application of principles has required a departure from the ordinary use of terms. In every such case, however, it is believed that the additional preciseness of nomenclature secured, has more than compensated for the inconveniences arising from such changes.

Lying, as this inquiry does, within the field of pure political speculation, the introduction of historical or descriptive matter has not been necessary, except for purposes of explanation and illustration. The only departures from this have been in the treatment of the Composite State, where the importance and complexity of the subject seemed to demand a somewhat particular description, and in the last chapter, where have been considered some of the political tendencies and problems apparent in modern life. With the Art of Government, or Politics properly so called, there has likewise been no concern.

It may be proper to add that this work is based upon a course of lectures given at the Leland Stanford Junior University, and later at the Johns Hopkins University.

W. W. W.

WASHINGTON, D.C.,
January, 1896.

TABLE OF CONTENTS

CHAPTER I
Introductory: Scope of the Work 1

CHAPTER II
Preliminary Definitions and Distinctions . . . 8

CHAPTER III
The Origin of the State 18

CHAPTER IV
The Origin of the State (*continued*); the Contract Theory 54

CHAPTER V
Criticism of the Contract Theory; Natural Law . 89

CHAPTER VI
The True Origin of the State 119

CHAPTER VII
The Nature of Law 142

CHAPTER VIII
Analytical Jurisprudence 160

CHAPTER IX

THE POWER OF THE STATE: SOVEREIGNTY 181

CHAPTER X

THE NATURE OF THE COMPOSITE STATE 232

CHAPTER XI

LOCATION OF SOVEREIGNTY IN THE BODY POLITIC . . 276

CHAPTER XII

THE AIMS OF THE STATE 309

CHAPTER XIII

GOVERNMENTS: THEIR CLASSIFICATION 351

CHAPTER XIV

RECAPITULATION: PRESENT POLITICAL CHARACTERISTICS AND TENDENCIES 380

INDEX 441

THE NATURE OF THE STATE

CHAPTER I

INTRODUCTORY: SCOPE OF THE WORK

The term "sociology" in its broadest meaning embraces the systematic treatment of all those interests that arise from the life of men in social aggregates. So considered, it includes within its general scope such particular branches of inquiry as Economics, Law, Politics, and the like. In these special departments of knowledge, the facts dealt with are largely the same, the differences consisting in the standpoints from which they are viewed. Thus, for example, the subject of crime is of particular interest to the economist as regards its cost to society, the extent to which it is due to economic conditions, and the manner in which it enters as a disturbing element into economic life by rendering insecure the possession of property. To the lawyer, the subject is one of importance as a violation of law, and as necessitating legal action for its punishment or prevention. To the student of Political Science, finally, it is of interest as being a revolt against the constituted authorities of the land, as an anarchistic element in the body politic, and, if widespread and continued, endangering the very existence of the State itself.

To distinguish then the domain of Political Science from the larger field of Sociology, and from the other special departments of knowledge embraced therein, we say that Political Science deals with society solely from its organized standpoint, — that is, as effectively organized under a supreme authority for the maintenance of an orderly and progressive existence.

We thus distinguish between the conception of an aggregate of men as politically organized — as constituting a body politic — and the same community of men as forming merely a group of individuals with mutual economic and social interests. The body politic is the social body plus the political organization. An aggregate of men living together and united by mutual interests and relationships we term a society. A human "society" is distinguished from the types of communal life exhibited by the lower beings, such as bees, wasps, and ants, in that there is in the minds of its members a common consciousness of mutual interests and aims. "Human society truly begins," says Giddings, "when social consciousness and tradition are so far developed that all social relations exist not only objectively as physical facts of association, but subjectively also, in the thought, feeling, and purpose of the associated individuals. It is this subjective fact that differentiates human from animal communities."[1] "In its social consciousness a community has a living bond

---

[1] *The Theory of Sociology.* Supplement to the Annals of the Am. Acad. Pol. and Soc. Sci., July, 1894, p. 60.

of union. The mutual aid and protection of individuals, operating in an unconscious way, are no longer the only means that preserve social cohesion: the community feels and perceives its unity. The feeling must be destroyed before rupture can occur."[1]

When this society becomes organized for the effectuation of certain general, or, as they are called, political interests, and with a magistracy into whose hands is entrusted the exercise of its controlling authority, it assumes a political form, and a State is said to exist; and the rules defining the contents of this authority and the manner of its exercise are collectively termed its constitution. As a preliminary definition of the State, we may therefore say that wherever there can be discovered in any community of men a supreme authority exercising a control over the social actions of individuals and groups of individuals, and itself subject to no such regulation, there we have a State. The definition given by Holland is that: "A State is a numerous assemblage of human beings generally occupying a certain territory amongst whom the will of the majority, or of an ascertainable class of persons, is, by the strength of such a majority or class, made to prevail against any of their number who oppose it."[2]

---

[1] *Idem*, p. 57.

[2] *Elements of Jurisprudence*, 6th ed. p. 40. Notice that the territorial element is not made essential, but is prefaced by the word "generally." Bluntschli, however, makes land a necessary element, and defines the State as "the politically organized national person of a definite country" (*Theory of the State*, trans. 2d ed. p. 23). Upon this point, see *post*, p. 27.

Ihering defines the State as "the form of a regulated and assured exercise of the compulsory force of society."[1] According to Lasson, "the State is a community of men which possesses an organized authority as the highest source of all force;"[2] while Burgess describes it less specifically as: "A particular portion of mankind viewed as an organized unit."[3]

Without, however, further multiplying these definitions, or more particularly explaining them, we may, at this preliminary stage, declare the essential elements of a State to be three in number. They are:

(1) A community of people socially united.

(2) A political machinery, termed a government, and administered by a corps of officials termed a magistracy.

(3) A body of rules or maxims, written or unwritten, determining the scope of this public authority and the manner of its exercise.

Just as the sciences of Economics and Jurisprudence may be further separated into distinct departments of inquiry, so does the domain of Political Science admit of further subdivision. Thus we may have: First, Descriptive Political Science, dealing with a description of the various forms of political organization; secondly, Historical Political Science, dealing with the inquiry as to the manner and order in which political forms or governments have appeared

---

[1] *Der Zweck im Recht,* I. p. 307.
[2] *System der Rechtsphilosophie,* p. 283.
[3] *Political Science and Constitutional Law,* Vol. I. p. 51.

and developed; thirdly, the Art of Government, or "Politics" properly so called, dealing with the principles that should properly control the administration of public affairs; finally, Political Theory or Philosophy, concerned with the philosophical examination of the various concepts upon which the whole science of politics rests.

It is wholly within the confines of this last-named field that the present treatise will lie. But even here, further subdivision suggests itself. First of all, Political Theory may be either particular or general; that is, as devoted to the theoretical explanation of the nature of particular political types, or as occupied with the deduction of principles of universal applicability. Again, the History of Political Theories may properly be held to constitute a distinct field of inquiry.

In this treatise we shall be concerned with the general postulates of Political Science, and incidentally with the History of Political Theories. History gives us, as it were, the third dimension to Political Science, and it will frequently be the case that we shall be very greatly aided in arriving at the proper comprehension of the principles with which we are engaged by a comparative study of the varying aspects in which they have been viewed at different times by different writers, and an examination of the extent to which the diverging views have been dependent upon the dissimilar political conditions by which their respective expounders have been surrounded.

The task that we have assigned ourselves in attempting to determine the exact nature of the State, will be by no means an easy one, for here, as in all branches of speculative inquiry, there will be required the clearest conception of, and the most rigid adherence to, the connotations of the terms used. A further difficulty, and one not inherent in the task, is the fact that it will be necessary to use words to which common usage has attached very general and therefore vague and overlapping significations. In this particular we shall be in much the same situation as are political economists who are still struggling to obtain generally acceptable and precise definitions of their most important terms, such as "value," "rent," "capital," and "wealth."

The conception of the State which we are to obtain, if it is to be satisfactory, must be one that will disclose its ultimate nature, including therein a sufficient reason for its existence, and an adequate justification of the right by which it exercises its authority. It must contain a statement of the attributes with which a State is necessarily endowed, and by the possession of which it may be distinguished from other corporations. It will thus afford us a general type rather than an empirical illustration. The origin of political authority, so far as it can be rationally determined, must receive satisfactory treatment; and the nature and location of sovereignty considered. Furthermore, the conception must be one upon which we can base a true philosophy of law, and in accordance with which may be satisfactorily interpreted the nature of the relations between different States, and between particular States and the individuals composing them.

It will thus happen that in the consideration of the various theories that have been held by political philosophers in the past, there will not be mentioned many of those whose names would properly appear in a general history of Political Science. Only those will be here referred to who have contributed by their writings to the development of the idea of the State as distinct from its organization or good administration. Thus, for example, the writings of Aristotle, Machiavelli, Montesquieu, and Sidgwick, which are devoted to the science of politics, will need comparatively scant mention. Nor shall we find it necessary to consider the works of that large body of writers who have devoted their attention either to the description of governmental forms or to the analysis of particular political types. During the Middle Ages, and indeed reaching well up into modern times, the relation between Church and State was the pivotal point around which political controversies raged. In all the writings which these struggles engendered theological dogma played an important part, and we shall find this literature of interest to us only in so far as doctrines of a general nature were evolved.

CHAPTER II

PRELIMINARY DEFINITIONS AND DISTINCTIONS

"**State**" **and** "**Government.**"—The first fundamental distinction that must be made, is that between "State" and "Government." By the term "Government" is designated the organization of the State,—the machinery through which its purposes are formulated and executed. Thus, as we shall see, while the term "State" is, when strictly considered, an abstract term, Government is emphatically concrete. More than that, Government is purely mechanical and governed by no general laws. Its varying forms are in all cases determined by political expediency, and the examination of its essential character involves no such philosophical considerations as will interest us in our present inquiry. The subject of Government thus lies almost wholly without the field of Political Theory, and is comprehended within the domains of descriptive and historical politics.

Simple and definite as is this distinction between the State and its governmental machinery (corresponding as it does very much to the distinction between a given person and the material bodily frame in which such person is organized), we shall find it to be one that has been but seldom made. In fact, it has been the confusion between these two terms that has led directly or indirectly to a great majority of the erroneous results reached by political philosophers in the past.

"Nation" and "People." — From the terms "Nation" and "People" the State is likewise to be dissociated.

In the use of the two former terms the greatest confusion exists. In Germany the word "People" (*Volk*) has primarily and predominantly a political signification, as denoting a body of individuals organized under a single government; while the term "Nation" (*Nation*) is reserved for a collection of individuals united by ethnic or other bonds, irrespective of political combination. According to this use "a Nation is an aggregate of men speaking the same language, having the same customs, and endowed with certain moral qualities which distinguish them from all other groups of like nature. . . . All people living under the same Government compose the 'People' of the State. In relation to the State, the Citizens constitute the People; in relation to the human race, they constitute the Nation."[1]

---

[1] Helie, in Lalor's *Encyclopædia of Political Science*, Vol. II. p. 923. Attention may also be called to the fact that the English word "government" is of wider meaning than the German term *Regierung*, which excludes the function of legislation, and frequently has no wider signification than that conveyed by our word "administration." The Germans have, however, a narrower term *Verwaltung*, which has especial reference to the details of executive action. Cf. Sarwey, *Allgemeines Verwaltungsrecht*, pp. 93, 94 (Marquardsen's *Handbuch des Oeffentlichen Rechts der Gegenwart*). See *post*, for the special use of the term "government" by Burgess.

As opposed to this usage, American and English publicists are wont to give to "Nation" the political meaning, and to signify by the word "People" an aggregate of men united by other than political bonds. Thus, as Bluntschli says in his *Theory of the State:* "In English the word 'People' and the French '*Peuple*' implies the notion of a civilization which the Germans (like the old Romans in the word '*Natio*') expressed by 'Nation.' The political idea is expressed in English by 'Nation' and in German by '*Volk*.' Etymology is in favor of German usage; for the word '*Natio*' (from *Nasci*) points to birth and race, *Volk* and *populus* rather to the public life of a State ($\pi \delta \lambda \iota \varsigma$)."[1]

At the same time, however, the English are not always consistent in making the use of these words the converse of that of the Germans. Commenting upon this paragraph of Bluntschli which we have cited, his translators say: "It will be found that he goes too far in supposing our use to be the exact converse of the German. The fact is, our word 'People,' though often less political in its signification than *Volk*, is more political than the German word *Nation*. Thus we must translate '*Volksvertretung*' by 'representation of the people,' and we can only render *Populus Romanus* by 'the Roman people.'"[2] They might also have added that the same indefiniteness surrounds the use of the word "Nation." For example, in the phrase "rights of nationality," there is the obvious postu-

[1] Trans. 2d ed. p. 86.   [2] *Idem*, p. vii.

late that nationality is nowise coterminous with political boundaries.

Notwithstanding, however, the confusion that thus exists in the English use of these terms, the translators of Bluntschli have seen fit to translate wherever possible the German word *Volk* by "Nation," and *Nation* by the English word "People." In this it would seem to the writer they have been unwise. The mere fact that they could not follow this rule in all cases condemns it. It would have been far better to have followed the German usage, and thus to have obtained, if not a perfect, at least a more definite and precise nomenclature. We shall therefore in the following pages denote by "People" an aggregate of men living under a single political control. The term "Nation" will be reserved for the more general and abstract use. That which welds a body of individuals into a national unity is no rigid political control, but ethnic and other factors largely sentimental or psychological in character.

Now when we say that it is these influences of race, religion, custom, language, and history that create a Nation, we mean that from these sources spring the feeling or sentiment that binds together a community of people, and constitutes from them a Nation. Each of these factors invites the formation of a Nation, but no one of them compels it. The essential principle is the feeling that is the result of one or more of these factors. Thus, as says Renan: "A Nation is a spiritual principle, resulting from the profound complications of history; a spiritual family, not a group determined by the configuration of the soil. . . . A Nation is, then, a great solidarity constituted by the sentiment of the sacrifices that have been made, and by those which the people are disposed to make. It supposes a past; it is, however, summed up in the present by a tangible fact: the consent, the clearly expressed desire of continuing the common life. The existence of a Nation is (if the metaphor be permissible) a continued *plebiscitum*, as the existence of the individual is a perpetual affirmation of life."[1] According to Mill, "a portion of mankind may be said to constitute a nationality if they are united among themselves by common sympathies which do not exist between them and others — which make them co-operate with each other more willingly than with other people, desire to be under the same government, and desire that it should be government by themselves, or a portion of themselves, exclusively."[2]

The tendency of course is, as indicated in Mill's definition, for Nations to constitute themselves as individual States, and it may be said that this demand for political unity constitutes the surest index to the existence of a national feeling. Hence, most publicists see in the national State the most perfect type of political development thus far attained.

The advancing enlightenment of the masses has been instrumental in creating the true feeling of

---

[1] Article *Nation* in Lalor's *Ency. Pol. Sci.*
[2] *Representative Government*, Chap. XVI.

nationality, that is to say, a demand for unity based upon some other ground than mere coercive political control; and the present century has seen the enormous influence that this principle has had in reforming the political map of Europe. At the same time the point may be made that it is not too much to expect that this same spirit of enlightenment that has thus given rise to this demand for a re-demarkation of political boundaries will, in turn, as civilization continues to advance, make this demand less imperative. And for this reason: While at first the enlightenment of the masses creates in them a consciousness of their own individuality and solidarity, and thus a national feeling; at the same time, as the culture of the people increases, their sympathies become more cosmopolitan, and their appreciation of the true unity of all humanity more real. Ethnic, lingual, and even political unity will thus exercise comparatively less and less influence as Nations find themselves drawn into a higher and more intellectual union. At the same time, also, economic interests will tend more and more to cross national and political boundaries, and thus unite with increasing closeness the material interests of different Peoples.

It may thus be entirely possible that the spirit of nationality at present so active in politics will prove to be a phase of civilization rather than a permanent product; and that while the realization of a true World-State may never be possible, we may yet look forward to a growth of internationality (*sit venia verbo*) that will largely deprive the feeling of nationality of its present force.[1]

State Abstractly Considered (*Staatsidee*). — Finally, as recognized by most modern publicists, and as already indicated, a distinction is to be made between the abstract idea of the State and its empiric conception. The one is the result of abstract speculation, the other of concrete thinking. The first is what the Germans designate "*Staatsidee*," being the idea of the State in its most general form. It is that idea which embraces all that is essential to, and which is possessed by all types of State life. It is the State reduced to its lowest terms. The empiric conception, on the other hand, is particular, and has reference to special civic types as historically manifested.

The State is an almost universal phenomenon. Everywhere, and in all times, we find men, as soon as their social life begins, submitting to the control of a public authority exercising its powers through an organization termed Government. In no two instances do we find the character or scope of this public authority identical or exercising its functions through precisely similar governmental organizations. We recognize, however, that no matter how organized, or in what manner their powers be exercised, there is in all States a substantial identity of purpose; and that underneath all these concrete appearances there

---

[1] Upon this question of Nationality, *vide* Bluntschli, *Theory of the State*, trans. 2d ed. Bk. II.; de Laveleye, *Le Gouvernement dans la Démocratie*, Vol. I. pp. 52-63; and Burgess, *Pol. Sci. and Const. Law*, Vol. I. Bk. I.

is to be found a substantial likeness in nature. If now we disregard all non-essential elements, and overlook inconsequential modifications, we shall be able to obtain those elements that appear in *all* types of State life, whether organized in the monarchical or republican, the despotic or limited, the federal or unitary form. We shall thus discover those characteristics that are of the very essence of the State's life, and which unfailingly distinguish it from other public bodies.

All concrete instances of State that are historically afforded us, are to be considered as embodying the *Staatsidee* as their principal essence. Variations in governmental organizations and administration are to be considered as merely differences in form that have arisen in response to demands of time, place, and peculiarities of political temperament of the people, but without disturbing the State's fundamental nature.

With this abstract, general conception of the State in our minds, we will be furnished with the criterion for distinguishing between mere variations and anomalous formations of civic life, and those public bodies that resemble, but do not possess this essential element, and are therefore not to be dignified with the title State.

It is to be observed, however, that this abstract conception of the State for which we seek, does not exactly correspond with the meaning given to the term *Staatsidee* by some writers. Thus, for example, Brie in his " *Theorie der Staatenverbindungen* " uses the term to express the ideally perfect State; that is, one possessing and itself directly exercising all the powers that properly belong to a State, rather than the general or universal idea of the State as we have above described it. For instance, he says: "Concrete States are ever more or less incomplete pictures of the *Staatsidee*, in that they do not possess and in themselves exercise all the powers that logically belong to them."[1] Professor Burgess likewise in his recent work makes a distinction between what he calls the "Idea" and the "Concept" of the State. Thus he says: "The idea of the State is the State perfect and complete. The concept of the State is the State developing and approaching perfection. From the standpoint of the idea, the State is mankind viewed as an organized unit. From the standpoint of the concept, it is a particular portion of mankind viewed as an organized unit. From the standpoint of the idea the territorial basis of the State is the world, and the principle of unity is humanity. From the standpoint of the concept, again, the territorial basis of the State is a particular portion of the earth's surface, and the principle of unity is that particular phase of human nature and of human need, which, at any particular stage in the development of that nature, is predominant and commanding. The former is the real State of the perfect future. The latter is the real State of the past, the present, and the imperfect future."[2]

[1] p. 7.
[2] *Pol. Sci. and Const. Law*, Vol. I. pp. 49, 50.

It is obvious that in the above, the distinction is not between the general or abstract conception of the State and its empiric manifestation. Not only this, but it would seem to the writer that there is an improper use of terms and a distinction attempted that may not properly be drawn. A given ruling organization either embodies and expresses the will of the State, or does not; but in no case can two or more States be spoken of as differing in degrees of perfection. States may differ as to the good or bad qualities of the governmental machinery in which they are organized and through which their wills find expression, but they themselves do not admit of comparative degrees of excellence. In other words, there can be no such thing as an imperfect State, and to maintain that there can be is only to confound again the ideas of State and Government. Professor Burgess himself sees the necessity of taking this ground when he comes to deal with the nature of the so-called non-sovereign State.[1]

[1] In his review of Laband's *Staatsrecht des Deutschen Reiches*, *Pol. Sci. Quar.*, Vol. III. p. 128.

CHAPTER III

THE ORIGIN OF THE STATE

In considering the origin of the State we shall be necessarily led into a much wider discussion of the nature of the State than this title would indicate. We shall find ourselves carried, indeed, almost directly into the heart of the subject to which this treatise is devoted; namely, to a general examination of the nature and justification of political authority. It is of course needless to repeat that in this chapter we shall be concerned with political authority in general, and, therefore, with no reference to the manner in which it may have been empirically manifested in the course of the world's history.

(A) *The Origin of the State from the Historical Standpoint*

Concerning the absolute origin of political authority among men, history does not afford definite information, nor does it appear possible that there will ever be furnished final light upon this subject. A study of origins is always an attractive one, and the work of many anthropologists has thrown a vast amount of light upon the early history of social and political institutions. The parts played by consanguinity, by religion (especially by the worship of ancestors), by the communal ownership of land and other economic interests, and, above all, by the influence of the family upon the development of social and political life, have been carefully considered. The significance of totem worship, of endogamy and exogamy, of polygamy, of polyandry, and of patriarchal life has been discussed in the light of the facts presented by the earliest literary and archeological records, and interpreted by analogy with the present customs of races now in the lowest stages of civilization. All of these facts have been compared and exhaustively studied, but the absolute origin of civic life has not been historically determined. The fact is, that the first subjection of man to public authority, of some sort or other, was practically and necessarily coeval with the beginning of his social life, and this carries us back to periods of human development anterior to those that furnish historical records.

The most prominent of the theories regarding the origin of political institutions that pretend to rest upon historical data, is the so-called "Patriarchal Theory," represented by the name of Sir Henry Maine as its propounder and chief advocate. "The patriarchal theory of society," to use Maine's own words, " is the theory of its origin in separate families, held together by the authority and protection of the eldest valid male ascendant."

Opposing the Patriarchal Theory is that of Morgan and McClennan, according to whom social life may be traced from the horde, or a condition of absolute promiscuity in sexual relations, from which, through various restrictions, the monogamous family and patriarchal State were subsequently reached.

Concerning these theories it may be said at once that they are social rather than political hypotheses. It is common to speak of the body politic as a development from the family and the State as the family "writ large." This, however, we conceive to be an error. It may, indeed, be true that in the earliest stages of political development, the family was such an all-important group that its interests dictated to a very great extent political action; that the father's authority was utilized for the enforcement of most of the then rules of conduct; and that, indeed, such authority of the father and the family organization suggested the establishment and manner of organization of the primitive State;—but admitting this, it would not be true to say that the State developed out of this small social unit. The two institutions are different in essence. In the family the location of authority is natural (*i.e.* in the father). In the State it is one of choice. Subordination is the principle of the family; equality that of the State. Furthermore, the functions or aims of the State are essentially different from, and often even contradictory to, those of the family. It is only by the necessarily primitive character of the patriarchal authority, and the extent to which the State in its early period of development recognized this power of the father, and utilized his authority for the obtaining of many of its aims, that countenance is given to the idea that the State developed from the family. So dissimilar are the aims of the two institutions, that one could not have owed its origin to the other. The family never was and never can become a subject of public law. Its interests are necessarily private.

Thus, as says Bentham: "It is true that every person must, for some time at least after his birth, necessarily be in a state of subjection with respect to his parents, or those who stand in the place of parents to him; and that a perfect one, or at least as near to being a perfect one as any that we can see. But for all this, the sort of society that is constituted by a state of subjection thus circumstanced, does not come up to the idea that, I believe, is generally entertained by those who speak of a *political* society. To constitute what is meant in general by that phrase, a greater number of members is required, or, at least, a duration capable of a longer continuance. Indeed, for this purpose nothing less, I take it, than an indefinite duration is required. A society, to come within the notion of what is originally meant by a *political* one, must be such as, in its nature, is not incapable of continuing forever in virtue of the principles which gave it birth. This, it is plain, is not the case with such a family society, of which a parent, or a pair of parents, are at the head. In such a society, the only principle of union which is certain and uniform in its operation is the natural weakness of those of its members that are in a state of subjection; that is, the children; a principle which has but a short and limited continuance. I question whether it be the case, even with a family society, subsisting in virtue of *collateral* consanguinity; and that for the like reason. Not but that even in this case a habit of obedience, as perfect as any we see examples of, may subsist for a time; to wit, in virtue of the same *moral* principles which may protract a habit of *filial* obedience beyond the continuance of the *physical* ones which gave birth to it: I mean affection, gratitude, awe, the force of habit, and the like. But it is not long, even in this case, before the bond of connection must either become imperceptible, or lose its influence by being too extended."[1]

The lucidity with which the above distinction is drawn will excuse the extended quotation that is given. It will be noticed that the emphasis is properly laid upon the inherent possibility of indefinite continuance as the criterion of political power. At the same time, Bentham mentions, though he does not dwell upon, the question of size; holding the fewness in numbers of the family to disqualify it as a political society.

This raises an interesting question as to what minimum limitation, if any, should be placed upon the number of citizens necessary to constitute a State. To our mind no minimum (short of one) can logically be placed. As our argument proceeds, it will appear that none of the essential elements of the State are such as cannot conceivably be predicated

[1] *Fragment on Government.* Ed. by Montague, 1891, p. 140 n.

as well of a small as of a large body of individuals. Aristotle would fix a limit below which the number of citizens should not go, but this, it will be found, is based, not so much upon logical grounds as upon the utilitarian principle that in a community too small there is not the possibility of that varied life which is essential to the true aim which the State should strive to attain. Austin denies the possibility of a State being constituted from a single family, upon the ground of its absurdity, and quotes Montesquieu as taking the same position.[1] After admitting that a single family living in total estrangement from every other community might exhibit all the traits of an independent political society, Austin, however, says: "But, since the number of its members is extremely minute, it would, I believe, be esteemed a society in a state of nature; that is, a society consisting of persons not in a state of subjection. Without an application of the terms, which would somewhat smack of the ridiculous, we could hardly style the society a society *political* and independent, the imperative father and chief a *monarch* or *sovereign*, or the obedient mother and children *subjects*."[2] Upon this says Clark:[3] "In this *dominion* so called (= ownership) of the original patriarch, law is *possible*. He *may*, that is, govern by *general rules*. It is not, however, *probable*, because he would have little interest in setting, or at least in adhering

---

[1] *Spirit of Laws*, Bk. I. Chap. III.
[2] *Province of Jurisprudence Determined*, 2d ed. 1861, Lect. VI. p. 183.
[3] *Practical Jurisprudence*, p. 147.

to, such rules. He would be more likely to govern by means of *occasional commands.*" In other words, though it is entirely improbable that a single, isolated family should ever become *politically* organized, it is not logically impossible. It is not the size but the lack of that element of possible perpetuity of dominion, that prevents the family from becoming, *as such*, a State.[1]

But whatever may be the proofs in support of these theories based upon family relationship and upon historical evidence, it is clearly improper to conceive of them as affording explanations of original and primitive conditions. The most that Maine and his school can properly say is that the earliest records, especially those of the Aryan race, point to the existence of patriarchal life. But this is not to say that the original type of political life even among the Aryans was of this character. As a recent writer has said: "The most archaic human society which we can picture to ourselves even by plausible conjecture is removed from the actual origin of mankind by a lapse of time demanding geological rather than historical measurement, and by a series of events of which we know nothing whatever."[2]

If thus, however, we are not able to obtain from history the absolute facts regarding the first appearance of political life among men, nevertheless it is not necessary to say that from this source we cannot

---

[1] For a comment upon the logical value of the argument based upon the ridiculous, see Maine, *Early History of Institutions*, p. 379.

[2] *Edinburgh Review*, July, 1893.

obtain facts throwing light upon the subject we are considering. Though we may not be able to obtain the facts regarding the actual origin of the State, yet we may be able to obtain from history and anthropology data from which, in combination with the operation of the natural and psychic forces working in societies of which we do know, we may be able to draw valuable conclusions regarding the conditions of early political society and the early stages of its development.

With the association of man with his kind, arise by necessity social interests. These interests not being in all cases identical with individual interests, and selfishness being an universal trait of mankind, there early comes the necessity for some means whereby the common welfare may be protected. To a certain extent at least it becomes necessary that there should be some means whereby the actions of men may be restrained in so far as they are directed to the satisfaction of individualistic desires that conflict with the common weal.

In addition to the task of preserving internal order is soon imposed that of maintaining the individual autonomy of a society as a political unit. Indeed, it is probable that it is this necessity that is first *consciously* felt. With communal life, and, to a large extent, communal goods, there naturally arises in the mind of each individual a feeling of interest in the welfare and continuance of the social unit of which he is a member. To these utilitarian grounds there are early added sentimental feelings that in the aggregate constitute what is known as Patriotism. Thus is begotten in the minds of the people not only a consciousness of their unity, but an appreciation of the necessity for some sort of organization through which they may continue their existence as a social unit against hostile interests from without, as well as from disintegrating forces from within. As has been said, it is probably this necessity for a military organization that is first consciously felt. Afterwards, when social development has proceeded further, the existence of this armed organization is utilized for the satisfaction of internal needs as their existence is recognized.

Whether by original force or by voluntary recognition and establishment, whether founded upon acknowledged supremacy of personal prowess and sagacity of the leader selected, or whether springing from patriarchal authority the public authority becomes established, cannot now be known and undoubtedly differed in different instances. *But however originated, a public authority once created, the State becomes an established fact.*[1]

With the permanent settlement of tribes upon definite areas of land, the territorial element becomes

---

[1] "That moment of the organization of every society," says Pulszky, "in which it presents itself as independent, dominant, and capable of asserting its own conditions of life *by force*, forms always a distinct phase in the process of association; and whenever any particular society assumes this form it appears as the State. The State is properly a law-creating and law-maintaining society which proclaims and asserts the conditions of its existence in connection with its own conduct and that of its subjects, through commanding, permissive, and prohibitory rules." — *Theory of Law and Civil Society*, p. 216.

embraced in the empiric conception of the State, and is henceforth an integral part of its life. The State now becomes a people politically organized in a particular territory, and the bonds of kinship and tribal relations become supplemented by geographical unity. The duties of the Government necessarily widen with the cultivation of land, and with the growth of personal property arises the necessity for increased duties of protection and regulation. Thus as civilization progresses, *pari passu*, social interests become greater, and, by necessity, the governing powers more elaborately organized and endowed with more extensive jurisdictions.

Together with this increasing elaboration of structure comes an increasing definiteness. The powers of the public authority become more strictly defined and their scope and manner of exercise more and more regulated by customs that have crystallized into fixed rules, — rules that collectively represent the jural ideal of the given society at its then stage of development.

There has been inclination on the part of many publicists to refuse the designation of " State " to the earlier types of political life, especially to those undeveloped organizations wherein the people have not yet obtained for themselves a settled abode. Those taking this ground must be considered as governed by an empiric conception of the State. We cannot refuse the designation of State to a society of men, if politically organized, even though it be in the nomadic stage. Low order of development cannot deprive an institution of its generic name. A society is politically organized if it have established within it and over it a public authority for the control of those interests that are connected with its orderly existence, and the enforcement of its jural ideal, however crude and limited that ideal may be. Thus organized, a society of men is properly embraced within the scope of the *Staatsidee* and is as truly a State as when in its more developed form.

To make this point clear, we can, for this particular purpose, liken the term "State" as used in Political Science, to the term "living being" as employed in Biological Science. The biologist does not refuse the designation of living being to the lowest orders of life, even though they be but mere splotches of protoplasm, so structureless and homogeneous in character, that different individuals can be scarcely distinguished, and in each of which the most powerful microscope is barely able to discover differentiation of parts. The point that is conclusive to the biologist is that such beings have crossed the line from the inorganic to the organic, from the inert to the living, that within them is contained a possible growth, a potential development.

Likewise, for purposes of illustration, we may compare, though not identify, the growth of the living being toward a higher life, with the development of political institutions. In both there appear an increasing differentiation of parts, and growth in variety of their needs. As the higher forms are assumed, the organism becomes more definitely and delicately constructed; its activities become increasingly self-directive, until finally the self-conscious individual appears. At the same time that this elaboration of structure has proceeded, varying influences and conditions of life have caused individuals to differ from one another until the number of classes, genera, and species becomes almost beyond estimate.

The development of political society is characterized by these same features. With the advance of civilization, come augmented social needs and activities. The governmental organization of the State becomes a more complex structure, and is endowed with wider, and, at the same time, more definite power. Also the exercise of these powers becomes more intelligently controlled, and in a sense self-directed, — that is, dictated rather by the interests of a State itself, than by the personal interests of the individuals in whom the exercise of the State's powers happens to be entrusted. Likewise, from substantial similarity of governmental organization, in the early stages, States, in the course of their development, assume diverging forms. Geographic, ethnic, economic, and moral conditions, all have their influence in determining the direction in which the development of political forms shall proceed. Distinctions arise as to the number of interests to be regulated by the State, as to the extent to which the people generally shall participate, either actively or by way of popular control, in the administration of their public affairs, and as to the manner in which the powers of the State shall be distributed among its several departments. Thus arise all those varieties of Governments running from the despotic Oriental State to the democracy of the Swiss communes. Later arise such forms as the feudal State, the constitutionally limited monarchy, the composite State, and the so-called national State. Within each of these classes are also to be found the members distinguished from each other by the greatest variety of internal organizations.

The manner and order in which these various forms have historically appeared, belong rather to historical and descriptive Political Science, than to Political Philosophy.

(B) *The Origin of the State from the Rational Standpoint*

Various attempts have been made to obtain, in a purely speculative way, a satisfactory explanation of the manner in which the State may be supposed to have come into existence.

It is to be observed that these theories are directed to the solution of a problem essentially different from that which has just been considered. The question now to be answered is, not the manner in which the State actually did originate, but the way in which it may reasonably be supposed to have been created, in order that it may be justified in the exercise of the authority that it wields. The question thus assumes a largely moral character. It is undoubtedly a fact, that many have believed States actually to have arisen in the manner in which such theories suppose, but a mere proof of the historical inaccuracy of this view does not touch the real point aimed at; such point being, as said, not how the State actually did originate, but its existence being granted, how its authority may be justified.[1]

The study of man in his social life reveals two conditions that are in apparent conflict. In the first place we recognize in him the ability to determine consciously his own actions; that is to say, a volitional capacity. It is the possession of this will that distinguishes the individual from his mere physical frame, that in fact makes him a *person* and not a *thing*. Now the possession of the power of willing which is given to man by his very nature endows him at the same time with a natural freedom — for free self-determination of action is of the essence of willing — and thus the oft-used expression "freedom of will" becomes, in this respect at least, mere tautology.

At the same time, an inspection of mundane conditions discovers these volitional subjects universally organized in political communities, in which they are subject to a coercive control by a general governing authority, whose power extends even to matters

---

[1] In this sense the problem much resembles the inquiry as to the origin of private property. To the followers of Henry George, it would be no answer to their claims, to demonstrate historically the manner in which private property in land arose. They would say that such would be an *explanation*, but not a *justification*. So likewise of the State.

of life and death. The universality, as well as the obvious utility, of this phenomenon of governing and governed, sovereign and subjects, lead naturally to the supposition that it is not an arbitrary injustice and immoral condition. But, at the same time, it does not relieve the philosopher from the desire of discovering if possible how this condition of affairs may be harmonized with the character of man as naturally gifted with powers of self-determination of action. How comes it that political power exists and is so universally acquiesced in? Is it simple usurpation, or does it owe its origin and existence to voluntary action on the part of those over whom its authority is exercised? If the latter, how has their consent been given? How explain the necessity for force to execute its commands? Is there, or can there be, any actual or theoretical limit placed to its power? Whence the right of particular persons to assume the prerogative of declaring and executing its will? Etc., etc.

We shall consider *seriatim* the various answers that have been given to these questions, and from a critical examination of them, seek to obtain the standing ground upon which to construct what we shall conceive to be the true solution.

The "Natural" or "Instinctive" Theory. — In the first place, it is no solution of the problem to rest the State upon the "Natural Sociability of Man," as is done by Bluntschli and many others. Thus says the author whom we have named, after considering and criticising the other theories: "We have still to discover the common cause of the rise of States as distinct from the manifold forces in which they appear. This we find in human nature, which, besides its individual diversity, has in it the tendencies of community and unity. These tendencies are developed and peoples feel themselves nations and seek a corresponding outward form. Thus the universal impulse to society (*Statstrieb*) produces external organizations of common life in the form of manly self-government, that is in the form of the State."[1] Here we have indeed the *cause* of the State, that is to say, the natural elements in human nature that urge its establishment and maintenance. But this is not that for which we are seeking. What we wish to discover is the justification of political authority as humanly exercised, and to harmonize it with predicated personal freedom.

To speak of the State as "naturally" created, makes of it an entity independent of man, uncreated by him, and, as such, not requiring justification in his eyes. In a general way, this was the view of the Greeks, who considered political authority almost as a metaphysical necessity arising from the social life of man, as existing in and of and for itself, and as determined by "the very nature of things." For this reason it did not occur to them to consider its essential nature and to vindicate its existence, in the manner in which later writers found it necessary. The State was not conceived by them

[1] *Theory of the State*, trans. 2d ed. p. 300.

as primarily the handiwork of men, and as such exercising a control over them that would require a philosophical interpretation.

It is of course apparent that such a view as this evades rather than solves the problem we are examining. Of course the State is natural in the same sense that everything that exists is natural. But the fact with which we are concerned is that political power is exercised through devices of human arrangement and construction, and its direction and scope humanly determined. To say that political authority is natural, neither answers the question as to how its empiric manifestation is brought about, nor shows the manner in which its control over the individual may be harmonized with the latter's natural freedom. Furthermore, we can properly conceive of, and in fact probably do know of, aggregates of men over whom no such control has been exercised. The State is, therefore, not a universal necessity at any rate, and hence the questions when, under what circumstances, and in what manner shall such control be established? While it is undoubtedly true that the communal life of man does necessarily give rise to mutual interests, which require for their realization the recognition of mutual rights and obligations, yet this does not of itself create a magistracy nor organize a governmental machinery such as is necessary for the creation of a State. The establishment of these instruments, together with the determination of the contents of their powers, requires conscious human action.

Aristotle says that "man is by nature a political being." But if we take the case of individuals who deny that they feel this so-called instinctive sociability or political sentiment, it would be no justification in their eyes to say that the general run of mankind is pervaded by this feeling. They would reply that "we do not feel so, and as to *us* there must be some other justification for the coercion that is exercised over us." And they would further add: "How does such a theory assist in determining the form in which the alleged political instinct shall find expression, and in whose hands this naturally given authority shall be vested?"

Allied, if not practically identical with this "natural" or "instinctive" theory, is that which sees in the State a natural organism, and as such governed by natural laws of development, decay, and death.

The State, strictly speaking, is not an organism. The analogy between a human society as politically organized and an organism is indeed striking, both as to structure and manner of development; but identity cannot be affirmed. Though the will of the State is not identical with the wills of its constituent units, yet, unlike the will of the natural organism, it is one that is influenced and largely determined by such individual volitions. Furthermore, the existence and activities of these units are not exhausted in the life and activity of the State. Not only is their organic life independent of the State's existence, but their entire spiritual being is uncontrolled by it. As we shall see in discussing the powers and aims of the State, this control is, by necessity, limited to the conduct of individuals only in so far as outward acts and material interests are concerned. Over motives, whether good or bad, the State has no control, though, through the environment which it provides, it may greatly influence indirectly the character of the motives that are formed. It cannot obtain this result by a direct command. Again, the body of the State (that is, the community of men as politically organized) is, as Spencer says, discrete rather than concrete. The form of governmental organization of any given State is in constant change, and at times undergoes radical alteration; its constituents move freely from place to place, and their numbers may be arbitrarily added to or lessened.

Contrasted with these characteristics, the living being is an aggregate whose parts exist solely to support and continue the life of the whole. The individual units have no life of their own, no independent powers of violation or action. Also, while in the organism the tendency is for the influence and control of the whole over the action of its parts to increase not only in exactness but in scope, this is not the necessary tendency in the State, whose control, though tending to become more and more perfect, at the same time secures to the individual a continually increasing sphere of free undetermined action.

Again, it is a universal rule that all natural organisms derive their life from pre-existing living beings; while, as we shall see later on, the State does not, and cannot, obtain its vitality from other political powers.

Finally, and what is absolutely conclusive upon the subject, is the fact that in the organism, the laws of development, though acting from within, are blindly and intuitively followed; while the growth of the State, though also from within, is, to a considerable extent at least, consciously felt, and the form of its organization self-directed. "A time arrives in the progress of social development," says Professor Cairnes, "when societies of men become conscious of a corporate existence, and when the improvement becomes for them an object of conscious and deliberate effort. We cannot, by taking thought, add a cubit to our stature. The species, in undergoing the process of improvement, is wholly unconscious of the influences that are determining its career. It is not so with human evolution. Civilized mankind are aware of the changes taking place in their social condition, and do consciously and deliberately take measures for its improvement."[1]

Thus the living individual of the biologic world is given no choice of the laws that shall govern its vegetative growth, though it may influence to some extent the direction of such growth. For it, the physical laws of assimilation and organic increase are rigidly fixed. The State, upon the contrary, though influenced, modified, and limited as to the

[1] *Fortnightly Review*, Vol. XXIII (January 1875), quoted by Ward; *Psychic Factors of Civilization*, p. 299. Cf. on this topic, Gunton, *Principles of Social Economics*, Pt. IV. Chap. II. Sec. 2.

form and development of its governmental organization by natural laws and objective influences, is yet itself possessed of a volitional power that so dominates its external manifestations, that of its own will it may change its form to an extent to which no theoretical limit can be placed.

In fine, as has been already said, the State, strictly considered, is essentially psychic rather than physical. It represents a will rather than a physical being; and thus, considered apart from the governmental machinery through which it acts, and the individuals organized under it, only psychological qualities are attributable to it.

It is also inaccurate to speak of the State as a "moral organism," as do many who refuse to it the designation of "natural organism." It is evident that an attempt is thus made to distinguish between a natural, or, we might say, physical or physiological organism, and a moral organism. The term "organism" does not admit of such use, and is applicable only in a physiological sense. Morality, on the other hand, is an attribute of a person, and not of a thing. A man may be moral, but his physical organic frame is not. To speak of a "moral organism" is thus a misuse of terms.

Utilitarian Theory.—When considered from the standpoint from which we are viewing it, the obvious utility of the State is not of itself a justification. So, as Dr. Taylor says: "When Mr. Morley tosses off Rousseau's problem by declaring that the State finds its justification in considerations of proved expediency with reference to the special case, it cannot be supposed that the author of *The Social Contract* would have admitted that this solution touches his real difficulty. Rousseau doubtless had as little question as Mr. Morley concerning the practical value of a really good government. But he had a very exalted idea of the sacredness of personality, and he found it difficult to reconcile with that idea the fact that in the State the individual is called on to submit to an alien will. He averred that no such high prerogative belongs to any man or set of men save in so far as the individual has granted it. In this he doubtless erred; but it surely would not help him to repeat time-worn truisms about the greatness and value of the State. You have a good thing, he would have said, but whence your authority to impose it on me? This same objection applies to any other theory which attempts to justify the State by justifying its mission."[1]

As a matter of fact, however, Dr. Taylor, while properly stating the question, does not himself escape entirely from the utilitarian view. His reasoning is as follows. Conceding to each individual the prerogative of rule, (*i.e.* the prerogative of coercively interfering with the liberty of other persons when necessary in order to maintain one's own version of the jural idea), he maintains this general prerogative to belong of right to the one best fitted to exercise such a power. Since, however,

[1] *The Right of the State to Be*, p. 46. This essay contains some very acute reasoning, and I have obtained many suggestions from it.

through the elimination in a large measure of individual and personal interests, and the increased wisdom obtained from the union of minds, persons acting collectively are manifestly better fitted to exercise this authority than when acting individually; and, since the whole community is evidently better qualified for this work than any other association of men; therefore, the prerogative of men acting in communities is the highest of all human prerogatives. The State, therefore, is justified in assuming and exercising final authority and control in the name of justice. Thus, according to this theory, the State is endowed with this prerogative of rule only because it is composed of individuals possessing the personal prerogative of rule. "It is the prerogative of man acting in and through communities." Furthermore, the authority of the State is not obtained by a process of delegation. The individual prerogative is not destroyed but suspended and controlled by a higher prerogative. In conclusion, the author says: "One need only reflect that the community is an association so extensive as to furnish an authority more nearly free from personal elements than any other association; that the sense of responsibility to a real public opinion makes the most reckless more thoughtful, lifts them out of their natural particularity, and enables them to realize in some degree the rationality which alone justifies their possession of authority; and, finally, that the community is an association which brings to the service of justice a physical force so overwhelming that the supremacy of justice is commonly assured without even a resort to that force. From these considerations the conclusion seems inevitable that, while the prerogative of men acting separately is high, and that of men acting in private association is higher, that of men acting through the community is highest of all."[1]

It is possible that we have not properly understood Mr. Taylor's theory, but so far as we have appreciated it, it seems to us to be essentially utilitarian. Prerogatives are distinctly regarded as relatively higher or lower according to utilitarian standards; and, in the paragraph last cited, this view is explicitly stated.

The Force Theory. — Thirdly, the so-called "Force Theory," that might *per se* is a warrant for coercion, is a futile attempt to avoid the question, and scarcely needs refutation. What causal connection can there be between "might" and "right"? Morality has reference only to a subject with powers of free self-determination of action. As Rousseau says, "Strength is physical power; I do not see what moral force could result from its action. To yield to force is an act of necessity, and not of will; it is at the most an act of prudence. In what sense could it be of duty? . . . If obedience must be rendered to strength, it is not necessary to obey from duty; and if obedience is not exacted, it is not necessary to obey. It may be seen then that the moral right adds nothing to strength; it has no significance here. Obey them that have the rule over you. If that means yield to force, the

[1] *Op. cit.* p. 95.

precept is good but superfluous; I answer for its never being violated."[1]

Dismissing, then, these various attempts to beg the question rather than to answer it, there would seem to be two other grounds upon which the justification of the State might conceivably rest. First, that it is an institution, which, though humanly administered, is yet created and justified by the will of God, and rests therefore upon a will higher than that of man, — a will which is itself the creator of man and of the entire universe, and the source of all justice. Secondly, the State may conceivably be regarded as a purely human institution, but resting upon the original consent of the individuals over whom its authority is exercised, and therefore, upon the principle of *volenti non fit injuria*, not oppressive to their freedom.

So important have been these two theories in the history of political ideas that we shall consider them with some degree of particularity.

The Divine Theory: History of. — During Antiquity and the Middle Ages, the State was generally viewed as of direct divine creation. In the ancient empires of the East, to such an extent were religion and law confused, that political science can scarcely be said to have existed as an independent branch of knowledge. The ultimate sanction of all law was supposed to be found in the sacred writings. In all of the vast Asiatic monarchies of early days the

[1] *The Social Contract*, Bk. I. Chap. III.

rulers claimed a divine right to control the affairs of the State, and this was submitted to by the people with but little question.

In the Shemitic races the theocratic theory was carried to the extent of not only maintaining the authority of their rulers to rest upon divine delegation and sanction, but of alleging a direct oversight and participation by the Almighty in the control of public affairs.

Among the Greeks, as already said, the State was considered as an institution existing in itself and of itself and as determined by the very nature of things. As such, it had a divine origin, as did all things in the phenomenal world. The State was not considered by them as primarily the handiwork of man, but as demanded by, and as a necessary outgrowth from, the very nature of man himself.

Thus while the political temperament of the Greeks, assisted by the topography of their country, led to the development of the "City State" rather than the "National State" as their civic ideal, their philosophical conception of the nature of the State led them to view it not so much as a *means* for furthering human development as an *end* in itself. Thus the State came to be considered as the all in all, and the citizens as of significance only as subjects of the State. These two elements, the practical and the philosophical, though not logically connected, became actually united, for it was only the comparatively small size of the City State that rendered practically possible the execution of that unlimited scope of governmental powers that logically followed from the conception of the State as "natural" and, therefore, indirectly divine. For its maintenance it was dependent upon the continuation of the Hellenic spirit in its full strength, — "when," as says Felix Dahn, " the subject without thought submitted himself to the substantial embodiment of the national spirit as traditionally expressed and represented in religion, customs, and the State, and thus submitted himself with a feeling that things could not be otherwise."[1] With the Macedonian and Roman conquests, this spirit began to die out. The old relations were dissolved, outside interests were introduced, disintegration of national and political life was rapid, and the independence of the Grecian States soon became a thing of the past.

With the Romans began in practice a clearer distinction between divine and civil authority. By them, law was considered as created by the State, and its final authority sought in the Roman people. They may thus be said to have been the first to attempt to give to the structure of the State a definite legal form, and thereby, while limiting its governmental power, to give to it greater stability and uniformity. At the same time, as is well known, the Romans were practical lawyers and administrators rather than philosophers, and, so far as they did indulge in philosophical speculations, followed closely Grecian thought, and made slight, if any,

---

[1] Lalor's *Ency. Pol. Sci.*, article *The Philosophy of Law*. Cf. Freeman, *Comparative Politics*, p. 93.

advances upon it. This is seen especially in the writings of Cicero.

Just as throughout the entire history of political philosophy we find specific theories evolved only as demanded by the events and conditions of the time, so did the question of the ultimate origin of temporal power fail to give rise to more than casual thought, as long as the origin of the State was of interest only as a part of political speculation, and unconnected with any practical question in the world of politics. Hence it was, that it was not until the rise of the temporal power of the Church, and the struggle between the Pope and the Emperor, that the divine or non-divine origin of political power became actively discussed.

In its early history the Church of Christ was distinctly and avowedly an organization claiming dominion over only the spiritual interests of mankind. In the patristic writings obedience to the State in all things not contrary to the law of God was distinctly taught. The supremacy of the civil power in all things temporal was freely admitted. The command to render unto Cæsar that which is Cæsar's was uniformly held during these earlier years as providing the principle according to which the relations between Church and State should be governed. "If the Emperor demand tribute," said Saint Ambrose, "we should not refuse. . . . If the Emperor desire our fields, he has the power to take them, no one of us can resist. . . . We will pay to Cæsar that which is Cæsar's." [1]

[1] *Epist. de basilicis tradendis*, 38, t. II. (Ed. Bened. p. 872).

In proclaiming the kingdom of God, the Church declared the liberty of conscience and gave to the individual a law in spiritual affairs outside of and superior to that of the State. As, however, the See of Rome increased in power and importance, it began to claim powers other than those embraced in this principle. It maintained its right to preserve the peace, to decide as to the justice of quarrels between temporal princes, to enforce the purity of morals with temporal might, to defend the oppressed, and to enforce its decisions by anathema and excommunication, and even by force of arms when necessary.

Thus, by degrees, the temporal power of the Church increased until it became itself a civic organization, promulgating laws and enforcing obedience thereto by military coercion, and contesting with the temporal rulers of Europe the right of supreme control. Dante,[1] Occam,[2] and Marsillius of Padua[3] defended in their writings the claims of the temporal powers in this controversy. Hincmar, Hildebrand, Thomas Aquinas,[4] and Giles of Rome[5] supported the papal pretensions.

In this great mediæval strife between papal and temporal power, both parties remained, however, united upon one point; namely, that this dualism of Church and State found an ultimate union in a divine order. They were not divided as to the ultimate

---

[1] *De Monarchia.*

[2] *Octo questiones super potestate summi pontificis. Dialogus Magistri.*

[3] *Defensor pacis.*

[4] *De regimine principium.*

[5] *De regimine principium. De ecclesiastica potestate.*

nature of all political authority, but as to the manner of its delegation by its supreme author to particular hands.

We would not expect, nor do we find in this polemical literature, systematic treatises upon the nature of the State. The writings deal with utilitarian interests, quote the patristic writings and the Scriptures as the highest authorities, and depend upon conflicting versions as to the historical relations between the Church and the Empire. Thus in all these writings we find political philosophy confused with religious dogma, and its results largely vitiated by the extent to which the minds of men were dominated by theological beliefs. Aquinas, for example, argues as follows: "The highest aim of mankind is eternal blessedness. To this chief aim all earthly aims must be subordinated. This chief aim cannot be realized through human direction alone, but must obtain divine assistance, which is only to be obtained through the Church. Therefore the State, through which earthly aims are attained, must be subordinated to the Church. Church and State are as of two swords which God has given to Christendom for its protection; both of these, however, are given by Him to the Pope and the temporal sword by him handed to the rulers of the States. Thus the Pope alone received his power directly from the Almighty, the Emperor his authority indirectly through the Pope's hands."[1]

Against this argument, the supporters of the supremacy of the temporal power replied: "Between

[1] See Janet, *Histoire de la Science Politique*, Vol. I. pp. 381–401.

spiritual and temporal affairs there is a distinction that cannot be destroyed. The control of temporal affairs belongs exclusively to the State, and the Roman Bishop possesses no power either to enact or to suspend laws regulating affairs other than those of the spirit. The kingdom is necessarily and avowedly declared by the Scriptures to be not of this earth, but of the world to come; not over the bodies of men, but over their souls."

The Protestant Reformation, rather than lessening this confusion of divine and political power, tended to increase it. All of its leaders, Luther, Melanchthon, Zwingli, and Calvin, reiterated the divine origin of civil authority and the necessity of the citizens' obedience thereto. The opponents of the Reformation, especially the Dominicans and Jesuits, directed all their energies to proving the purely mundane character of the State. This they did in order to give to the Church the sole claim to spiritual origin and divine authority, and hence to the placing of political power upon a lower basis as compared with it. It was at this time and in the writings of these ecclesiastics that the doctrine of *naturrecht* was given a prominence in political speculations that it was henceforth to maintain until the present century.[1]

When however the contest became no longer one between Pope and Emperor, ecclesiastical and temporal power, but between ruler and ruled; and the scope and legitimacy of political rule in particular

---

[1] Upon this point see especially Gierke, *Johannes Althusius u. die Entwicklung der naturrechtlichen Staatstheorien*, pp. 61 et seq.

hands became questioned, the controversy assumed a new shape. The point in dispute then came to be, not so much the origin of political power itself, as the hands by which, and the manner in which, it could rightfully be exercised. By the end of the thirteenth century it had become an axiom accepted by all parties, that the will of God or the nature of man were to be considered only as *causæ remotæ*, and that all ownership lay in the free contractual gift of the community (*per viam voluntariæ subjectionis et consensus*), the debated point being only as to the effect of such a popular contract; that is, whether resulting in a total alienation or merely a revocable delegation of the supreme political power.

We now find the temporal princes, who, in their contests with the Pope, had been willing enough to separate entirely their rule from the sanction or support of the Church, looking to the Church to uphold them in their rule, by declaring tyrannicide and popular deposition impious; while the Clergy, especially in France and other countries whose rulers remained loyal to Rome, we discover refusing to accept the full consequences of the theories of Contract and Natural Law which they had been willing enough to support in the Church's struggles against the Empire.[1]

[1] During the counter-revolutionary period that followed the Congress of Vienna, the absolutist attitude of the Church was very pronounced. Ex-President Andrew D. White, in the *Papers of the Am. Hist. Ass'n* (Vol. IV. Part I.), gives an extreme instance of this in an article entitled "A Catechism of the Revolutionary Reaction." It is unnecessary to say that at present the Church at Rome supports the French Republic, and is apparently in full sympathy with true democratic thought.

E

It is only in the absurd and extravagant patriarchal theory of Filmer,[1] according to which royal authority is based upon the dominion given by God to Adam at the time of his expulsion from Eden, and in the subservient writings of Bossuet,[2] that we find the divine theory again openly argued.

At the same time, it cannot be denied that the idea of a "divinity that doth hedge a King" continued to be of great actual influence upon the ideas of the people — an influence that, though crushed in the French Revolution, revived during the counter-revolutionary period that followed 1815, and still lives in the thought of the commoner people of Europe, especially of those under the more autocratic of rulers. But for all purposes of political philosophy, the divine theory disappeared before that of natural law and contract, and received its *coup de grace* on the continent, from the writings of Hugo Grotius, and in England from those of Hobbes and Locke.[3]

Criticism of the Divine Theory. — It will be seen that the application of this theory to political condi-

---

[1] *Patriarcha, or the Natural Power of Kings*, published in 1680. For refutation of Filmer's views, see Sidney, *Discourses on Government*, and Locke, *Two Treatises of Government*, Book I.

[2] *Politique tirée de l'Ecriture sainte.*

[3] Mr. Spencer remarks how remarkable it is that a system of thought may often be seen going about in high spirits after having committed suicide. Thus it is that the divine theory, though killed and buried, is from time to time revived and seen going about in habiliments changed, to be sure, but so thin as to but slightly hide its true self. Instances of this are to be seen in Stahl, *Die Philosophie des Rechts*, Haller, *Restauration der Staatswissenschaft*, and Mulford's Apocalyptic rhapsody (as Professor Dunning terms it), *The Nation*.

tions has been of a twofold order: first, as justifying political authority in general; and secondly, as legitimizing the exercise of such political authority in particular hands by viewing *de facto* rulers as either direct agents of the Almighty, or as wielding a power indirectly delegated. But, however understood, the theory is devoid of value, and open to much of the same logical criticism as that applied to the theory of the State as a purely "natural" institution. To those who are not theists, the two theories are not, in fact, separable. The theist must hold that all power is from God, and if this be so, the individual may, with a propriety equal to that of the State, maintain that his inclinations and powers are of divine origin and entitled to recognition irrespective of law or custom. Divine laws being at most only partially revealed to us in the Scriptures, there still remains a very large portion of human conduct that must be regulated by rules resting upon human experience and reason.

Were it, indeed, a fact that the actual presence and activity of divine action, as distinguished from human action, could be seen in the enactment and enforcement of the law of the State, it would be another thing; but that which we do see, whatever may be its ultimate metaphysical basis, is the State acting through human agencies. Now whence the prerogative of rule of these human agencies, whoever or whatever they may be? Even though the substance of the State, or rather the tendency to political life, be implanted by Nature or by God in human nature, the realization of this political tendency, its actual manifestation and operation, has been left to human agencies, and it is the justification of the authority exercised by these human agencies for which we are seeking. Grant all that the divine theory necessarily maintains; that ultimately all power is from God; that by Him is implanted in the nature of man the need and demand for the State, and we get no nearer to knowing why in any particular case there should exist in a community a definite set of individuals arrogating to themselves the right of exercise of this divine prerogative of rule. All that necessarily follows from the divine theory is that political rule of some sort or other is divinely justified. No test, or suggestion of a test, is thereby afforded for determining whether any particular empiric manifestation of such order is exercised according to this divine purpose, or by the hands divinely appointed; unless, indeed, we say that the mere fact that the given State does exist and that its government is in the hands that it is, such a condition must therefore be according to the will of Him who is omnipotent and directs all human things. But of course this is nothing more than saying that "whatever is, is right," which is also the motto of the Force Theory. Thus, instead of affording a basis for true political authority, it logically justifies every conceivable act, whether such act tends to uphold or subvert the existing state of rule.

It is in fact quite superfluous to show in this age that from their own inherent nature, divine or moral sanctions can have no application to political matters. That compulsion for which we are seeking, and which is described as political, is a compulsion that is backed by outward human physical force, and its sanctions have reference to actual fear of physical evil. Its application is thus necessarily limited to external acts. Contrary to this, the laws of God and the rules of morality have their authority upon the intention rather than the outward act, and, in fact, the very application of morality to actions predicates a freedom of outward action. Thus says Green, in distinguishing the two realms occupied by morality and political Sovereignty: "The question sometimes put, whether moral duties should be enforced by law, is really an unmeaning one; for they simply cannot be enforced. They are duties to act, it is true, and an act can be enforced; but they are duties to act from certain dispositions and with certain motives, and these cannot be enforced. Nay, the enforcement of an outward act, the moral character of which depends on a certain motive and disposition, may often contribute to render that motive and disposition impossible."[1]

The two domains of political and divine obligations are thus not only exclusive (not necessarily exclusive as relating to particular acts, but only as to the character of the sanction applied), but, from the individual standpoint, often contradictory. For the solution of this difficulty, the premise that all power is from God, gives no assistance.

[1] *Philosophical Works*, Vol. II. p. 310.

CHAPTER IV

THE ORIGIN OF THE STATE, CONTINUED: THE CONTRACT THEORY

In our search for a justification of the authority of the State, we have thus far been forced to reject as invalid the answers given by the "force," "instinctive," "utilitarian," "natural," and "divine" theories. There yet remains to be considered the so-called "Contract Theory," or that theory which founds the State upon an original agreement entered into by the individuals of a society, who, prior to that time, have been entirely independent of political control.

Now, aside from the conception of a superhuman spirit, there is no other reason, understanding, or will than that existing in individual human beings. If, then, we premise in these individuals an inherent right of self-determination of action as the foundation of all morality, it would seem necessarily to follow, that the only way in which an authority that coercively restrains these individuals can justifiably exist, is by the consent of the subjects in some way given to the imposition of such control over them. It remains to be seen, however, whether this consent is of a sort that may be given in such an original compact as is embraced in the Contract

Theory, and whether, in fact, such a compact is logically possible.

Before proceeding directly to this point, it will be necessary to state in a general way the various forms in which this theory has been held by different writers. In giving the views of these writers, we shall state at considerable length not only their theories as to the origin of the State, but also the deductions drawn by them, from this premise, regarding the proper scope of the State's power, and the nature of the relations that exist between the governed and the governing. This we do, because it is pre-eminently in these writers that we find an entire philosophy of the State. From their positions we shall thus be able to obtain points from which to develop our own conception of the State, not only as regards its origin, but as to its various attributes.

History of the Contract Theory. — It is to be noticed in the beginning that the term "contract"[1] as found in political theory, is used in a double sense : —

First: as descriptive of an agreement between rulers and subjects, according to which the power of rule is placed in particular hands. This we may term the "Governmental Compact."

Secondly: as descriptive of an agreement between individuals of a particular community according to which such community first becomes politically

---

[1] There are some writers who attempt to distinguish between the terms "contract" and "compact." In this work they are used synonymously.

organized; and in which agreement there is no necessary reference to the manner in which, or the persons by whom, the political power is to be exercised. This is more usually termed the "Social Contract," but might more properly be named the "Political Contract," for by it is supposed to be created a body *politic* where before had existed only an unorganized aggregate of men, or, at most, merely a social body.

By contract as used in the first sense, the legitimacy of existing governments is determined, and the validity of the titles of their rulers established. As understood in the second sense, the origin of the State, that is, of the political power itself, is explained. We shall treat briefly and separately of the history of the Contract Theory as understood in these two ways, and first of the Governmental Compact.

The Governmental Compact. — The idea of resting the authority of rulers upon an original compact with their subjects is of very ancient origin, occurring not only in the writings of political philosophers, but apparently exhibited in frequent historical instances.

As regards its use in theory, we find a suggestion of it in Plato;[1] the Roman jurists universally rested the power of the Emperor upon an original explicit, or subsequent implicit, consent of the populace; and mediæval and early modern writers generally took

---

[1] *Republic*, p. 359, and *Crito*, p. 51 (Jowett's translation). Cited by Professor Ritchie in the *Pol. Sci. Quar.* VI. p. 657.

this view. In our history of the Divine Theory we have already spoken of the manner in which the idea of national law supplanted that of divine law as the basis of political authority. This predication of a State of Nature governed by Natural Law logically necessitated the introduction of some sort of contract or agreement whereby civil rule might be substituted for natural freedom.

As for historical instances in which a governmental compact appears, or is alleged to have been entered into, we have that of King David making a covenant with the Elders before the Lord;[1] the formula used by the nobles in the election of the King of Aragon, mentioned by Hallam[2]; and Locke quotes[3] the words of even King James himself, contained in a speech to Parliament, in 1609, in which the Contract Theory is plainly expressed. The idea was also prominent in the contests over investitures; and numerous historical instances abounded in German history in which political compacts had been made between the several Estates.

But it is hardly worth while to attempt to enumerate more instances of this sort. The fact is, that the whole feudal system was saturated with ideas of contract. Thus, as says Sir Henry Maine: "The

---

[1] II. Samuel v. 3.

[2] *Middle Ages*, Vol. I. Chap. II. The form being: "We who are as good as you choose you for our king and lord, provided that you observe our laws and privileges; and if not, not."

[3] *Two Treatises of Government*, Bk. II. § 200. See especially a very able article upon "The Social Contract Theory," contributed by Professor D. G. Ritchie to the *Pol. Sci. Quar.* December, 1891.

earliest feudal communities were neither bound together by mere sentiment nor recruited by a fiction. The tie which united them was a Contract, and they obtained new associates by contracting with them. The relation of the lord to the vassals had originally been settled by express engagement, and a person wishing to engraft himself in the brotherhood by commendation or infeudation came to a distinct understanding as to the conditions on which he was to be admitted. It is therefore the sphere occupied in them by Contract which principally distinguishes the feudal institutions from the unadulterated usages of primitive races. The lord had many of the characteristics of a patriarchal chieftain, but his prerogative was limited by a variety of settled customs traceable to the express conditions which had been agreed upon when the infeudation took place." [1]

Absolutists and their opponents alike held the thesis of an original sovereign capacity of the people, and the transfer of this power to their rulers by a compact. The point at issue was as to the character and scope of this compact.

Upon the one side it was held that the surrender of this supreme power by the people was necessarily entire, and resulted in a total and irrevocable alienation of their political rights. This was the view held by the Roman jurists, by Suarez and other Jesuitical writers, and later, as we shall see, by Grotius and Pufendorf.

[1] *Ancient Law*, p. 353.

Upon the other side, it was maintained that this governmental part effected nothing more than a delegation of power to the rulers, such power to be used by them only for the purposes for which granted, and liable to be recalled upon being misused.

Suarez, whose development of the idea of Sovereignty was especially profound for his time, likens the birth of the State to that of a child, and from that analogy derives its necessarily absolute character. Just as man, says he, is free and has full power over all his members, as soon as he exists, so is the political body. Just as the father of the child only gives to it existence, while God gives it freedom, reason, and power, so the Sovereignty of the community is created by the free will of men uniting; and, just as the father can procreate the child or not, as he sees fit, but if created, cannot deny it full power and freedom; so, likewise, the community may or may not create the body politic at its option, but when created cannot refuse it freedom from all control. Again, Suarez likens the temporal powers of the prince to the spiritual power of the Pope. The sovereign pontiff, he says, although holding his power from God is able to abdicate it, and, in the same way, the republic, though receiving the legislative (*i.e.* sovereign) power from God, is able to abandon it, if it see fit, and to transfer it to another person.[1] Grotius

---

[1] *Tractatus de legibus et legislatore*, Bk. III. Chap. III. Cf. Gierke, *Althusius u. die Entwicklung der naturrechtlichen Staatstheorien*, pp. 67 et seq.

endeavored to maintain the possibility of a people surrendering its Sovereignty without reservation or power of revocation, upon the ground that the conquered may purchase their lives at the hands of their conquerors by an acceptance of political slavery, — a doctrine that excites the especial indignation of Rousseau, who clearly shows the impossibility of founding a "right" of control upon such a basis, not to speak of the false principle of international law that it contains.[1]

By those whose views differed from the above, it was variously held, either that it was inherently impossible for a people to alienate its Sovereignty; or, that, if it could be done, the presumption would be, in absence of any exact knowledge of such a compact, that the surrender of power would be coupled with the condition that its exercise should be directed to the general welfare of the community.

In accordance with these views we find many of the political discussions of these centuries turning upon such points as the power of the people to offer resistance to tyrants *absque titulo* and to tyrants *ab exercitio*, that is, to tyrants without legitimate title to power, and to those who, though possessed of proper title, exercise their control in an oppressive manner. The general view held was, that towards tyrants of the first class both natural right and civil right permitted resistance, as there was really no compact on the part of the people with them. But as regards those of the second class, views differed, some hold-

---

[1] *The Social Contract*, Bk. I. Chap. IV.

ing that citizens were individually bound, but that collectively they had the right of resistance; while others held that implicit obedience was in all cases demanded.

Regarding the school of writers who would have limited the power of kings, we shall speak further when we come to consider the development of the idea of "Popular Sovereignty."

The Social or Political Compact. — In accepting the contractual origin of governments, even the absolutists had to concede an original sovereign power of the people; for the people must, of course, have first had that which they are conceived as granting away. But this surrender of power could only be imagined as being performed by a community acting as a single body in a corporate capacity. That is to say, it was necessary that it should first assume the character of a legal subject. Hence, it was early agreed that a given aggregate of men must first constitute a single social or political body, as distinguished from a mere horde or arithmetical sum of persons, before they could contract with the particular rulers to whom the political power was to be given. It thus became necessary to account for the manner in which this transition from a sum of individuals to a united community was effected.

In the earlier and more theological times, society was held by some to be as much a direct creation of God as was man himself. In general, however, God was considered simply as the *causa remota*, and Nature, or the "instinctive sociability" of man viewed as the proximate cause. That is to say, the Aristotelian doctrine was maintained. This was the general view until the end of the sixteenth century. We thus find no mention of an original Social Compact in the writings of Bodin, the body politic being considered by him as an aggregation of families. Nor did the *Monarchomachi* advance beyond this point.

The first writer upon the Continent to make the idea of an original Social Compact a necessary antecedent to the Governmental Compact was Johannes Althusius, who wrote at the beginning of the seventeenth century. This idea he fully developed and made a constructive principle in his system; applying it also to the smaller social units, and even to the family.[1]

In England, the first definite statement that we find of the Social Compact is in the writings of an English clergyman. In his *Ecclesiastical Polity*, published in 1594, Richard Hooker attempted the defence of the established church of England, by denying that the church was necessarily subject to direct divine regulation in all matters; but that for its government laws might be made by men, so long as they were not contrary to the Scriptures. In sustaining this thesis, he was led to an inquiry regarding the origin of all authority, and found it in the consent of the governed. A pre-civic condition of man was distinctly premised, and, to escape from this

---

[1] *Politica methodice digesta atque exemplis sacris et profanis illustrata,* pub. in 1603.

state, which was one of lawlessness and war, the Social Compact was entered into. Hooker did not follow out to its various consequences the theory thus advanced, but left this task to his successors Hobbes, Locke, and Rousseau.

The full acceptance of the Social Compact theory upon the Continent was secured, when Hugo Grotius adopted it as one of the bases of his work *De jure belli et pacis;* in which he was followed by Pufendorf. This latter writer, however, interpolated between the social and governmental compacts a "resolution" of the people whereby was determined the *form* of government to be established, *i.e.*, whether monarchic, aristocratic, or democratic.[1]

But in none of the works of the writers whom we have mentioned was there any attempt to deduce the various results that logically follow from the premises assumed. This was first done by the Englishmen Hobbes and Locke, and the Genevese Frenchman Rousseau. Their systems we shall now consider with some degree of particularity, as in them we shall be able to find, though

---

[1] *De jure naturæ et gentium*, pub. in 1672, and *De officio hominis et civis*. An advance made by Pufendorf upon Grotius and Hobbes was as to the distinction to be made between the act or will of the sovereign when acting as such, and when as a private individual; and the consequent possibility of a subject suffering injustice at the hands of the sovereign. Furthermore, he practically limits the power of the ruler in the assertion that his rule to be legitimate must be orderly and for the general good, and hence differs from Hobbes, who, as we shall see, would say that *any* act of the sovereign, however capricious, irregular, or arbitrary, is entirely legal. The views of Pufendorf were closely followed by Thomasius in his *Fundamenta juris naturalis ex sensu communi deducta*, and his *Institutiones jurisprudentiæ*.

mixed with many errors, many of the components of a correct system of political philosophy. In thus carefully sifting these principles from the chaff by which they are surrounded, we shall be at the same time advancing the constructive portion of our work.

Hobbes.—In the writings of the philosopher Hobbes we come to clearly expressed principles. Conceiving the State of Nature to be one of war—*homo homini lupus*—in which there exist no legal rights either of person or property, but only natural rights founded upon morality and utility, Hobbes based the State upon a compact between individuals, whereby each of them gave up a part of his own natural liberty in order that all might be protected by the strength of all. Thus, says he:—

> The State is established by a "covenant of every man with every man, in such manner, as if every man should say to every man 'I authorize and give up my right of governing myself, to this man, or to this assembly of men, on this condition, that thou give up thy right to him, and authorize all his actions in like manner.' This done, the multitude so united in one person is called a 'commonwealth,' in Latin *civitas*. This is the generation of that great 'leviathan,' or rather, to speak more reverently, of that 'mortal God,' to which we owe, under the 'immortal God,' our peace and defence. For by this authority, given him by every particular man in the commonwealth, he hath the use of so much power and strength conferred on him, that by terror thereof, he is enabled to perform the wills of them all, to peace at home, and mutual aid against their enemies abroad. And in him consisteth the essence of the commonwealth, which, to define it, is one person, of whose acts a great multitude, by mutual covenants one

with another, have made themselves every one the author, to the end he may use the strength and means of them all, as he shall think expedient, for their peace and common defence.

"And he that carrieth this person is called 'sovereign,' and said to have 'sovereign power'; and every one besides, his subject."[1]

From this contract the rights of absolute monarchy are deduced. The contract once made, not only does the power of the ruler become absolute, but all right of revolution on the part of the people is, according to Hobbes, forever lost.

"They [he continues] that have already instituted a commonwealth, being thereby bound by covenant to own the actions and judgments of one, cannot lawfully make a new covenant amongst themselves to be obedient to any other, in anything whatsoever, without his permission. And therefore, they that are subjects to a monarch, cannot without his leave cast off monarchy, and return to the confusion of a disunited multitude; nor transfer their person from him that beareth it, to another man, or other assembly of men; for they are bound every man to every man, to own, and be reputed author of all, that he that already is their sovereign, shall do, and judge fair to be done; so that any one man dissenting, all the rest should break their covenant made to that man, which is injustice: and they have also every man given the sovereignty to him that beareth their person; and therefore if they depose him they take from him that which is his own, and so again it is injustice. Besides, if he that attempteth to depose his sovereign be killed, or punished by him for such attempt, he is author of his own punishment, as being by the institution, author of all his sovereign shall do: and because it is injustice for a man to do anything for which he may be punished by his own authority, he is also upon that title unjust. And

[1] *Leviathan*, Morley ed. p. 81.

whereas some men have pretended for their disobedience to their sovereign, a new covenant, made not with men, but with God; this also is unjust: for there is no covenant with God but by mediation of somebody that representeth God's person; which none doth but God's lieutenant, who hath the sovereignty under God. But this pretence of covenant with God is so evident a lie, even in the pretenders' own consciences, that it is not only an act of an unjust, but also of a vile and unmanly disposition.

"Secondly, because the right of bearing the person of them all is given to him they make sovereign, by covenant only of one to another, and not of him to any of them, there can happen no breach of covenant on the part of the sovereign: and consequently none of his subjects, by any pretence of forfeiture, can be freed from his subjection. That he which is made sovereign maketh no covenant with his subjects beforehand, is evident; because either he must make it with the whole multitude as one party to the covenant; or he must make a several covenant with every man. With the whole, as one party it is impossible; because as yet they are not one person; and if he makes so many several covenants as there be men, those covenants after he hath the sovereignty are void; because what act soever can be pretended by any one of them for breach thereof is the act both of himself, and of all the rest, because done in the person, and by the right of every one of them in particular. Besides, if any one, or more of them, pretend a breach of the covenant made by the sovereign at his institution; and others, or one other of his subjects, or himself alone, pretend there was no such breach, there is in this case no judge to decide the controversy; it returns therefore to the sword again; and every man recovereth the right of protecting himself by his own strength, contrary to the design they had in the institution. It is, therefore, vain to grant sovereignty by way of precedent covenant. The opinion that any monarch receiveth his power by covenant, that is to say, on condition, proceedeth from want of understanding this easy truth, that covenants being words and breath, have no force to oblige, contain, constrain, or protect any man, but what it has (*sic*) from the public sword: that is, from the united hands of that man, or assembly of men that hath the sovereignty, and whose actions are avouched by them all, and performed by the strength of them all, in him united. . . . Because every subject is by this institution author of all the actions, and judgments of the sovereign instituted, it follows, that whatsoever he doth, it can be no injury to any of his subjects; nor ought he to be by any of them accused of injustice. For he that doth anything by authority from another, doth therein no injury to him by whose authority he acted."[1]

From this form of dominion, termed "sovereignty by institution," Hobbes next turns to dominion acquired by conquest or victory in war. "This power of rule is acquired," says he, " when the vanquished, to avoid the present stroke of death, covenanteth either in express words, or by other sufficient signs of the will, that so long as his life and the liberty of his body is allowed him, the victor shall have the use thereof at his pleasure. . . . It is not, therefore, the victor that giveth the right of dominion over the vanquished but his own covenant. . . . In sum, the rights and consequences of both paternal and despotical dominion" (*i.e.* dominion by conquest) "are the very same with those of a sovereign by institution."[2]

It would thus seem that, setting aside the primitive contract, Hobbes would legitimize existing governments upon the basis of force. Indeed, he becomes still more explicit in regard to this in treating of the cases in which the subjects are absolved

[1] *Leviathan*, Chap. XVIII.   [2] *Idem*, Chap. XX.

from their obedience to the sovereign. Thus he says, "The obligation of subjects to the sovereign is understood to last as long, and no longer, than the power lasteth, by which he is able to protect them. For the right men have by nature to protect themselves, when none else can protect them, can by no covenant be relinquished." He, however, saves himself from the obvious inconsistency by basing the duty of the citizens' obedience upon the two contradictory principles of force and of covenant, by impliedly holding that this dissolution of the sovereign power can only come from foreign force or voluntary act of the ruler, and never rightfully from the citizens themselves, who are rigidly bound by the terms of their own contract.

Spinoza, who accepted the contractual theory of the origin of political authority, disregarded the above distinction and founded the right of the *de facto* government to rule, upon its power to maintain itself against force from any quarter whatsoever. Thus, if it be asked as to the difference between his system and that of Hobbes, it may be replied, that that which distinguishes his opinions from those of Hobbes is, that he preserves the natural law, even in the civil state, and accords right to the sovereign only in proportion to his actual power.[1]

In other words, Spinoza held, and logically, as we shall see, that a compact entered into between individuals in a then State of Nature could have no

---

[1] *Tractatus politicus*, Chap. II. *Tractatus theologico politicus*, Chap. XVI.

efficiency in giving greater legal or moral validity to rules based on it, than such rules would have in an entirely unpolitical state of society. Hobbes, however, though his contractual thesis would not warrant it, made a clear distinction between so-called natural law, and civil or political law, and thus laid the foundation for that system of Analytical Jurisprudence that was afterwards elaborated by Bentham and Austin. "Natural laws" (which he identifies also with divine laws), says he, "doth always and everywhere oblige in the internal court or that of conscience; but not always in the external court, but then only when it may be done with safety."[1] "Civil law," on the contrary, says he, "is to every subject those rules which the commonwealth hath commanded him, by word, writing, or other sufficient sign of the will to make use of, for the distinction of right and wrong; that is to say, of what is contrary, and what is not contrary to the rule."[2] "The law of nature and the civil law," he continues, "contain each other and are of equal extent. For the laws of nature, which consist in equity, justice, gratitude, and other moral virtues on these depending, in the condition of mere nature, . . . are not properly laws but qualities that dispose men to peace and obedience. When the commonwealth is once settled, then are they actual laws, and not before; as being then the commands of the common-

---

[1] *Philosophical Rudiments Concerning Government and Society,* Chap. III.
[2] *Leviathan,* Chap. XXVI.

wealth; and therefore also civil laws; for it is the sovereign power that obliges men to obey them. . . . But every subject in a commonwealth hath covenanted to obey the civil law; either one with another, as when they assembled to make a common representative, or with the representative itself one by one, when subdued by the sword they promise obedience, that they may receive life; and therefore obedience to the civil law as part also of the law of nature. Civil and natural law are not different kinds, but different parts of law; whereof one part being written, is called civil, the other unwritten, called natural. But the right of nature, that is, the natural liberty of man, may by the civil law be obliged and restrained; nay, the end of making laws is no other but such restraint; without the which there cannot be any peace. And law was brought into the world for nothing else, but to limit the natural liberty of particular men, in such manner as they might not hurt but assist one another, and join together against a common enemy."[1] Furthermore, " All laws, written and unwritten, have their authority and force from the will of the commonwealth." . . . " By the virtue of natural law which forbids breach of covenant, the law of nature commands us to keep all the civil laws. For where we are tied to obedience before we know what will be commanded of us" (*i.e.* by the original compact), " there we are universally tied to obey in all things. Whence it follows

[1] *Leviathan*, Chap. XXVI.

that no civil law whatsoever, which tends not to a reproach of the Deity (in respect of whom cities themselves have no right of their own, and cannot be said to make laws), can possibly be against the law of nature. For though the law of nature forbids theft, adultery, etc.; yet if the civil law command us to invade anything, that invasion is not theft, adultery, etc." [1]

The sovereign, then, possesses unlimited power; and no matter how arbitrarily or oppressively this power be exercised, obedience on the part of the people is demanded. To resist the sovereign is to return to a state of anarchy. The rights transferred to the sovereign cannot be withdrawn without his consent; for, though not a party to the contract he has obtained indefeasible rights under it. There is no contract between the people and the sovereign, but only of all between all, in which contract there is a sovereign necessarily established. That is to say, Sovereignty, which before the union did not exist, springs into being of necessity by the very act of union, and he to whom this authority is then given, is henceforth the sovereign.

In his *Leviathan* Hobbes is not explicit as to just the manner in which this supreme power is conferred upon this specific person or these specific persons. In his *De Corpore Politico*, however, he is more definite. Of the various forms of government, "the first in order of time," says he, " is democracy; and it must be so of necessity, because an aristocracy and

[1] *Philosophical Rudiments*, Chap. XIV. § 10.

a monarchy require the nomination of persons agreed upon, which agreement in a great multitude of men must consist in the consent of the major part; and where the votes of the major part involve the votes of the rest there is actually a democracy."[1] And again, he says, "And seeing a democracy is by institution, the beginning both of aristocracy and monarchy, we are to consider next how aristocracy is derived from it. When the particular members of the commonwealth, growing weary of attendance at public courts as dwelling far off, or being attentive to their private businesses, and withal displeased with the government of the people, assemble themselves to make an aristocracy, there is no more required to the making thereof but putting to the question one by one the names of such men as it shall consist of, and assenting to their election; and by plurality of vote to transfer that power, which before the people had, to the number of men so named and chosen."[2]

When so chosen, however, this aristocracy has the same unlimited and illimitable rights as the original sovereign. "And from this manner of erecting an aristocracy," Hobbes continues, "it is manifest that the few, or *optimates*, have entered into no covenant with any of the particular members of the commonwealth, whereof they are sovereign; and consequently cannot do anything to any private man, that can be called injury to him, howsoever their acts be wicked before Almighty God, according to

[1] Chap. II.   [2] *Idem.*

that which has been said before. Further, it is impossible that the people, as one body politic, should covenant with the aristocracy or *optimates*, on whom they intend to transfer their sovereignty. For no sooner is the aristocracy erected but the democracy is annihilated and the covenants made unto them void."[1]

Without proceeding at this point to consider the historical or legal impossibility of such an original compact as Hobbes predicates, it will be seen that the cardinal fault of this writer is the utter failure to distinguish between the two conceptions of the State and Government, — between the sovereign power itself and the personal hands into which its exercise is entrusted. That is, while he rightfully holds that the birth of Sovereignty is synchronous with that of the body politic, he does not separate this event from the delegation of this power to governmental agencies, — an act independent of and posterior to it. Thus he says in the sentence last quoted, that it is impossible that the *demos* should covenant with the aristocracy to whom it is about to hand the sovereign power, because aristocracy once established the democracy is annihilated, and hence the agreement that might have been made to it lapses. He does not see that democracies and aristocracies are but forms of government, and that the change from the one to the other or to monarchy involves no death or re-creation of the

[1] *Idem.*

Sovereignty, that is to say, of the State. Concerning his views as to the impossibility of subjecting Sovereignty to legal limitation, and as to the distinguishing of natural and civil law, — these we shall find to be correct, though based upon an untenable theory. Aside from this, the one trouble in his political system is that everywhere this legal absolutism of the State is confounded with governmental absolutism, — the subjection of the people to particular rules identified with their subordination to civil authority.

Locke. — Starting with the premise of an original non-civic condition of mankind, Locke considered this state to have been one of natural equality and freedom, and the individual to be endowed by nature with certain rights; as, for example, those of property and self-defence. The origin of government he conceived to have been by a compact wherein the individual voluntarily surrendered into the hands of a general authority certain rights and powers, whereby his remaining liberties and rights should be protected and preserved. The State is thus conceived as created to protect rights already in existence. Moreover, these rights (and here he differs fundamentally from Hobbes) remain in the individual even after the contract, and have the same binding force as in the non-civic State. In other words, the governing power created is in no case absolute and thenceforth independent of the individual and his rights, but is limited by these rights. The power of the ruling authorities is a fiduciary one, and when abused may be revoked by the people who have granted it. Thus says Locke: "The State of Nature has a law of nature to govern it, which obliges every one; and reason, which is that law, teaches all mankind who will but consult it, that being all equal and independent, no one ought to harm another in his life, health, liberty, or possessions."[1] The disadvantages that arise, however, from allowing to each individual the power of determination and enforcement of his own rights, lead to the necessity for some sort of control that shall act as a common arbiter of individual rights, and which shall be endowed with sufficient power to enforce its decrees. Men are thus led to the establishment of a political authority. "Wherever, therefore," says Locke, "any number of men so unite into one society as to quit every one his executive power of the law of nature, and to resign it to the public, there, and there only, is a political or civil society. And this is done wherever any number of men in the State of Nature enter into society to make one People, one body politic under one supreme Government; or else when any one joins himself to, and incorporates with, any Government already made."[2]

"But though men when they enter into society give up the equality, liberty, and executive power they had in the State of Nature into the hands of the society, to be so far disposed of by the legislative as the good of the society shall require, yet it being only with an intention in every one the better to

[1] *Two Treatises of Government*, Bk. II. Chap. II.
[2] *Idem*, Bk. II. § 89.

preserve himself, his liberty and property (for no rational creature can be supposed to change his condition with an intention to be worse), the power of the society or legislative constituted by them can never be supposed to extend further than the common good, but is obliged to secure every one's property by providing against those three defects above mentioned that made the State of Nature so unsafe and uneasy."[1]

"Whensoever, therefore, the legislative shall transgress this fundamental rule of society, and either by ambition, fear, folly, or corruption, endeavor to group themselves, or put into the hands of any other, an absolute power over the lives, liberties, and estates of the people; by this breach of trust they forfeit the power the people had put into their hands for quite contrary ends, and it devolves to the people, who have a right to resume their original liberty, and by the establishment of a new legislative (such as they shall think fit) provide for their own safety and security, which is the end for which they are in society."[2]

The above citations are sufficient to make it plain that Locke does not draw the line between moral and civil laws with the same degree of accuracy that did Hobbes. He nowhere clearly distinguishes between the rights and obligations created by the command of a political superior, and the general moral rights and duties that arise independently of a common authority. Thus, while with Hobbes

[1] *Two Treatises of Government*, Bk. II. § 131.   [2] *Idem*, Bk. II. § 222.

a rule commanded by the governing power is legally valid, whatever its character, when judged by moral or utilitarian grounds; with Locke, it has but a hypothetical validity, dependent upon its consonance with natural rights of person and property. In other words, while Hobbes could not conceive of an instance in which the person or persons possessing the sovereign power could act in an illegal manner, Locke could not conceive of a case in which the ruler might legally oppress his people. From the strictly juristic standpoint, we shall see that Hobbes was nearer right as to the legal omnipotence of the sovereign power; but what he did not see was, as we have already said, that this sovereign power represents the will of the State rather than the will of the individual or individuals to whom the governing powers are entrusted; and that in any given case, while it may not be possible to place a legal limit to the will of the sovereign State, it is possible to limit the legal competence of governmental agents. In other words, that which Locke did not sufficiently recognize, or at least explicitly state, was the possibility of endowing kings or other governing agents with such power as would enable them to oppress the people in a strictly legal manner; and that therefore the right of revolution against such government is a moral rather than legal right. In so far, however, as Locke recognized that rulers are of limited powers, and act in but a representative fiduciary capacity, he made an enormous advance over Hobbes. He thus prepared the way for, if he did not himself reach, the full distinction between Government and State.

Where he failed was in not sufficiently distinguishing between the community as simply a social aggregate, and as a political body; and that Sovereignty in its true legal sense resides in the latter and not in the former. He fully recognized that a government is but the political machinery of the State, and public officials but agents of the political power, but he did not fully appreciate that this political power belongs not to society as such, but to it as a body politic. Thus, when he says that "there remains still in the people a supreme power to remove or alter the legislative, when they find the legislative act contrary to the trust imposed in them," the context shows that he does not recognize that this right of a community of men as such to use the force which their number gives them to dictate the manner in which their public affairs shall be administered, is not a legal but a moral right; and that, in so far as their will is expressed in ways other than those provided for by law, it is not the will of the State.

As we shall have occasion subsequently to maintain, every State is completely organized in its government, and therefore the aggregate of governmental powers comprehends in its entirety the State's Sovereignty. Therefore, when it shall be said that governmental powers are capable of legal limitation, reference will be had to their exercise by particular organs, and not to their exercise as a totality. Hence it follows that Sovereignty may be exercised only in a legal manner, that is, according to rules prescribed by existing law. In one of his closing paragraphs, Locke explicitly says, that the superior "right" of the people (impliedly, as organized in England) to change their rulers can never be enforced through or by means of the then existing government, but he does not then immediately conclude, as he should have done, that, therefore, such act cannot be an act of the State, which can only operate through the governmental apparatus in which it is organized. In curtailing the power of political rulers, Locke in fact limits the power of the State. Of this we shall speak at greater length in connection with the nature of Sovereignty and its location in the body politic.

Rousseau. — In the writings of Rousseau, the doctrine of Popular Sovereignty was carried to its extreme extent, — to an extent that rendered practically impossible the existence of a true State. The distinction between State and Government is clearly made (though Government has with him a more limited meaning than that which we have ascribed to it[1]); but that between the Sovereignty of the State and the power of the people as a community is hopelessly confused. Thus, while he makes Government but the servant for executing the will of the State, he makes this will practically identical with popular demand. The permanence of all Government and its authority is thus practically destroyed. While Locke limited the power of Government, Rousseau annihilates it. He absolutely refuses to

[1] That is, as excluding the true legislative function.

any governmental authority the power of expressing the will of the State. Its duties are, according to him, strictly limited to executive acts. It is thus in no true sense an organ of Sovereignty. "What, then," he asks, "is the Government? An intermediate body established between subjects and sovereign for their mutual intercourse, charged with the execution of the laws and the maintenance of liberty — civil as well as political."[1] But even this limited power is at any moment subject to be withdrawn. "The instant that the people is legitimately assembled in a sovereign body," says he, "all jurisdiction of Government ceases."[2]

The natural freedom of man is presupposed, and the purpose for which the State is established is "to find a form of association which shall defend and protect with the public force the person and property of each associate, and by means of which each, uniting with all, shall obey, however, only himself, and remain as free as before."[3] This purpose is obtained by a Social Contract entered into between individuals of a community, according to which each person "gives in common his person and all his power under the supreme direction of the General Will, and receives again each member as indivisible part of the whole." The individual in giving himself to the control of all gives himself to no particular person. Each person in himself possesses an indivisible and inalienable portion of the

---

[1] *The Social Contract*, Bk. III. Chap. I.
[2] *Idem*, Bk. III. Chap. XIV.   [3] *Idem*, Bk. I. Chap. VI.

Sovereignty of the whole. The contractual origin of Government is expressly disavowed. The original compact is between individuals and creates the body politic, of which Government is but the servant. "Those who contend," says Rousseau, "that the act by which a people submit to chiefs is not a contract, are quite right. It is absolutely only a commission, in which, as simple officers of the sovereign, they exercise in his name the power of which he has made them the depositary, and which he can limit, modify, and take away when he wishes."[1]

The legislative or volitional power must always remain with the people, for while power may be delegated, will cannot. The people are thus left as free as before the contract, and owe obedience to the acts of the *de facto* Government only so long as it pleases them to do so. Only that is law and has a binding force which accords with the General Will; and this General Will can only be expressed directly by an assembly in which every citizen has a personal vote. Representative Government is thus condemned; and, according to him, the English, though believing themselves free, are only free when electing a new Parliament. A Parliament once elected, they become its slaves. The true political sovereign is thus the totality of the citizens. Its powers are necessarily unlimited, for the original contract which is the "foundation of all rights" is entered into by and between the whole people, who as the sovereign

[1] *Idem*, Bk. III. Chap. I.

cannot enter into a contract with itself. Thus, "As nature gives to man absolute power over his members, the social compact gives to the body politic absolute power over its members; and it is this same power which, directed by the General Will, bears, as I have said, the name of Sovereignty."[1]

Such political absolutism is not, however, oppressive of the liberty of the citizens either individually or as a People. Obviously not of them as a People, for they are themselves the possessors of Sovereignty. Nor individually, because "the constant will of all the members of the State is the General Will."[2] This General Will, however, is not necessarily the result of the unanimous will of the citizens. The only agreement needing absolutely unanimous consent is the original compact. "There is but one law," says Rousseau, "which, from its nature, requires unanimous consent; it is the social compact; for civil association is the most voluntary act in the world; every man being born free and master of himself, no one can, under any pretext whatever, enslave him without his consent." But "when the State is established, consent is in residence; to dwell in a territory is to submit to its Government."[3] Within the State, however, a majority vote is sufficient to control. The manner in which Rousseau harmonizes this subjection of the minority to the majority with his declaration that all men should be free, is as follows:—

[1] *The Social Contract*, Bk. II. Chap. IV.   [2] *Idem*, Bk. IV. Chap. II.
[3] *Idem*, Bk. IV. Chap. II.

"When," says he, "a law is proposed in an assembly of the people, what is asked of them is not exactly whether they approve of the proposition or whether they reject it, but whether or not it conforms to the General Will, which is theirs; each one in giving his vote gives his opinion upon it, and from the counting of the votes is deduced the declaration of the General Will. When, however, the opinion contrary to mine prevails, it shows only that I was mistaken, and that what I had supposed to be the General Will was not general. If my individual opinion had prevailed, I should have done something other than I had intended, and then I should not have been free."[1]

Upon this point it will be seen that the reasoning is substantially the same as that of Hobbes; namely, that the consent given to the original compact makes all acts of the power established by that contract the acts of the contracting party. Thus in Book I. Rousseau says: "In fact each individual can, as man, have an individual will contrary to or different from the General Will which he has as a citizen. In order then that the social compact may not be an idle formula, it includes tacitly this agreement. which alone can give force to the others, that whoever shall refuse to obey the General Will shall be compelled to it by the whole body, which signifies nothing if not that he will be forced to be free."

But "it is only the General Will which is obligatory upon individuals, and it is never certain that an in-

[1] *Idem*, Bk. IV. Chap. III.

dividual will will conform to the General Will until after it has been submitted to the free suffrages of the people." Thus, as he says in a previous note, though unanimity be not necessary in the formation of a General Will, it is necessary that all votes be counted.

Comparison. — Having stated now the positions of Hobbes, Locke, and Rousseau, each of whom, starting with an original compact as the origin of political society, deduces such different results, it will be convenient, by way of summary, to compare and contrast their views.

Hobbes and Rousseau agree in maintaining the absolutism of Sovereignty. But the latter considers the exercise of this power possible only by the whole community, and that law is a formulation of the General Will which can be expressed only in a direct manner by the people; for, while power can be transmitted, will cannot. With Hobbes, however, the sovereign power can be placed in the hands of one, the few, or all, but once conferred, such sovereign power cannot be recalled by the people into their own hands. Rousseau makes a distinction between *de facto* Governments and Governments *de jure;* while with Hobbes, the *de facto* Government is always, because of its existence, a *de jure* Government as well.

Hobbes thus makes no distinction between Government and State, both being conceived as at once created by the original compact, the ground being taken that the only way that a society of men can become politically organized is by handing over entirely and forever the sovereign power to some sovereign one, few or all.

Hobbes differs from Locke in holding that a change in Government necessitates a dissolution of political society and a return to anarchy; the latter holding that such change only signifies that the people exercise their sovereign and legal right of selecting their own public servants.

Locke and Rousseau agree in limiting the power of Government. Hence they agree in placing in the hands of the people the power to determine in whose hands political rule shall be placed or allowed to remain. With Locke, however, a legal validity is granted to all acts of the governing power except those plainly in violation of the rights of the individual, and oppressive to such an extent as to justify revolutionary measures. With Rousseau, on the other hand, all laws require the direct participation of the people in their formulation and expression. Thus, that sovereign power which Locke considered as held in reserve by the people, and only to be exercised in extreme cases, Rousseau held to be in continual and constant exercise by the people. According to Rousseau, by the original compact the people themselves in their collective capacity became the sovereign and continued so. The General Will and political Sovereignty are thus completely identified.

Contract Theory in Germany and America. — The

Contract Theory had a very considerable influence upon German publicists during the period immediately following Rousseau; but the development given to it by them was not such as will make it necessary for us to spend more than a few moments upon their views. Kant and Fichte both accepted the Contract Theory as a good working hypothesis, but denied its historic possibility. Moreover, Kant held this view merely as one that furnishes the best rule by which to test the justice of laws, not as one by which to determine their legality. That is, according to him, laws should be such as a people might consent to; and if not such, they are unjust. But whatever the law is, it is the duty of subjects to obey.

Fichte, likewise, accepted the Contract Theory as furnishing the best theoretical basis upon which to found rules of justice, and, in his earlier writings, pushed the rights of the individual, in some directions to a greater extent than had done Rousseau, maintaining the right of the individual to withdraw at any time from the State of which he is a citizen. But in a later work his political views became more absolute, and the sphere of the State which he had at first, like Kant, limited to the negative functions of preservation of life and property (*Rechtsstaat*), became, in his later work (*Der Geschlossene Handelsstaat*) almost communistic.

In addition to the great influence which the theories of Locke and Rousseau had upon English and European thought and politics, a most profound influence was exercised upon political thought in America. The compact theory is recognized in the preamble of the Declaration of Independence, and is explicitly accepted in nearly all of the Bills of Rights of the Constitutions of the various commonwealths of our Union. Thus, for example, in that of New Hampshire it is declared that "all men are born equally free and independent. Therefore all government of right originates from the people, is founded in consent, and instituted for the general good." In the preamble to the Constitution of Massachusetts it is said, "the body politic is formed by a voluntary association of individuals. It is a social compact, by which the whole people covenants with each citizen, and each citizen with the whole people, that all shall be governed by certain laws for the general good."

Also in the private writings of Jefferson and Madison and other statesmen of that period, we find the social contract theory accepted in its purest form. Jefferson goes to the extent of holding that one generation cannot bind another, and, based upon a calculation as to average length of life, says, "every constitution, then, and every law naturally expires at the end of thirty-four years." At a later date he reduces this period to nineteen years, thus making the natural life of political States, as some one has said, shorter than that of a horse. Madison, to whom these views were expressed, while not accepting this deduction, yet, in his answer to Jefferson, maintains the contractual origin of political society, and asserts that the continued validity of constitutions and laws rests upon tacit acceptance through the fact of their not being explicitly revoked.[1]

[1] See, upon this point, an article by Professor G. P. Fisher, entitled "Jefferson and the Social Compact Theory," in the Annual Report of the American Historical Association for 1893; and Borgeaud, *Adoption and Amendment of Constitutions in Europe and America*, Chaps. II. and III.

CHAPTER V

CRITICISM OF THE CONTRACT THEORY: NATURAL LAW

IN examining the logical grounds upon which the various theories of contract rest, it is observed that the necessary postulate to them all is an original, pre-civic, non-political condition of mankind. This condition is termed the "State of Nature," and in it there are conceived to be no rules regulative of human conduct, save those afforded by the so-called "Laws of Nature," or "Natural Laws." The results flowing from such a state of life are variously described as happy or the reverse, according to the disposition of the writer. According to Locke, Nature teaches men "that being all equal and independent, no one ought to harm another in his life, health, liberty, or possession." The natural state is one of peace, the only inconvenience being that every man is necessarily at once his own judge and executive in cases where his natural rights appear to be in conflict with those of others. Hence the necessity for the establishment of some sort of authority that shall be common judge and executive agent. The conception of Rousseau is quite similar to that of Locke's, though he sees in the "State of Nature" an ideal, rather than a primitive historical, condition.

The Monarchist Hobbes, however, more intent on proving the legitimacy and necessity of absolute political authority than in demonstrating individual rights, places more emphasis upon man's individualistic impulses, and pictures the non-political state as one of anarchy. The interests of men, says he, are so mutually antagonistic as to give rise to constant war of every one against his neighbour; for the right of nature is, in fact, nothing more than "the liberty that each man hath to use his own power for the preservation of his own nature." The unrestricted application of this principle necessarily makes man the wolf of man (*homo homini lupus*).

But reason soon tells man, says Hobbes, that the rule of self-preservation thus defeats itself, and that the end will be better attained by uniting in some sort of general agreement whereby, through a union of individual powers, a supreme power may be obtained, which will have the strength to compel the obedience of individuals to its orders, and thereby to introduce peace. Thus the Social Contract is entered into for the better preservation of life, and is hence validated by natural right, which, as said, commands each man to use his power "for the preservation of his own nature."

Now, it is obvious that if we would criticise upon logical grounds the views of these contract writers, it is necessary that we should first of all examine the character and validity of these so-called "Natural Laws" and "Rights" upon which they so confidently base their reasoning. In doing this we shall likewise be preparing ourselves for a consideration of the doctrines of constitutional government and popular sovereignty with which we shall be later concerned.

Distinctions. — The term "Laws of Nature" we find used in various senses, and our first task will be to distinguish between those that have figured in, and served to confuse, political speculations.

I. First of all, "Natural Law" is employed to indicate mere sequences of cause and effect in the phenomenal world.

It is only in a borrowed sense that the term "law" is here applicable. There is here no element of a command addressed to rational beings, and in fact no possibility of an infraction of the principles stated. Such "laws" are only statements of observed operations in the world, which, in accordance with the principle of nature's uniformity, may be confidently expected to re-occur whenever certain given conditions are present.

It will be seen that in conceiving these uniformities of nature as due to pre-ordained "laws," nature is viewed as an active legislative principle and as itself, by its own will, and as a living entity, dictating the manner in which its operations shall proceed. In this aspect it is thus distinguished from nature as simply a sum or series of particular phenomena. "This is the distinction," says Ritchie, "which in scholastic phraseology is known as that between (a) *Natura naturans*, and (b) *Natura naturata*. We may indeed speak of nature doing this or that, personifying and unifying the forces of the universe, without intending to commit ourselves to any definite theory as to the ultimate explanation of things; but whenever we speak of nature in such a way, we are more or less consciously speaking of *natura naturans*, of nature as dynamic, as operating and operating for definite purposes, however much we may qualify our personification by warning others and ourselves that our language is metaphorical. When we speak of nature as simply a collection of objects, in whose presence we find ourselves and which form the materials for scientific inquiry as to how they stand related to one another, we are speaking of *natura naturata*."[1]

II. The term "Laws of Nature" is likewise used to indicate the instinctive conduct of living beings — men and animals alike.

The most general principle under this head, and the one upon which all other principles are based, is that of the "natural" or instinctive effort of all living beings to preserve their own existence, and to satisfy the desires to which their own nature gives rise.

In this sense, also, the "Laws of Nature" are not commands to do or refrain from doing particular acts. They contain, in reality, "nothing but a statement of that which a given being tends to do under the circumstances of its existence, and which, in the case of a living being, it is necessitated to do if it is to escape certain kinds of disability, pain, and ultimate dissolution."[2]

---

[1] *Natural Rights*, pp. 71, 72.
[2] Huxley, "Natural and Political Rights," *Essays*, Vol. I. p. 349.

Mr. Huxley, in the essay from which the preceding sentence is taken, has developed with his characteristic lucidity the exact nature of "Natural Laws" and "Natural Rights," in the sense we are now treating them, and the consequences that flow therefrom. Thus, it is the natural right of the tiger, as based upon the characteristics of its own being, to seek its prey, and this without distinction as to whether that prey consists of animal or human meat. "If, therefore, we deny that tigers have the right to torment and devour man, we really impeach, not the conduct of tigers, but the order of nature." "The natural right deduced from such a law of nature is simply a way of stating the fact; and there is in the nature of things, no reason why a being possessing such and such tendencies to action should not carry them into effect. . . . The ceaseless and pitiless 'struggle for existence' which obtains throughout the whole world of living beings is, in truth, the inevitable consequence of the circumstance that each living being strives knowingly, or ignorantly, to exert all its powers for the satisfaction of its needs; and asserts a tacit claim to possess (to the exclusion of all other beings) all the space on the earth's surface which it can occupy and to appropriate all the subsistence which it can utilize. The state of sentient nature, at any given time, is the resultant of the momentarily balanced oppositions of millions upon millions of individuals, each doing its best to get all it can and to keep what it gets; each, in short, zealously obeying the law of nature and fighting tooth and nail for its natural rights. This is the *ne plus ultra* of individualism; and whenever individualism has unchecked sway, a polity can no more exist than it can among the tigers who inhabit the jungle. It is, in fact, the sum of all possible anti-social and anarchistic tendencies." [1]

Long before, however, Mr. Huxley so clearly developed this subject, Spinoza had laid bare its essential character, and followed it out to its extreme and logical consequences: "By the right and ordinance of nature," says he, "I merely mean those natural laws wherewith we conceive every individual to be conditioned by nature, so as to live and act in a given way. For instance, fishes are naturally conditioned for swimming, the greater for devouring the less, therefore fishes enjoy the water, and the greater devour the less *by sovereign natural right. For it is certain that nature taken in the abstract has sovereign right to do anything she can; in other words, her right is coextensive with her powers.*" [2] Furthermore, he says: "We do not here acknowledge any difference between mankind and other individual natural entities, nor between men endowed with reason, and those to whom reason is unknown, nor between fools, madmen, and sane men. Whatsoever an individual does by the laws of its nature it has a sovereign right to do, inasmuch as it acts as it was conditioned by nature, and cannot act otherwise." [3]

[1] Huxley, "Natural and Political Rights," *Essays*, I. pp. 349–351.
[2] *Tractatus-theologico-politicus* (Bohn's trans.), Chap. XVI. p. 200.
[3] *Idem*, p. 201.

III. The third meaning ascribed to the term "Laws of Nature," with which we need to concern ourselves, is that of hypothetical commands, guiding human conduct, which commands are supposed to derive their validity from divine intention, or from universal nature itself. Hence, as independent of human enactment, laws thus conceived are necessarily of absolute and universal validity, binding at all times, in all places, and over all peoples. The belief in the existence of these laws is not necessarily bound up in the acceptance of the view that there once existed a "State of Nature," in which perfect state these laws supplied the entire regulative force, but in history it has been largely identified with such a view.[1]

It is especially in this third sense that we meet with the theory of Natural Law in juridical and political speculation. Before, however, proceeding to a critical consideration of the logical principles involved in the acceptance of these metaphysical, divine, or natural rules of human conduct, it will pay us to consider shortly the history of the manner in which this element has entered into the systems of political writers.

History of the Theory of the Law of Nature.[2] — As already known, divine law, pure and simple,

---

[1] See article by Professor Taylor, on "Law of Nature," in the *Annals of the Am. Acad. Pol. and Soc. Sci.*, April, 1891.

[2] In beginning this division of our subject, it is proper that special mention should be made of the extremely able and lucid treatment of this subject by Mr. John W. Salmond (*Law Quarterly Re-*

swallowed up, in the beginning, all ideas of law. Though necessarily uttered and enforced by human agents, a supermundane sanction was conceived to attach to all rules to which the obedience of the people was demanded. This was the condition that existed in all the Oriental countries, and during the Heroic period of Grecian history.

It is first in the time of the Sophists, representing, as Janet says, the period of enlightenment (*aufklärung*) of Greece, that we find the question raised whether there be fixed canons of right and wrong that are settled for all time by God, or Nature, or only provisions changeable at the caprice of men. The Sophists, however, did not recognize the distinction between the *idea* of legal right and wrong, and the *forms* in which it may be embodied; and because they saw those forms differing among different peoples and at different times, they rejected the whole *idea* of right and the good. Thus "they maintained that every nation, every epoch, as well as every individual, from motives of caprice or interest, might prescribe to itself or himself what it or he should consider lawful or unlawful, and might act accordingly. In this manner subjectivity finally passed all bounds."[1]

view, April, 1895, article "Law of Nature") as well as of the recent work of Professor Ritchie, entitled *Natural Rights*. From these two sources has been derived much of the historical matter contained in the next following paragraphs. Other valuable sources are Gierke, *Johannes Althusius u. die Entwicklung der naturrechtlichen Staatstheorien;* Lasson, *Rechtsphilosophie;* and of course Maine, *Ancient Law,* Chap. III.

[1] Janet, in Lalor's *Ency. Pol. Sci.*, article "Philosophy of Law."

At the hand of the Cynics, the appeal to the State of Nature took the form of a protest against human conventionalities and so-called artificialities of life, as opposed to simple primitive conditions. This principle they applied not only in their philosophic thought, but in their practice of life. In the conduct of Diogenes, who disowns the State, becomes a "citizen of the world," lives in a tub, and discards all superfluous clothing, we see the practical results obtained. In many respects, Rousseau's conception of "naturalness" corresponds to this Cynic view, and as we shall also see, Mr. Herbert Spencer does not escape from the same error.[1]

Coming now to Plato, we find the pre-existence of eternal ideas again upheld. In fact, the chief object of his Republic is the demonstration of a natural justice apart from human origination, and of which human justice is but an imperfect image. The idea, however, of a natural *law* declaring and rendering practically valid this natural justice, is not made prominent. In the writings of Aristotle we find a correction of the Cynic view that had characterized the civilized, conventional life of man, as unnatural, and as morally inferior to simpler and cruder forms. A natural law as well as a natural justice is spoken of, but so far as this law is made to apply to human conduct, it is practically identified with divine, original, unwritten law.

---

[1] A very entertaining revival of this doctrine is likewise to be found in Mr. Edward Carpenter's essay, *Civilization: Its Cause and Cure*.

In the systems of the Stoics we at last find a well-defined philosophical meaning given to the term "Nature," according to which it appears as the "manifestation of the single and homogeneous spirit of the world, whose several phenomena are connected together through the common law of right reason. The Law of Nature is therefore that common, universal, divine, and good rule of reason which governs creatures combined in a natural association, regarding it as a reflection of the process of nature, in instinct as well as in the human understanding: it is the harmony of human justice with the law of the world, which results from the identity of moral and of material nature, independently of any positive institution." [1]

By this postulation of human reason as the revealer of the laws of nature, and as thus the judge of right conduct, the Stoics avoided the absurdities of the Cynic maxims and made their application to ordinary life conformable to the practical and reasonable conditions by which man is surrounded. Thus "Nature to the Stoics is not the mere chaos of sensible things *minus* whatever results from man's rational efforts. It is objective reason; it is, as with Aristotle, the divine element in the Universe, the reason of the individual man is only a partial manifestation of it; his reason is a divine element in him, and it is in virtue of this divine element in him that man can understand the reason that is in the Universe and can live the life according to

[1] Pulszky, *Theory of Law and Civil Society*, p. 79.

nature. Thus, reason is not something that separates the judgment of one man from that of another. The appeal to reason is an appeal to the common reason of mankind. Human laws and institutions, therefore, are no longer despised as merely conventional. They are a realization, however imperfect, of the Law of Nature which is behind and above them."[1]

It was in the Stoic form that the idea of "Law of Nature" was introduced into Roman Law. It will not be necessary to trace the manner in which Rome was obliged to recognize laws not emanating primarily from her own will in the administration of justice between members of her Latin provinces who were not entitled to the benefit of his own peculiar *jus civile;* how from those laws, found to be common to all the Latin tribes, a body of *jus gentium* was formed; how, subsequently, under the Stoic influence, the Roman jurists began gradually to see in these laws, so uniformly accepted by independent tribes, the lost "code of nature"; nor, finally, how this conception once accepted, the Roman Law avoided all danger of arrest of development by her code, and became furnished with an ideal, in the effort for the attainment of which, unlimited possibilities of development were contained.[2]

[1] Ritchie, *Natural Rights*, p. 34.
[2] See the account of Maine in his *Ancient Law*, Chaps. III. and IV. Maine also calls especial attention to the service of the *jus naturale* in France as supplying general principles through which the diverse elements of her law were partially harmonized and unified.

With the spread of Christianity it was but natural that the views of law and civil society should be somewhat changed.

The influence of the *jus naturale* upon the *jus civile* of Rome, it is to be noticed, was not so much in the supplying of specific principles of adjudication, as in the harmonizing, simplifying, and, above all, the *equalizing* influence that it exerted. The Romans did not distinctly affirm the historical reality of a "State of Nature" in which Natural Law held full sway. For them, *jus naturale* was founded on empiric law (*jus gentium*), and as such was not actually superior to their own *jus civile*. That is, the Natural Law was not held by them, as at any time actually valid until accepted and adopted by Rome as her own, whereby, in fact, it thus became a part of the *jus civile* proper. In other words, this hypothetical Natural Law was received as an ideal towards which the civil law should tend; not as a code which had actual, present inherent validity. Its actual applicability depended upon the peculiar conditions of a civil society, and, until these were favorable, the civil law prevailed.

But with the Christian conception of the world, the State of Nature was received as the original state of sinlessness and grace, from which man had fallen by Adam's sin. It was thus only the corruptness of this world that made the political power and the civil law a necessary evil. This is especially the conception developed by St. Augustine in his *Civitas*

Dei. Natural law now becomes divine law (*lex æterna*) and is held by the Church to be actually applicable, so that disobedience to it on the part of the temporal powers may be punished by deposition, or justify regicide.

As might be expected, the doctrine of Natural Law did not escape further analysis in the keen dialectics of the Schoolmen. In their hands, the Natural Law in general, or *lex æterna*, becomes distinguished from that particular part of it which applies to man alone (*lex naturalis*). According to this, the *lex æterna* has its source in divine reason, and the *lex naturalis* immediately in man's reason. Thus the *lex naturalis* governs man's actions only. Though revealed by his reason, it is not, however, commanded by such reason, but by the divine reason, of which man's reason is only a partial manifestation. Thus the *lex æterna* says to beasts and all non-reasoning beings, you *must;* while to man, because of his reasoning faculties and his moral nature, you *ought*. It is of course apparent that this distinction is very nearly identical with that between the second and third conceptions that we have stated at the beginning of this chapter.

The reign of Scholasticism may be roughly said to have lasted from the eleventh to the sixteenth century, its greatest influence being in the thirteenth century. During these years the distinctions that we have given dominated European thought.

With Grotius and Hobbes, however, began a new period, characterized by the severance of natural and divine laws; that is, a return to the principle of nature as *natura naturans*, as itself legislative, as it were, and providing rules for human conduct binding upon man by his very own nature. As such, the obligatory character of these rules was made independent of a belief or disbelief in a deity to which this nature might be ultimately referable. The reasonableness of these laws, as founded upon considerations of utility, rather than their ascription to a divine source, served to give validity to them. In practical politics, the writings of the Florentine, Machiavelli, had, before this, served to free the temporal princes from the obligatory force of divine law even upon the conscience, and the bald utilitarian principle of *salus populi*, boldly maintained as justifying every act of whatever character.

We have already traced the history of the Contract Theory, and in connection therewith seen the part played by Natural Law as affording a basis thereto. When, however, we come to consider the history of the theories of Constitutional Government and Popular Sovereignty, we shall find that long after the Contract Theory had been generally discredited and discarded, the theory of Natural Law maintained its influence in the form of so-called "natural," "inalienable," "imprescriptible" rights of man. In fact, in this guise, it is still widely held at the present day.

The influence of the doctrine of Natural Law upon the development of International Law, through the work of Grotius and his school, was immediate and all-important. By a mistranslation, the *jus gentium* of the Romans was made to mean the law *between* nations. By thus ascribing to it a source in Nature itself, a fictitious validity was given to it, which went far towards securing its recognition at the hands of sovereign rulers. States were viewed as independent individuals, as without a common superior for the enunciation of mutually binding rules of intercourse, and hence, as in a "State of Nature" towards each other — a State of Nature governed, however, as said, by Natural Law. Thus Vattell distinguishes between "the *necessary* law of nations, which consists in the application of the law of nature to nations" (being *necessary* "because nations are absolutely bound to observe it"); and the *positive* or *arbitrary* law of nations, which he again divides into *Voluntary*, *Conventional*, and *Customary*.[1] What Vattell calls the "necessary" law of nations, Grotius terms the "internal law of nations" because obligatory in point of conscience. He also terms it the "natural law of nations."

Criticism of the Theory of Natural Law. — In the first place, the idea of the civilized life of man being in any sense non-natural or unnatural, — a position taken, as we have seen, by the Cynics, substantially by Rousseau, and revived by Spencer and Carpenter, — is false. Man is himself a part of Nature, and his actions, whatever they may be, are

[1] The title of Vattell's work is *The Law of Nations, or Principles of the Law of Nature Applied to the Conduct and Affairs of Nations and Subjects*. The quotations are taken from the Preface, p. lvii, of the 4th Am. ed. 1835.

necessarily "natural." In fact, to state that a thing *is*, is equivalent to stating that it is *natural*, for everything that exists is a part of *natura naturata*, and everything that happens is a part of the decree of nature as *natura naturans*. When we come to consider the "Aims of the State," we shall see what bearing this alleged distinction between the "natural" and "unnatural," or conventional life of man, has upon that problem.

Secondly, the idea of Natural Law as supplying definite, absolute rules of conduct is impossible. Though conceived as absolute, its rules are necessarily relative, that is, dependent upon the particular interpretation of Nature's will obtained through man's reason. What this interpretation will be, obviously depends upon the given *data* from which men reason; and these, in turn, are only supplied by objective conditions of social, economic, and political life. Hence Natural Law, so far as it is viewed as *lex naturalis* rather than *lex æterna* generally (which is the only sense in which it is pertinent to our inquiry), is by necessity practically identical with the "law of reason," even if it be not so philosophically conceived. Thus in fact, with Kant, who, as we have seen, accepts the Contract Theory as the only foundation upon which to base a just criterion of law, the Law of Nature becomes practically identical with the categorical imperative of practical reason. As Mr. Salmond points out, there is, however, this essential difference between the view of Kant and the position of Aquinas and the Schoolmen generally.

When Aquinas speaks of the dictates of practical reason, he means principally the reason of God, not of man; *i.e.* he holds that man's reason is not in itself possessed of legislative, commanding authority. Kant, however, proclaims the autonomy of human reason as itself possessing a law-giving faculty, and declares its commands to constitute the Moral Law. "This law," says he, "is the single isolated fact of the practical reason, announcing itself as originally legislative. *Sic volo, sic jubeo.* Reason is spontaneously practical and gives that universal law which is called Moral Law." We thus see the *a priori* element in law carried to its extreme extent. The ascription to reason of the capacity for something more than mere generalization, comparison, and judging of the *data* furnished it from outside, and the giving to it of the capacity to evolve not only form but subject-matter, necessarily renders the law to that extent independent of actual experience and historic relativity.[1]

Thirdly, though Natural Laws are conceived as commands either of the Deity or of Nature herself (*natura naturans*), there exists no means of actual coercion in case of disobedience. Hence their actual binding force can only be upon the conscience. That is, Natural Laws, from their inherent nature, must necessarily be moral laws, and moral laws only. They may serve to represent what *should be*, but not what *is*. When they obtain actual acceptance and enforcement at the hands of

[1] Cf. Pulszky, *Theory of Law and Civil Society*, pp. 75 *et seq.*

a political power, they become *ipso facto* civil or positive laws. But of this more anon.

It is its character as *ideal*, rather than *actual*, that has caused Natural Law to be appealed to by those desiring a change from what is, and it has thus made it ever the instrument of reform. It is its character as being revealed only in the reason, and not in the explicit command of a human authority, that has given to it its influence against all customs and institutions that have lost their sacredness or outlived their usefulness. Thus, as Ritchie well points out, the appeal to Natural Law is an appeal from established authority and judgment to the individual conscience as such, — the demand for a justification that is based upon grounds, utilitarian and moral, that will satisfy the practical reason of the individual making the demand.[1]

Fourthly: Having now reduced so-called Natural Law to its proper ideal, relative, moral character, we have finally to show, that, even in this sense, the term is not applicable to any form of regulation that can conceivably exist in such a completely non-political "State of Nature" as is necessarily postulated by Contract writers as the condition from which the establishment of political life relieved mankind. That is to say, we have to demonstrate that, when in a "State of Nature" men are said to be ruled by "Laws of Nature," these laws cannot be held to be even of a moral validity. That, therefore, when, as Hobbes says, the original

[1] Cf. Ritchie, *Natural Rights*, pp. 6 *et seq.*

contract is held to rest upon that Law of Nature, "that men perform their covenants made,"[1] an assumption is made that cannot be logically justified.

That this is so, we may see by picturing again to ourselves just what would be the condition of mankind in a completely non-political State. In such a "State of Nature," there is, if not *ex hypothesi*, logically, at least, an utter and entire absence of human association and concert of action, the only rules for the regulation of conduct that can possibly obtain being Natural Laws as used in the second sense which we have given them above: — namely, that which identifies them with the natural instincts of all living beings, men and brutes alike, to maintain their own existences, and to satisfy the desires that their own natures give rise to. Under such a regime, passion and momentary inclination necessarily have full sway, and, as we have seen, an unmitigated and pitiless struggle for existence must prevail.

It need not be said, then, that under such conditions there could not arise in the minds of individuals any recognition of "rights" on the part of other individuals which should be respected by them independently of their power to maintain them. Thus defining "right" as a man's capacity of influencing the acts of another by means other than his own strength, we may agree with Green that "natural right as right in a State of Nature which is not a state of society, is a contradiction. There can be no right without a consciousness of common interest on

[1] *Leviathan*, Chap. XV.

the part of members of a society. Without this there might be certain *powers* on the part of individuals, but no recognition of these powers by others as powers of which they should allow the exercise, nor any claim to such recognition; and without this recognition or claim to recognition there can be no right."[1] Thus Green criticises Spinoza, who fully accepts the above view, for retaining, nevertheless, the term "*jus naturale.*" "As it is," says Green, "the term '*jus naturale*' is with him really unmeaning. If it means no more than *potentia*, why call it *jus?* Jus might have a meaning distinct from that of *potentia* in the sense of a power which a certain *imperium* enables one man to exercise as against another. This is what Spinoza understands by *jus civile.* But there is no need to qualify it as *civile*, unless *jus* may be employed with some other qualification and with a distinctive meaning. But the *jus naturale*, as he understands it, has no meaning other than that of *potentia*, and his theory as it stands would have been clearly expressed if, instead of *jus naturale* and *jus civile*, he had spoken of *potentia* and *jus*, explaining that the latter was a power on the part of one man against others, maintained by means of an *imperium* which itself results from a combination of powers."[2]

---

[1] "Lectures on the Principles of Political Obligation," *Phil. Works*, Vol. II. p. 354.

[2] *Op. cit.* II. p. 361. Thus the definition of a "legal right" is "a capacity residing in one man of controlling with the assent and assistance of the State the actions of others" (Holland, *Elements of Jurisprudence*, 6th ed., p. 72).

In the absence, then, of "rights," as distinct from "powers," the term "morality" can have no application to a State of Nature as above considered. For morality, in at least its social aspect, has no other basis than the recognition and respect of others' rights. The same is true of the term "justice," by which is meant the giving to each one his proper "rights." Hence follows the truth of the thesis stated above, that in such a non-civic state there could not arise even the sense of a moral obligation to observe covenants entered into.

Thus the entire difficulty in answering the question with which we have been so long dealing, is the false manner in which the problem has been stated. "Given," it has been said, "individuals endowed by nature with a right to freedom of action, how can the compulsion that the State exercises be justified?" But, as we have seen, the individual is not endowed with a natural right to freedom. Nature gives to him only powers, and in any non-political state, the amount of compulsion that he would suffer at the hands of others would far exceed that exercised by any government. By the creation of a political authority, there is merely a substitution of a general, definite, paramount force, for an uncertain, arbitrary, individual force. With the social life of men, antagonism between their respective interests and spheres of activity is an absolute necessity. Complete freedom of every one to do as he likes is, therefore, out of the question. The only question is, whether these conflicts shall be settled by the particular strength given by Nature to each individual, or whether the compulsion shall be supplied by a general authority created by a union of strengths. Thus the only rational meaning that the word "freedom" has in reference to the individual, apart from freedom of the will, or of conscience, is in respect to a certain sphere of activity within which the individual claims the "right" to act as he pleases, undisturbed by others. As already said, however, neither the recognition nor claim to recognition of such a "right" can exist in a simple State of Nature. It is, therefore, only in a civil state that such a "right" can be secured. In fact, the mere propounding of the question, "Why should I be forced to do this or that?" implies that I claim a certain freedom that should be respected by others independently of my power to maintain it.

By what might at first seem a paradox, it thus appears that *freedom* exists only because there is restraint. That is, civil freedom has necessarily a positive and a negative sense:— positive, as regards freedom to perform certain acts unhindered by others; negative, as regards the necessity laid upon the individual to refrain from interference with the like freedom of others. Freedom and restraint are thus but obverse sides of the same shield. The fallacy of that school of anarchists who seek to abolish coercion by the substitution of so-called voluntary co-operation for political authority, we shall examine in another place.[1]

[1] *Vide post*, Chap. XII.

In conclusion, then, of this entire subject, we find that the demand for a moral justification of the State is an unnecessary one. If the political government does not render the individual any less free than he would be without it, its authority does not require a moral justification. There is no presumption of unwarranted interference to be rebutted. (In fact, the real reason why the demand for a moral basis for the State has been so persistently urged, is because of the confusion that has existed between State and Government, — between the political power itself, and the particular agents in whose hands its exercise happens to be vested.) So long as this confusion existed, it was but natural that people, in demanding a *quo warranto* for irresponsible monarchs, should have largely identified this with the demand for the right of the State itself to be.

(The positive basis, then, upon which the State rests, is its utility.) It will be remembered that we have before this apparently repudiated the utilitarian doctrine, but this was only when it was urged as a justification for coercion over individuals endowed with a natural right to freedom; that is, where the presumption was against the right of political authority. We there held that if the individual *did* have a natural or moral "right" to freedom, no doctrine of utility could justify the imposition of the coercive power of the State upon an individual who, so far as he himself was concerned, denied its usefulness. But, as it is needless to again repeat, in the new and correct light in which we are to view the character of political control, such reasoning does not apply.

The State is thus justified by its manifest potency as an agent for the progress of mankind. The only way in which the moral element enters, is as to the manner in, and extent to, which the power of the State shall be exercised. The "code of morality" of a given community, as including those rules of human conduct that satisfy the general sense of moral right and justice of that community, whether founded on eternal immutable principles of right and wrong, upon the dictates of man's conscience as completely autonomous, upon reason, or upon utility as revealed by inherited experience, is necessarily relative to the state of enlightenment, character of religion, economic conditions, and civilization in general of the particular people by whom its provisions are recognized. Taking any code of morality at any one time, the laws of a State are, in this light, morally justified just to the extent to which they coincide with its provisions. But even in this respect, it is to be noticed that in approximating law to ethical commands, reference must be had not only to the abstract ethical end to be obtained, but to the practical possibility of attaining that end by the physical compulsion supplied by the law, and the very rough means at its disposal for evaluating moral merit or guilt. Also, the still further question is to be considered, whether or not the substitution of legal compulsion for voluntary action, while possibly securing more general conformity to the principle indicated, may not lessen man's feeling of moral obligation in the premises. For where men obey from necessity, the ethical duty is easily forgotten.

Thus we find lying outside of the law's proper province two classes of actions. *First*, those that do not admit of legal enforcement, *i.e.* of external compulsion; and, *secondly*, those that, while possible of legal enforcement, are better left to the individual conscience because of the reasons above indicated.[1]

[1] There is no one thing that renders the study of Continental jurisprudence so difficult to the English and American student as the extent to which moral and legal principles are there confused. It will be certainly, therefore, not out of place to call attention here to the manner in which this confusion is created by and reflected in the terminology employed. This point is clearly elucidated in the article of Mr. Salmond, to which I have already referred, and from that source the substance of this note is taken. Upon the Continent, ethics is divided into two parts, the one dealing with actions which may or can be enforced by external compulsion, forming the subject-matter of *Jurisprudence* or *Rechtslehre*, or the science of *Droit* or *Recht*; the other dealing with those actions that cannot be so compelled, but must be left to the individual conscience, forming the subject-matter of *Morale* or *Tugendlehre* or *Ethik* in a narrower sense, or the science of *Moralité* or *Tugend*. It will be thus seen that in France and Germany *Droit* and *Recht* have both an ethical and legal application. That is, *Droit* and *Recht* are applied not only to actions that actually are enforced by the State, and which the English and American jurist designates as positive law, or law proper, but to all actions capable of such enforcement whether or not they are as a fact so enforced. In like manner *Morale* and *Tugendlehre* are not made applicable to all portions of right conduct, but simply and solely to those actions that do not admit of external compulsion. This distinction between the English and Continental nomenclatures may be diagrammatically represented as follows:—

Let the quadrangle $ABDC$ represent the entire field of conduct; $GBDH$ that portion not enforceable by law; $AGHC$ that portion capable of legal enforcement; and $FEHC$ that portion actually so

As for the propriety of the expression "Natural Law," which figures in the title of this chapter, it would appear that, excluded from applicability in a "State of Nature," except as meaning mere animal instinct, the only sense in which its use can possibly be justified, is as indicating a moral ideal towards which the civil law should tend. But thus driven from one position after another, even here in its last stand, the relativity of its provisions would seem to destroy any definiteness or claim to absolute moral authority. The trail of its *a priori* character is over it all. Professor Taylor, who is the most recent champion of Natural Law, attempts to explain its relativity as apparent rather than real by the logom-

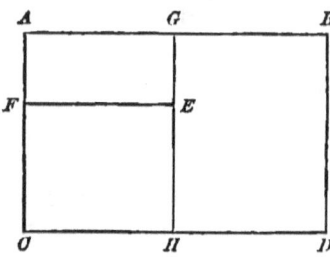

enforced. *AGEF* will then, of course, represent that portion of human conduct capable of legal enforcement, but not as a matter of fact so enforced. Then, according to Continental usage, *GBDH* would constitute the field of *Moralité* or *Tugend*, or the science of *Morale* or *Tugendlehre*; *AGHC* would be the field of *Droit* or *Recht* (*Jurisprudence* or *Rechtslehre*), thus including *AGEF* as well as *FEHC*. According to English usage, on the other hand, the whole field *ABDC* constitutes the field of "Rights" in its unqualified or moral sense, and the science of ethics is correspondingly inclusive. But between that portion of human conduct possible of legal control, and as thus potentially law, and that part of such portion of human conduct as actually is thus enforced, a distinct line is drawn, and the terms "law," "legal rights," and "jurisprudence" definitely limited to this field. Thus is obtained a preciseness of connotation to the terms "law" and "morals," "legal right" and "moral right," that Continental publicists have never been able to secure. It may perhaps be just to Mr. Salmond to say that he is not responsible for the diagrammatic illustration given above.

achy that "if the nature of men and circumstances change, we are wont to say that the law changes. But to speak exactly, we should say that a different law applies; but a law like its predecessor, eternal and unchangeable, because determined by the new nature of men and circumstances."[1] Without stopping to ask what he means by the "new nature" of men and circumstances, it thus appears, according to Professor Taylor, that there *is* an eternal, unchangeable law of nature that should govern men's conduct, but the determination as to which of its provisions shall apply depends upon the given conditions. In different conditions, different laws apply. Surely this is reducing the eternal immutable character of the alleged Natural Law to little but a name.

To the writer's mind, the continuance of the use of the term in political or legal science is improper in any sense, and, if retained, sure to introduce confusion of thought. The only possible value that it can have in any field of thought is in ethics proper, where it may sometimes be used by those who wish to emphasize an alleged pantheistic origin of moral precepts.

In the foregoing criticism of the Contract Theory nothing has been said either as to its legal or historical invalidity. So far as it is necessary to make any argument upon these grounds, it may be done in

---

[1] "The Law of Nature," in the *Annals of the Am. Acad. Pol. and Soc. Sci.*, April, 1891.

very few words. That such a contract could have no legal force, is obvious, for *ex hypothesi* there is no antecedent political power or civil law to determine contractual rights. And the contract not being itself legally binding, could not, of course, serve as a foundation for subsequent legal rights and obligations. But, as this chapter has shown, such a criticism goes but little way towards invalidating the essential position assumed by the Contract Theory writers. They rely not so much on the legality as the moral force of the alleged contract, their object being the moral justification of the right of the State to be. As a matter of fact, as we have seen, it was Hobbes himself who first emphasized the distinction between moral and legal rules, and prepared the way for the present accepted definition of positive law.

From the historical standpoint, the Contract Theory of the origin of political authority is untenable, and confessedly so by some of its adherents. Not only are historical records wanting as to those early times when, if at all, such compacts must have been entered into; but what historical evidence there is, from which, by analogy and inference, primitive conditions may be imagined, are such as to show its impossibility. The theory presupposes individuals as contracting, when the researches of Maine and others show that in early times law was applicable not so much to the individual as to the family, and that, in fact, in these early times the individual as such counted for almost nothing, either in the eyes of the law or of the political authority. There was thus, at that time, no idea of individuals, as such, having either the right or power of severally entering into a covenant or covenants. As Maine says, "Whether they (*i.e.* early laws) retain their primitive character as Themistes or whether they advance to the condition of customs or codified texts, they are binding, not on individuals but on families. . . . The movement of progressive societies has been uniform in one respect. Through all its course it has been distinguished by the gradual dissolution of family dependency and the growth of individual obligation in its place. The individual has been steadily substituted for the family as the unit of which civil laws take account."[1] Or, as he sums up this law in a single sentence, "The movement has been from one of *status* to one of *contract*." Researches also show that the further we go back in civilization, the more does communal property tend to swallow up private property; while the Contract Theory speaks of men submitting their property and other rights to the State for its protection. If, now, these are the conditions that prevailed at the time at which history first catches glimpse of man, analogy and inference would show that in the primitive period anterior to this, at which the contract is conceived to have been entered into, the conditions would be still less favorable to the execution of such an agreement. In addition to this, there is of course a manifest absurdity in conceiving a sufficient mental qualification, for such a

[1] *Ancient Law*, pp. 161, 163.

formal act on the part of a people in the very first stages of civilization.

It is, however, a waste of words and a misapplication of energy to demonstrate the unhistorical character of this theory. As has been already said, that which is sought by the propounders of this explanation of the origin of the State, is not so much the manner in which the State actually did originate, as the determination of such a theoretical foundation for the establishment of political life as will permit such political authority to be harmonized with a predicated individual right to free self-determination of action.

CHAPTER VI

THE TRUE ORIGIN OF THE STATE

JUST as we have shown that it is, at the bottom, an idea or sentiment that creates a Nation out of an aggregate of men; that where without this sentimental element we have only a mechanical union, or complexus of atoms, with it, we have a higher, more intimate, permanent, psychological unity; so, in like manner, it is true that in the State, in the body politic, we have a unity created out of a mere sum of individuals by means of a sentiment of community of feeling and mutuality of interest, and this sentiment finds expression in the creation of a political power, and the subjection of the community to its authority. As the eminent Austrian publicist, Jellinek, has put it, "The inner ground of the origin of the State is the fact that an aggregate of persons has a conscious feeling of its unity, and gives expression to this unity by organizing itself as a collective personality, and constituting itself as a volitional and active subject."[1] That is to say, in effect, that this essential psychological element must first exist subjectively in the minds of the people, and then become objective in laws and political institutions. It thus follows that while this subjec-

[1] *Die Lehre von den Staatenverbindungen,* p. 257.

tive element of unity is the essential element of the State, it alone is not sufficient to constitute a State. The body politic cannot be said to be created until the desires that this feeling engenders have become outwardly realized by the erection of a common governing authority. Other conditions favoring, or at least not hindering, the objective realization will always follow the subjective inclination. But, except in rare cases, there is not this utter absence of hindrance. The political *status quo ante* has always to be considered. Existing political institutions and methods have the support of tradition, backed by the natural indisposition of men to change their habits and manner of life, especially when they cannot foresee with absolute precision the results that will follow from such a change. But, most of all, an existing political authority is always supported by an enormous weight of selfish interest. To the desire to rule, which is almost universal in the human breast, is added the pecuniary and social interests and honors that are bound up in an existing Government, thus making those in power reluctant to consent even to a change in administration, much less to the establishment of a new body politic.

It thus frequently happens that there exists in the minds of a community of people a desire for a political unity of a particular sort, and that this desire is of sufficient strength to maintain the unity of a State, were it once established and organized, but that objective conditions prevent for many years the realization of such an end. It is only when this pent-up flood of feeling rises to sufficient height and strength to burst the existing political barriers that hold it in, that a new State is created.

As has been said, the natural tendency of the feeling of Nationality is to find expression in political unity. The two sentiments, then, that lie at the basis of the Nation and of the State are largely similar. The same conditions that tend to create the feeling of Nationality tend also, in most cases, to demand the establishment of the State. Absolute identity of these two sentiments, however, cannot be affirmed. It is possible, in other words, to have present a well-developed feeling of Nationality, with but slight desire for political unity. On the other hand, we find instances in which the establishment of political unity is clearly demanded by a People, among whom there is no other claim of Nationality. The factors that create the feeling of Nationality are community of race, language, historical tradition, mutuality of economic interests, and like degree of civilization. That which calls for the establishment of political control over definite territory and community may be nothing more than political expediency, — the necessity for self-defence or offensive strength. Certainly the feelings of common Nationality were very strong at the time of the severance of the American colonies from their mother country, yet independent political organization was demanded and obtained. Strong feelings of Nationality were frequently displayed by the Greeks, especially when combating a common foe, yet at no time during the height of Grecian prosperity was political unity called for. At the present day we see three distinct Nationalities organized under the Swiss Government, with no demand for separate political autonomy.

To those who would say that a national feeling does not truly exist unless there be demanded political unity; that, in fact, the desire for such unity is a *necessary* consequence of the feeling of Nationality, it is to be replied, that to take such a view is to give a more intensive and exacting definition to the sentiment of Nationality than is usually ascribed to it. It is an obvious fact that we often have instances of political unions in which there is an absence of such elements as community of race, language, custom, and historical tradition. It is, therefore, impossible to identify the desire for political unity, even before it obtains realization, with the sentiment of Nationality, unless we assume the position that political expediency alone is able to create the feeling of Nationality. But to do this is not only to go counter to all accepted usage of terms, but in fact entirely to destroy the very idea of Nationality, which is supposed to rest upon other than political foundations.

Though intimately connected, it seems best, then, to distinguish from each other the feelings of National and Political unity. In fine, to recognize that though the desire for political unity does, as a rule, arise from and out of a sentiment of Nationality, yet it may arise independently of it.

Now, as has already been made evident, the only validity which could be ascribed to a social compact would have to be based upon a consciousness, on the part of the individuals consenting to it, of a moral duty to keep one's engagements to another; — in fact, upon the recognition of mutual rights and obligations. But given in a community this feeling of mutual rights and duties, and have we not already existing that feeling of unity, that sentiment that creates the State? If, then, such a compact were thus entered into, it would not be a creative act, but only a formal declaration of the sentiments of community of interests and feelings that have already existed.[1]

It therefore appears that the origin of the State must be conceived as an act of a People rather than of individuals. The existence of a common or "General Will" must be predicated, and the creation of the State held to be due to its volition.

Now a General Will is something much different from the sum of particular wills. Rousseau himself recognized this, though he did not see that it was logically destructive of his theory. Thus he says, "There is often a great difference between the will of one and the General Will: one regards the common

---

[1] "How can the consciousness of obligation arise," says Green, "without recognition by the individual of claims on the part of others — social claims of some sort or other — which may be opposed to his momentary inclinations? Given a society of men capable of such consciousness of obligation, constituting a law, according to which the members of this society are free and equal, in what does it differ from a political society?" Green, *Philosophical Works*, Vol. II. p. 377.

interest only, the other regards private interests, and is only the sum of individual wills."[1] Hence, by adding together a sum of private interests, we can never get a public interest, nor from a sum of private rights obtain a public right. The General Will, as distinguished from the sum of individual wills, is rather a volitional unit that is obtained by extracting from each of the individual wills certain sentiments and inclinations that concern general interests, and from a combination, equating, and balancing of them obtaining a single result that is based upon elements that exist in the individual wills, but is thus distinct from their sum. But even this is a more mechanical description of the General Will than its essentially unitary character properly permits.

Therefore when it is attempted to create or conceive of the creation of a General Will superior to the individual will by simply joining together these wills, the undertaking is foredoomed to failure. By simply uniting wills of a single class we cannot hope to create a will of a higher order. In the absence of such higher will, then, that very capacity of individuals which would enable them to enter into a social compact would empower them to withdraw from it at any time, or to refuse assent to commands based upon it. The same moral force that would urge men to a compact would urge them to break it when its continuance would threaten their welfare.[2]

[1] *The Social Contract*, Bk. II. Chap. III.

[2] Hobbes himself says: "Contracts being words and breath, have no force to oblige, contain, constrain, or protect any man, but what it (*sic*) has from the public sword."

The Contract Theory errs in conceiving the State as created by individuals rather than by a People. It is thus atomistic and entirely destructive of political authority, for as long as such authority is made to rest upon individual consent, just so long may such consent be withdrawn.

It is true that Hobbes correctly outlined the necessarily absolute character of the State from the legal standpoint, but it was a result that could not logically be based upon the Social Compact which he predicated. The result of both Locke's and Rousseau's system is, if carried out to the logical end, subversive of all true political authority; and for much the same reason. Locke's, because it admits a right on the part of the people to resist the enforcement of law in certain cases. Since, however, the determination of these cases is necessarily with the people, there can be no case in which they may not assert this right. All laws have, hence, only a hypothetical validity, *i.e.* a validity dependent upon their acceptance as just and expedient by the people whose actions they are intended to control. Rousseau's system is directly destructive of the State, because it openly refuses to governmental agencies any volitional power, and explicitly declares the validity of all legislative acts to be dependent upon an absolutely popular consent.

In a political society every human being may be regarded in a double aspect; as an independent individual endowed with freedom of self-determination of action; and as a citizen, or member of the body politic in which he lives. As a citizen, he can never be considered apart from the whole, of which he is an integral and inseparable part. Nor, consequently, can his will, as such, be separated from the General Will. It is in this second capacity that he is related to the State, and contributes by his will to the formation of its sovereign will. And it is upon him in this same capacity that the authority of the State is exercised. He is coerced by the law, not as a free autonomous person, but as a constituent element of the authority that coerces him. He is an integral and inseparable part of the political body, and his will cannot be separated from its will.

The existence of the State is *rationally* justified because the result of the exercise of its authority is in all cases, as a matter of fact, to preserve freedom rather than to destroy it, to enforce rights rather than to crush them, to check certain acts in order that more important and more numerous acts may be made freely possible. In a society of men, mutual interests are an absolute necessity. Freedom in society has, hence, both a positive and a negative side. Positive, or the right of free self-determination of action; negative, or the restraint from the interference with a like freedom of others. To protect positive freedom, the power of the State is exercised in restraining the actions of the individuals in so far as they would interfere with this positive liberty.

To repeat, then, what was made plain in the

last chapter, there is no *onus* upon the State to justify its existence as an infringement upon a predicated natural freedom *of the individual*. Such a freedom we have shown to be a myth and an impossibility. Liberty, as equivalent to a condition in which there exists a certain sphere of activity in which the individual is protected from outside interference by some power other than that based upon his own physical strength, is only possible in a political community. Hence, if there be a necessity to demonstrate the moral right of the State to be, apart from, and in addition to, the question whether it subserves the ends for which it was established, such a right of existence may be said to rest upon the consent of the People collectively expressed. That this is so, is obvious from the fact that should the entire community, or a dominant portion thereof, decisively determine, in any given case to abolish all civil control and to re-establish a regime of complete animality, it could do so.

As to the particular individual, therefore, civic subordination is one of necessity and force; for *nolens volens* he must submit to political power. As Hume says in one of his essays in answer to those who maintain that the individual can, when dissatisfied with his State, leave it for another; this right of emigration cannot mean anything to a poor peasant or artisan. "We may as well assert," says he, "that a man by remaining in a vessel, freely consents to the dominion of the master, although he was carried on board while asleep and must leap into the ocean and perish the moment he leaves her ... The original establishment (of Government) was formed by violence and submitted to from necessity. The subsequent administration is also supported by power and acquiesced in by the people not as a matter of choice but of obligation."[1]

[1] From the individual standpoint, the power of the State over the lives of its citizens is the highest power possessed by it, — right to life being obviously the necessary basis of all other rights. The exercise of such a power of itself refutes the idea that a moral justification of the right of the State to be can be founded upon individual consent, impliedly or explicitly given. For the sake of securing other rights, we cannot rationally conceive of an individual consenting to place within the will of another a control over that right which must necessarily be possessed in order to enjoy the benefit of all other rights. Even the absolute Hobbes excepted (though illogically) from the surrender of individual rights to the State the right of self-defence, which he held to be inalienable. Rousseau, in order to defend the right of the sovereign power to condemn the criminal to death, is forced to resort to the palpable quibble of maintaining that "it is for the sake of not being killed by an assassin that we consent to be killed if we become assassins" (*Social Contract*, Bk. II. Chap. V.), — an assertion as sensible as the one that he elsewhere makes, that one may be "compelled to be free."

Of course the necessity for such explanations of the control of the State over the life of the individual becomes unnecessary when, as we have seen, the political power is not founded upon the will of the individual, but upon that of the People as a unit. The right of the State to punish for crime, even to the extent of inflicting the death penalty, is the same as that by which any of its activities are exercised. Lawlessness is punished by the State, not for the sake of vengeance or retribution based upon a breach of contract of the individual with the community, but for the preservation of the State's own orderly existence. For this reason penal law is ordinarily designed to be not only punitive, but, as far as possible, reformatory and preventive in its effect. Were it designed to be purely retributive, it would be necessary to apportion punishment as nearly as possible to moral guilt alone. But, as we know, this aim is in very many cases avowedly subordinated to such other factors as, for example, the nature of the consequences directly resulting from the act, the

It has been said that an aggregate of men only becomes a "People" when politically organized. It might therefore be said, that a State cannot be considered as created by a People, for that would necessitate a pre-existence of this creating factor. Strictly speaking, this is true. The creation of a State and of a People are necessarily synchronous. It is, therefore, more precise to say that a State is created by a community of men, which, by reason of a sentiment of unity, is *potentially* a People, and that this community becomes *actually* such when the State is established.

It follows from what has been said, that this transformation of a community or of a society into a People, potentially or actually considered, cannot be due to any formal act on their part. Sentiments and desires are not thus formed. The necessity for the existence of the subjective condition prior to the objective creation of a political organization,

---

example that it will set to others, its bearing upon existing political conditions, etc. All of these elements, that have no bearing upon the moral guilt of the offender, often determine the severity of the punishment. In like manner, because of the impossibility of the State exercising a direct control over man's motives, the political power is not properly concerned with religious beliefs, nor with religious customs, except in so far as they lead to actions that affect the existence and prosperity of the State. Thus, in the much debated problem regarding the proper province of State and Church, we may say that the delimitation of their functions is not determined by the objects or actions over which their respective controls are exercised, but by the nature of the sanctions supplied to their commands, and the aims sought to be attained. The one is necessarily limited to the imposition of material physical sanctions, and the attainment of material physical aims; the other to the declaration of moral or ethical ideals, and the securing of spiritual ends.

makes impossible the assumption of a formal origin of the State. The logical result, therefore, is, that it is impossible to ascribe, even in modern times, a formal or juristic origin to the State. The adoption of a formal constitution cannot be considered as a creative act. The State is not, thereby, brought into existence, though from the historical standpoint it is for convenience properly so considered. The solemn adoption by a people of such a fundamental instrument is but the act through which that which has formerly existed in a more or less undefined and vague state, is brought into definite and positive statement.

It may be the fact, indeed, that the origin of the State (as, for example, the creation of a federal State, by the union of formerly independent States) is apparently synchronous with the adoption of the written constitution by which such union is effected. But it cannot be said that such federal State was created by such instrument. The creating cause was the feeling of national unity which found its formal and juristic expression in the articles of union. The constitution is the instrument that definitely creates and defines the organs through which the State, already subjectively in existence, is henceforth to exercise its activities. The essence of the State is the national feeling that unites its People, and its written constitution is but the formal expression of the fundamental principles according to which this People propose to conduct their political life. The truth of this is seen in the fact that a written constitution is by no means essential to State life, and is, indeed, of very recent invention. Its *raison d'être* is no deeper than a political expediency that is based upon the definiteness thus obtained, and the added stability acquired by the restrictions that these written instruments ordinarily impose upon hasty and constant amendment.

From the standpoint of Public Law, it may not be necessary to go back of a written constitution; but from the philosophical standpoint the more teleological view is demanded. Viewed in this latter aspect, the true constitution of the State may be said to date from the earliest beginnings of State life, when first the feeling of unity began to be felt by the people, and to have developed *pari passu* as the feelings of national life have grown and found expression in political organization and control.

The State not Artificial: not a Mechanism. — Leaving now this subject, which has already too long detained us, we turn to one or two collateral propositions that flow from it.

It is clearly apparent that the State is not to be considered as in any sense "artificial," or as a "mechanism." The political life of man is as "natural" to him as is an individualistic existence, and his emergence from the savage condition or so-called "State of Nature" into political life, is not to be termed a change from a natural life to an artificial one. The feelings that unite men into social and political units are as natural to them as are any of their individualistic impulses. Government, on the other hand, is mechanical. It is the artificial means consciously created for formulating and executing the will of the State. Its form is in all cases an arbitrary one, and liable to radical change by a single definite fiat of the State's will. Thus, the State, while not a conscious creation of the individuals composing it, nevertheless operates through devices mechanically and consciously created, and is influenced in its structure and in many of its activities by objective conditions.

A mechanism has been defined as "a functional totality, the construction, regulation, and energizing of which is from without."[1] Such is Government; for the General Will which actuates it is not created by, but sustains, it. There is no innate life either in its parts or in the whole. The State, on the other hand, as we have seen, has a will of its own; its actions are self-determined. There is life and volition both in itself and in its members. A common, conscious, animating purpose pervades and vivifies it. It is moreover in a continual state of change and growth. Its organized form is in process of constant modification. At no two periods of its history is the manifestation of its life the same.

By the above it is of course not intended to return to the instinctive or purely natural theory of the origin of the State, which we have criticised in an earlier portion of the work, and which would make

[1] F. M. Taylor, *The Right of the State to Be*, p. 30.

of the political power an entity independent of man. We readily grant that there are in man's nature certain appearances and characteristics that naturally lead (that is, reasonably may be expected to lead) to the development of a political life. In fact, the point that we are here making is, that so natural is the development of this political sentiment, that it is not until the State's rise into actual being that the process becomes a conscious one to the individuals embraced within it. The State is born when the common consciousness of a community reaches a certain degree of preciseness; but since the fact of this point having been reached is only recognizable by the outward manifestations to which it leads, and which are necessarily subsequent to it, it is no more possible for a community to fix the instant of its creation as a body politic than it is for the individual to determine by memory the moment at which he became conscious of his own identity and personality.

For these reasons we speak of the State as natural, though not independent of man's agency. For man, as himself a part of Nature, supplies the forces that generate and maintain the State. The necessary governmental organs must be created through conscious, human agency. Furthermore, once generated, the continued existence of the State is almost wholly dependent upon man's own efforts and determination. It is this fact — the perception by men that the continuance of political rule is dependent upon their own will, and that it would be a physical possibility upon their part to destroy and live without it — that leads them to demand a justification for it, if it be allowed to remain.

In describing, then, the State as natural, and not artificial, we emphasize the largely unconscious manner of its growth and its dependence upon certain essential human attributes; and, at the same time differentiate it from Government, which is purely mechanical. We also anticipate an argument that we shall hereafter make against that school of thinkers who see in the persistence of political power a necessary evil, and view its regulation as an interference with what they are pleased to term the "natural" laws of human life and development.

The Personality of the State. — The organic theory of the State is to be distinguished from that theory which predicates personality of the State. Though refusing to the State an organic character, it may properly be described as a juristic person; and, indeed, the idea of its personality is the cornerstone of the science of public law.

The State is a person because it has a will of its own, that is recognized in the national consciousness in a manner very similar to that by which the feelings of an individual organism are recognized by the animal consciousness. Thus, the law-making organs of government are the instruments through which this will is expressed.

Psychology shows us that the will of a conscious being is in all cases the result of the action and inter-action of numerous forces, — of physical and psychical tendencies, of objective influences, of habits,

— and that the simplest acts of volition are thus found to be, when analyzed, of a most complicated nature. So it is with the will of the State; resulting, as it does, from the operation of innumerable forces, from motives selfish and unselfish, moral and unmoral, from material conditions, from tendencies, customs, inherited usages, racial characteristics, and intellectual impulses.

Jellinek, in his valuable work entitled *Gesetz und Verordnung*, has treated this subject of the personality of the State as springing from its possession of a unified will and purpose, with such lucid and cogent reasoning, that in the two following paragraphs his words are almost literally translated.

Personality, he says, is no figurative attribute of the State, as is so often maintained. It exists in the same sense as that of any other person. A person, truly speaking, is no concrete being, but an abstraction; and personality is not identical with physical individuality. Personality signifies the capacity for unified, continuous, reasoning volition. There are two kinds of unity, a physical and an ideal one of purpose. Now it is unity of purpose which is the principal factor of individuation for all human things; and individuality, in all practical thinking, furnishes the teleological criterion for a division between persons. Without the application of this idea of purpose, there exists in any individual a complexus of molecules, but no person; for the mere mechanical conception gives us only atoms and unions of atoms.

A teleological unity can be recognized in a complexus of atoms when they are conceived as held together by a common aim, even where there does not exist a continuous physical connection between its parts. All things that we designate as individuals are, if considered from the purely materialistic standpoint, a collection of small units or atoms. The natural unit, the atom, has no perceptible existence. It is thus nothing more than the application of a common principle of thought, to ascribe unity to a plurality of men bound together by a common purpose.[1]

Applying these principles to a human community, we find that it is the unity of political purpose that gives to the State its attribute of personality, and that it is in this aspect as a person, that the State is distinguished from the individuals organized under it. To be sure, the State is always and necessarily composed of the citizens united under it, and without citizens there would be no State; but, as thus considered, the State is something more than the sum of its parts. It has an ideal existence apart from them, in exactly the same sense that the human individual is something more than a determinate amount of water, carbon, and a few other elements. This is really the point that was missed by those who have held to the possibility of a contract between individuals as the origin of the State; for by no union or surrender of purely private rights is it possible to create public rights;

---

[1] Jellinek, *Gesetz und Verordnung*, pp. 192 *et seq.*

nor from a combination of private persons to create a public person. The attributes of personality are not thus to be obtained. "From individuals as such," as Bluntschli says, "only an individual development can be obtained. Upon private individuals only private interests and relations can be grounded. A sum of individuals never is and never can be a unit, any more than can a heap of sand become a statue. If only the individual spirit and will existed and worked in the individual, the existence of the State as a collective body which lives and is determined by a common spirit and a unified collective will would be inconceivable." [1]

The legal personality of the State is especially evident in its Public Law as distinguished from Private Law. There the State appears as endowed with legal rights and duties analogous to those possessed by individuals. To be sure, as we shall see, all law is of the State, but not all law has relation directly to the State. So far as the rules of conduct that authoritatively obtain in a political community are devoted to the regulation of interests between individuals as such, they create only private rights and obligations, and the State appears only as their enunciator, and, if need be, their enforcer. Such law is therefore termed by publicists, Private Law. Distinguished from this class of rules are those that concern either the organization of the State and the delimitation of the powers of government, or the direct relations of the State and the

[1] *Geschichte der neueren Staatswissenschaft*, p. 348.

individual. These are termed Public Laws. In Private Laws, as Holland points out, "the parties concerned are private individuals, above and between whom stands the State as an impartial arbiter. In Public Law also the State is present as arbiter, although it is at the same time one of the parties interested."[1]

At the same time it is, of course, to be recognized that this attribute of personality, thus ascribed to the State, is a juristic conception, and is to be distinguished from the same term as ordinarily applied to man as a moral being. But in so far as a human being is recognized by the State as having "rights" that it will enforce and protect, his individual personality is of a character precisely similar to that enjoyed by the State. Thus the individual is a person in the juristic sense only because he has legal rights, and does not have legal rights because he is a person. This we made sufficiently plain in our criticism of the doctrine of Natural Rights. In this juristic sense there can be human beings who are not at the same time persons, as, for example, slaves. On the other hand, there may be legal personality apart from physical individuality; as, for example, corporations, or the State itself.

When, however, we come to apply the attribute of personality to man as a moral being; that is, to him considered as not only responsible for outward acts but for inward intentions and motives, we have, of course, a different conception. Man is

[1] *Elements of Jurisprudence*, 6th ed. p. 117.

then conceived as an independent individual, apart from the body politic, and as setting himself the standard to which his actions shall conform. His personality is then an ethical conception. Thus, while in the State we have simply a legal personality, we have in the human being a double personality; first, as an individual endowed with rights and obligations as regards his relations to other individuals and to the political community in which he lives; and, secondly, as an individual endowed with reason and volitional power, and recognizing a duty to strive disinterestedly to make his life conform to the highest moral and ethical ideals.

That which, moreover, further distinguishes the State as a juristic person from the human being as a person, is the fact that for the realization of its aims the State must depend upon the services of these human beings. That is to say, the State's personality is not embodied in a concrete physical frame of its own, as is man's. For the attainment of the will of this discreet person, it is therefore necessary that certain individuals shall serve as its mouthpieces and executive agents. When so officiating, these persons give expression and execution to no will of their own, but purely and simply to the will of the State. Therefore, governmental agents acting in conformity to law are but passive agents, mere organs. The instant that they exceed the legal competence of their powers, they no longer represent the State's will, nor are they its organs. They then appear but as private individuals, and, as such, are individually responsible for their acts.

Any public official from the lowest to the highest has, then, in addition to his moral personality, a twofold being; as a private individual with legal rights and obligations, and as an organ of the State. In the one he has a will of his own; in the other, he is but the medium through which the supreme political will is expressed or executed. Only in the case of the completely autocratic sovereign is this representative will so wide as to be in practical, if not actual, identity with his individual will. All constitutional law, therefore, in so far as it delimits the competence of governmental officials, fixes thereby the boundaries beyond which their actions are no longer to be considered as those of the State, but as actions of their own.

It is, thus, sufficiently accurate for present purposes to characterize the whole Government of a politically organized community, as the organ of political consciousness, and as the means through which the political will is expressed. The existence of defects in its organization, and the intermediation of selfish and corrupt influences, prevent, in all States, the formulation of a *general* will free from the admixture of *particular* elements; and hinder the exact performance of that will when formulated. Hence it is, that there is ever a disparity between the real political ideas of a community and the actual utterances of the State as contained in its law. The test of good Government is the facility it affords for the formulation of an enlightened and intelligent General Will, and the nearness with which its action harmonizes with such Will when so formulated. The advance of constitutional and popular Government means that this result is being achieved to an increasing extent. As Professor Ward says, "Government is becoming more and more the organ of social consciousness, and more and more the servant of the Social Will. Our Declaration of Independence, which recites that Government derives its just powers from the consent of the governed, has already been outgrown. It is no longer the consent, but the positively known will of the governed, from which Government now derives its powers." [1]

[1] *The Psychic Factors of Civilization*, p. 304.

CHAPTER VII

THE NATURE OF LAW

THE State has been defined as a society viewed from its organized side, that is, considered in its aspect as a political organization for the attainment of an orderly existence and a possible development. In the effectuation of these purposes its activities are largely manifested in the utterance and enforcement of commands addressed to its citizens. Such commands we designate laws, and in the aggregate they constitute what is known as "the law of the land."

It is recognized, however, that in any given community this body of legal principles is by no means a homogeneous whole, but composed of elements that vary not only as to their manner of statement, but especially as to their source.

First of all, there are those principles which are to be found embodied in the formal legislative acts of the State, and termed Statutes. *Secondly*, there is that large body of legal principles that are enforced by the judicial tribunals of a country, but whose origin it is impossible to discover in any formal declarations of the will of the State, and whose validity is commonly considered to rest upon custom. *Thirdly*, there is in every State that body of fundamental principles, written or unwritten, that controls the organization of the State itself and the scope and manner of exercise of its governmental powers. These principles are termed constitutional laws, and though not, as a rule, when written, enunciated through the ordinary legislative mouthpiece of the State, are considered as expressing the highest will of the State. They differ from statutory and customary law, not only as to their formal source, but also as to their prevailing power when in apparent contradiction to them. *Fourthly*, and finally, there is that aggregate of rules that control the relations of a State to other States, commonly known as International Law. These last differ from the three preceding classes of principles not only as to their source, but as to their manner of enforcement. It will be necessary, indeed, to consider whether they may be properly termed laws at all.

It is the purpose of this chapter to consider in a general way these various jural elements; to investigate their origin and legal validity, and thus, finally, to discover, so far as it is possible, the part played by the State in their creation. There are of course other questions of a theoretical importance that arise in connection with an analysis of the legal ideas of a community; as, for example, the distinctions between law and ordinance, between laws general and particular, public and private law, civil and criminal, permanent and temporary laws, laws passed by bodies of unlimited or original competence, and those enacted by bodies of limited or delegated authority, etc., etc. All these questions, and many others, have to be considered in a general treatise upon the nature of law, but for the purpose of this essay it is necessary to consider only the nature of law in general, and to determine the part played by the State in its creation. Especially in connection with this last inquiry it will be important to consider whether it is enforcement by the State that elevates certain principles of conduct to the title of law, or whether the distinguishing characteristic is to be elsewhere discovered.

There are two ways in which we may approach this examination.

First, by a historical inquiry into the manner in which these principles have arisen; and,

Secondly, by an analysis of these rules as they now exist, and a classification of them according to their form of expression, their comparative validity and their method of ascertainment.

From both of these methods we can obtain information that will assist us in our inquiry, but neither alone is sufficient. The results obtained by the first will afford the substantial grounds upon which to proceed to the analysis demanded by the second.

The Growth of Law. — The early history of societies and of the ideals and rules according to which their interests were regulated, demonstrates that custom has been, the world over, the earliest means of social regulation. The rules of conduct thus provided were not consciously created, but came into existence by an imperceptible process of growth as a reflex from the feelings of order, justice, and utility that existed in the minds of the people. So far then as the creation of first legal principles is concerned, no direct action of the State is to be discovered.

Now it may be conceived that with the earliest stages of social evolution, regulation of private conduct such as is afforded by custom alone is of sufficient force to produce results, if not satisfactory, at least endurable. In such primitive stages of social development common interests are few, and of the simplest character, and the utility and the justice of the customary rules that control them, are clearly apparent to all. Furthermore, the disorder that arises from their occasional violation, and the personal retaliation that usually follows, is not seriously grievous to a community in which the sense of order has been but slightly cultivated, and whose political organization is of the crudest and most unsensitive character.

But such conditions can be maintained only as long as social relations remain comparatively simple, and while their development is gradual and uninterrupted by sudden or violent changes, such as are introduced by migration, by conquest, or by a transition from a hunting and fishing stage of life to an agricultural one, or from a previously peaceful to a warlike mode of existence.

With the very first steps in social development, then, custom, from its inherent nature, must prove inadequate for the regulation of social interests.

This in two ways. In the first place, regulation of conduct by customary law wholly, is suited only to a community whose interests are not only simple, but homogeneous and apparent. When either conflicting interests arise, or controversies spring up in which there is doubt concerning the usual mode of conduct, the force of custom, such as it has, is lost. There are then required the services of the judge who shall decide as to the comparative merits of the interests that conflict, and determine what customary principle is applicable. Secondly, as social relations become complex, custom fails to satisfy the demands laid upon it, because of its inability to provide with sufficient promptness new rules for the regulation of new interests as they arise. The growth of customary rules is necessarily very slow, their age giving to them an essential credential for recognition; and where, as civilization advances, new interests are arising in increasing number, it necessarily results that conditions arise with greater frequency in which some regulation is necessary, and yet which are so suddenly born, so novel, or so intricate, that custom has not provided or cannot provide rules for their regulation. Thus custom early fails as a creator of law.

Thus the very first appearance of social complexity makes apparent the indefiniteness of customary law, and at the same time the increasing sense of order and justice that attends increasing civilization, makes consciously felt the evils and injustice resulting from the uncertain and the irregular sanction supplied by public opinion and private might. The appreciation, however, that there is needed the deliberate creation of general jural ideals other than those provided by tradition and customary conduct, involves a species of reasoning that arises only at a later date, and in a more advanced state of civilization.

The manner in which the State first enters this field is as the interpreter and enforcer of custom, rather than as the creator of new rules of conduct.[1] We may conceive how, as contested cases arise in primitive communities, in which there is no customary law apparent as applicable, these cases are naturally referred for decision to those whose judgments will be of such weight as to carry with them the prospect of their being accepted. Known wisdom and impartiality of mind will be qualities that will be sought for in such judges, but that which will be most desired will be a decision from those in whom lies the power of coercively enforcing their decisions if necessary. Such judges will of course be found in those having authority in the community, and representing the State. The decisions of such will be at first but expressions regarding the justice and rights involved in the particular cases. There will then be no idea of the judge formally interpreting and declaring general rules. Each case will be passed upon ac-

[1] In the few following paragraphs, in which is sketched the development of law, the author has been greatly indebted to the luminous account given in Lightwood, *The Nature of Positive Law*, Chap. II.

cording to its own merits as they appear in the eyes of the judge. This we may term the purely empiric stage of the law, in which particular facts alone determine the decisions to be rendered.

By degrees, however, as substantially similar cases arise, former decisions will naturally have their weight. Thus, gradually, general rules will be established, according to which all cases of similar nature will be governed. These rules will also constitute the material from which, by analogy, still other legal rules will be deduced. As time goes on, these judicially determined rules will continually augment in number, and, at the same time, by a perfectly natural process, increase in definiteness and rigidity as well.

This very definiteness and rigidity, however, (so essential to order in the earliest stages of social development, when the great need is not so much for good law as for definite and acknowledged law) necessitates a new phase of legal growth. With the advance of civilization new conditions and new interests of life arise, and in many cases the rules that have been thus definitely established become in a greater or less degree inapplicable; and, when strictly applied, fail to satisfy the better sense of justice that has developed in the minds of the people. When such cases arise, the judge is placed between two alternatives; either to modify the existing rule of law in behalf of justice in the particular case, and thereby to introduce uncertainty into the law; or, to apply the rule in all its severity, and thereby to inflict present injustice. Of these two evils, the tendency will of course be to select the lesser. If the circumstances of the case be exceptional and unlikely often to occur again, or the interest involved be a small one, the probability is that the existing law will be strictly applied. If, however, large and numerous interests are concerned, and the question is one likely to be repeatedly raised, the application of the rule will generally be modified, if by any strained construction it may be so altered in effect if not in form, that justice may be done, and the law brought into harmony with the sense of right residing in the community and into accord with the demands of social utility. In extreme cases also new rules will often be created by the simple *dicta* of the judges, without reference to the old rule.

Thus, through the establishment of new principles by analogy from old ones, by strained constructions, and by the independent *dicta* of judges, the strictness of the old law is corrected, and opportunity given for the introduction of new principles of law that conform more nearly with the changed conditions of developing social life.

This process of legal development is perfectly represented by the growth of the equity jurisdiction in the English Law, and by the modification of the strict *jus civile* of the Romans by the Prætorian legislation, and the application of what was termed *jus singulare*.

Still another instrumentality through which the

courts have broadened the application of old laws to meet new cases, while ostensibly and avowedly exercising only the judicial function of interpreting and applying existing law, has been the use of *legal fictions*. Such, for example, was the fiction of the Roman law according to which the wife was considered the legal daughter of the husband; and that of the English law, that she and her husband constitute but one person. Of similar character, in the English law, are the fictions of fine and recovery, that of considering the defendant as in the custody of the Marshal of the court, whereby the Court of Queen's Bench established its jurisdiction in Common Pleas, the fictitious parties in actions of ejectment, etc.

It is impossible to overestimate the influence of this element in the growth of law. As is well known, so powerful an instrument did this become in the hands of the English judges that acts of Parliament were frequently nullified and in some instances made to have an effect exactly opposite to that intended by their enactors. Jeremy Bentham, who most strongly reprobated this method of manufacturing law, described a legal fiction as " a wilful falsehood, having for its object the stealing legislative power by and for hands which could not or durst not openly claim it, and but for the delusion thus produced could not exercise it." This, however, is harsh criticism, its use being in almost all cases founded upon the desire of the courts to obtain necessary reform without entirely and openly repudiating the abrogated law. The value of fictions is more correctly stated by Blackstone, when he says, "This maxim is ever invariably observed, that no fiction shall extend to work an injury; its proper operation being to prevent a mischief or remedy an inconvenience that might result from the general rule of law. So true it is that *in fictione juris semper subsistit æquitas.*"

It is to be remembered, moreover, that throughout all this course of manufacture of laws, both substantive and adjective, the courts have never openly claimed this creative power. They have ever veiled their originative action under the guise of judicial interpretation of laws that are presumed to be already created by custom or by sovereign command. They have ever avowed themselves as controlled by the law as it is at the time of the accruing of the cause of action. However novel the principle of law enunciated, it has always been claimed to rest upon prior determined legal principles. Judge Cooley has stated this method of growth in the following words, which we give *in extenso :* —

"The code of to-day is therefore to be traced rather in the spirit of judicial decisions than in the letter of the statute. The process of growth has been something like the following: Every principle declared by a court in giving judgment is supposed to be a principle more or less general in its application, and which is applied under the facts of the case, because, in the opinion of the court, the facts bring the case within the principle. The case is not the measure of the principle; it does not limit and confine it within the exact facts, but it furnishes an illustration of the principle which perhaps might still have been applied had some of the facts been different. Thus, one by one, important principles become recognized through adjudications, which illustrate them, and which constitute authoritative evidence of what the law is when other cases shall arise. But cases are seldom exactly alike in their facts; they are, on the contrary, infinite in their diversities. And as numerous controversies on different facts are found to be within the reach of the same general principle, the principle seems to grow and expand, and does actually become more comprehensive, though so steadily and insensibly under legitimate judicial treatment that for the time the expansion passes unobserved. But new and peculiar cases must also arise from time to time, for which the courts must find the governing principle; and these may either be referred to some principle previously declared, or to some one which now for the first time there is occasion to apply. But a principle newly applied is not supposed to be a new principle; on the contrary, it is assumed that from time immemorial it has constituted a part of the common law of the land, and that it has only not been applied before because no occasion has arisen for its application. This assumption is the very groundwork and justification for its being applied at all, because the creation of new rules of law, by whatsoever authority, can be nothing else than legislation; and the principle now announced for the first time must always be so far in harmony with the great body of the law that it may naturally be taken and deemed to be a component part of it, as the decision assumes it to be." [1]

In addition to these instrumentalities for the creation of legal principles, is also another agency by

[1] *Torts*, pp. 12, 13. For a careful study of "Case-Law," see Clark, *Practical Jurisprudence*, Part II. Chaps. III. to VI. inclusive. Well worthy of notice is also the essay of Mr. E. R. Thayer entitled "Judicial Legislation: its Legitimate Function in the Development of the Common Law," contributed to the *Harvard Law Review*, V. p. 172.

no means unimportant. We refer to scientific commentaries upon law. The work of jurists in this respect is of two kinds, logical and creative. In the first place, they collect and arrange in systematic order, customs, adjudications, and enactments, and from them deduce rules of a more general and therefore philosophical character than have hitherto been recognized by the courts. They thus, as it were, crystallize into definite and logical statement those feelings of order and justice which have previously existed only in a vague and indefinite way. The systematic arrangement of these established laws serves also to indicate the gaps that remain to be filled by subsequent enactment. At the same time, by giving the philosophical grounds upon which these rules are based, the premises are furnished from which, by analogy and logical deduction, the rules so needed may be obtained. In the second place, in so far as these scientific law writers enunciate rules not based on previously determined jural principles, but merely upon their own conceptions of justice and utility, and these rules are accepted and enforced by the courts, to that extent their work may be described as not only illuminative of present and suggestive of future law, but as itself creative of principles of law.

The time comes, however, when even all of these methods of legal growth, co-operating, no longer satisfy the demands of developing political life. A more adequate means is demanded for the creation of legal rights and legal obligations, — one that shall be more direct and more immediate in its action. Thus, in response to this demand, has arisen the legislative function proper of the State, — a function in every case historically shown to have been posterior in point of assumption by the State to that of legal interpretation and application.

A study of the growth of legislation reveals the comparative recency of the State's entrance into this field, to any considerable extent, as the avowed and direct creator of law. Especially is this true of Private Law. We may say, indeed, that until the seventeenth century A.D. the law-making powers of Governments were exercised almost solely in the field of public and administrative law; the private relations between subjects being left to the control of custom and the courts, or to local administrative agents acting in their judicial capacities.

It is true that in despotic Governments, before political powers were limited by definite provisions, those in authority claimed a control over the citizen and all his private rights. But such control was commonly exercised, not with the purpose of creating general rules, but only in particular and exceptional instances, where individual interests happened to touch the interests of those in power. It was only tentatively, and by degrees, that the central law-making bodies began to undertake the general and uniform control of matters other than those directly concerned with the dignity, military strength, and fiscal prosperity of the State. Even where legislative bodies of a representative character were early established, as in England, the original purposes for which they were created were those of advice to, and control of, the executive in matters of public administration, (especially of taxation) rather than for the regulation of private rights; and for many years their activities were almost solely limited to the attainment of these ends.

As, however, these legislative bodies broadened the representative basis upon which they rested, and as the consciousness of their own power, which followed from knowledge that they acted for the entire nation and had its support, increased in extent, the inevitable tendency was for them to exercise in fuller degree this power thus knowingly possessed. Thus it is that the enormous increase in legislative activity that has characterized modern times has been intimately connected with the growth of popular representative Government.

The vastly superior efficiency in the creation of law of legislative enactment over custom or judicial interpretation is easily apparent. By means of a single statutory enactment, a legal regulation of complicated interests is established, that it would take custom many years to create, even were it ever able to evolve satisfactory principles. Even judge-made law, though more directly created than customary law, does not obtain absolute stability until repeatedly accepted by other courts.

Utility and propriety of exercise of this legislative power once granted, and its efficiency once recognized, all the conditions of modern life tend to encourage its wider use. The increasing specialization of governmental functions, the greater appreciation of the danger of injustice involved in permitting those entrusted with the application of law to manufacture it (not to speak of the uncertainty introduced into the law by such means), the perfection of legislative methods (as, for example, standing committees and other contrivances), and, finally, the enormous increase in the complexity and number of social interests to be regulated; — all these causes tend more and more to cast the burden of creating law upon the formal law-making branch of the State. To such an extent has this movement already gone, that at the present day, so accustomed are we to look to our legislatures for our laws, the part played by custom and courts in the development of our jural ideals is largely overlooked.

In a general way, the sources of Law have now been indicated. Defining the law of the land, as we have thus far used the term, as that body of principles applied by the courts in the exercise of their jurisdictions, we have seen its sources to be custom, judicial construction and precedent, scientific commentary, and legislative enactment. As we have seen, the recent tendency has been, and will undoubtedly continue to be, for the last source to become relatively more and more important. At the same time, it is to be remembered, that the other agencies will be ever present. Custom with its slow tread will render obsolete laws that have become anachronistic, and will create new principles that will force their recognition upon the legislatures and courts. Scientific commentaries and text-books will continue their influence, and courts, too, of necessity, will never be freed from the task of producing judge-made law. All statutory law, from its formal and definite statement, is rigid in character, and, in its application to changing conditions, must be softened by the judge, if the sense of justice be not outraged.

In the development of law, custom is the conservative element, legislative enactment the radical. The task of the true statesman is to give to both of these elements their due importance. It was the great merit of the work of Savigny that he showed that the task of the legislator should be largely limited to the statutory confirmation of principles that common usage has already established, rather than the invention of laws according to individual caprice or judgment. As Count Portalis has expressed it, "the legislature should not invent law, but only write it."

At the same time, however, it is undoubtedly true, that there should be, especially in these modern times, a more active principle than this in legislation. The opportunities enjoyed by legislatures should be used for the creation of rules that custom cannot supply. The necessity often arises, also, for the release of society from rules which custom has itself created, but which no longer comport with the best interests of all. This is an element that Savigny did not sufficiently recognize. The civilization of the East, and especially of the Chinese Empire, testifies to the result of the rigid reign of custom. Thus, says Bluntschli, in commenting upon the work of Savigny: "While it may be true that the present rests upon the past and cannot be entirely separated from it, yet it is none the less true that the forms of different ages are variable, and out of the depths of Man's nature, and brought forth by the mutations in the spirit of the ages, new forms are created. The critical examination of the past is necessary in order to discover the grounds upon which we rest, but the consideration of the future is none the less necessary in order to determine whither we are going. All law (*Recht*) is truly of the present; the past is no more, except in so far as its forces continue to operate in the present; and the future is not yet, except in so far as it is already a condition in the present. The present is therefore a union of the past and future. It alone is real. There is something that is often not sufficiently recognized by the historical school." [1]

In our day, however, the danger seems to be that our legislatures will go to the other extreme, and give expression to that spirit of innovation which, acting without reference to the past, or sufficient consideration for the future, seems to characterize popular bodies. The dictates of prudence and the feelings of personal responsibility that restrain the monarch from too hasty action are both wanting in a large representative assembly. The responsibility in case

---

[1] *Geschichte der neueren Staatswissenschaft*, p. 625.

of ill success, when distributed among a large number, is reduced to a minimum, and, at the same time, the feeling on the part of such a body that it represents in itself the entire nation, gives to it a feeling of power that is necessarily intoxicating.

CHAPTER VIII

ANALYTICAL JURISPRUDENCE

In the beginning of the last chapter we spoke of two ways in which one may approach the examination of law: *first*, by a historical inquiry into the manner in which legal principles have arisen; and, *secondly*, by an analysis of these rules as they now exist, and a classification of them according to their forms of expression, their comparative validity, and their method of ascertainment and enforcement. We have just considered the results to be obtained from the first method. Armed with them, we are now prepared for an intelligent and comprehensive estimate of the results to be obtained from the second, or analytical method.

First of all, it is to be remarked, we are no longer concerned with the moral obligation of the individual to yield obedience to the rules of conduct that obtain in the political community of which he is a member, but have to do solely and simply with the question of how those rules have obtained their coercive force.

The ambiguity which attaches to the word "law" makes it necessary to distinguish carefully the sense in which the word will be here used. As opposed to that use of the word which causes it to be applied to the sequence of cause and effect in the empiric universe, and thus to indicate an inevitable result that necessarily follows from given conditions — a necessity arising from an undiscoverable first cause, and independent of the will of mankind — it will be here used as expressing a rule of human action and indicating a principle of conduct which shall govern the actions of men for the attainment of certain ends. The characteristic of a law in this sense, is that it is capable of being expressed as a distinct proposition to rational beings. Furthermore, it is a command. That is, it is not merely a statement of advice, but an expression of the will of one who has the power to enforce it in case of disobedience. Thus, then, in a general sense, all rules of human conduct are defined as being " propositions commanding the doing, or abstaining from, certain classes of actions; disobedience to which is followed, or is likely to be followed, by some sort of penalty or inconvenience." [1]

Continuing the examination of the nature of laws as thus stated, we have yet to classify them according to the nature of the one by whose will they are stated, and the character of the sanction by which enforced. According to the character of the lawgiver they are of two kinds: first. laws set by God to man, which may be revealed or unrevealed; and second. laws set by men to men. As regards the character of the sanction applied, they may affect either the moral or physical side of man.

[1] Holland, *Elements of Jurisprudence*, 6th ed. p. 21.

The insufficiency of the doctrines of Divine or Natural Laws has already been shown in our discussion of the Contract and Divine Theories. Divine Laws, as such, are applicable only to motives or internal acts, and their sanction is a purely moral one. In so far as they may be held to control outward acts they not only need to be humanly cognized but to be enforced by physical or humanly determined means. As such, they become human rules, or rules set by men to men. The same is true of so-called Natural Laws. Except as purely moral or divine principles, the term "Natural Law," as we have seen, has no other meaning than as referring to those ideal rules of external action that are fitted to be enforced by some human power, and are only cognizable as such by human reason.

As we have previously shown, it was Hobbes who first made distinct the difference between these so-called laws of nature, which necessarily, in the absence of a general authority, can have no other than a moral sanction, and no greater guarantee of enforcement than individual might; and civil laws, whose enunciation and enforcement are by a political superior. It was this distinction thus made by Hobbes that was subsequently seized upon by Bentham and Austin, and so developed as to form the logical basis of what has since been termed the English Analytical School of Jurisprudence.

Austin's definition of Law is as follows: "Every positive law or every law simply and strictly so called is set directly or circuitously by a sovereign person or body, to a member or members of the independent political society wherein that person or body is sovereign or supreme. Or (changing the expression) it is set directly or circuitously by a monarch or sovereign number, to a person or persons in a state of subjection to its author." [1]

The first point to be noticed in this Austinian definition of law is that all law is considered as a command of the sovereign, which, for present purposes, we may consider as meaning the State.

It was of course obvious to Austin that, as our historical inquiry has shown, the law of a country as administered in its courts is never by any means to be wholly found in the formal expressions of the will of the State, but has its source largely in custom. That this objection to his position is only apparent, not real, he explains in the following way: "Now," says he, "when judges construe a custom into a legal rule (or make a rule not suggested by a custom) the legal rule which they establish is established by the sovereign legislature. A subordinate or subject judge is merely a minister. The portion of the sovereign power which lies at his disposition is merely delegated. The rules which he makes derive their legal force from authority given by the State: an authority which the State may confer expressly, and which it commonly imparts by way of acquiescence. For, since the State may reverse the rules which he makes, and yet permits him to enforce them by the power of the political community, its sovereign will

[1] *The Province of Jurisprudence Determined*, ed. 1861, Lecture VI.

that the rules shall obtain as law, is clearly evinced by its conduct though not by its express declaration. . . . Like other significations of desire, a command is express or tacit. If the desire be signified by words (written or spoken), the command is express. If the desire is signified by conduct (or by any signs of desire which are not words) the command is tacit. Now when customs are turned into legal rules by decisions of subject judges, the legal rules which emerge from the customs are tacit commands of the sovereign legislature. The State which is able to abolish, permits its members to express them; and it therefore signifies its pleasure by that its voluntary acquiescence, that they shall serve as a law to the governed."

Austin thus excludes from the domain of positive law all rules of conduct that look for their sanction merely to the pressure of public opinion and to the prevailing codes of public morality. Not until a principle has been declared by the legislative mouthpiece of the State or judicially accepted by the courts, and the courts' rulings in turn acquiesced in by the ruling authorities, as evidenced by the enforcement thereof, does such a principle become stamped with the quality of law in the Austinian sense.

It is generally agreed that the positive law of a State may be said to be contained in those rules that are accepted by its judicial tribunals. But it is by no means equally admitted by all, that all of these rules may be said to owe their establishment to the State either directly or indirectly, as stated by Austin and his school. It is vigorously contended that the State does not enjoy the sole prerogative of creator of positive law, either as acting through its special legislative mouthpieces or through its courts, but that it must share this honor with the people. In other words, it is claimed that that large body of legal principles commonly called customary law and accepted by the courts, does not, by such acceptance, then, for the first time, become invested with a legal character; but that such character has been previously established by the general recognition of its binding force by the people.

This, it need not be said, is a fundamental point in any political theory, for upon it depends the question not only as to the essential character of positive law, but as to the extent, and therefore the character, of the State's Sovereignty. The question is whether it is to be admitted that rules of legally binding force may be created independently of the State's action and therefore in limitation of it, or whether the political Sovereignty is to be viewed as the sole source whence all legal obligation springs.

In general, we may denominate as the Historical School that party of writers who are opposed to the Austinian conception of law. In England this school is headed by the name of Sir Henry Maine, and upon the Continent by Savigny and Puchta. In general, American writers are also of this latter school, a fact that is undoubtedly owing to the course of our political history. Resting, as we do, our origin as an independent nation on a forcible separation from England, and founding the justification for such action upon so-called natural or inalienable rights of liberty, we have not been disposed to see in political authority the sole source of legal rights, nor to concede to its Sovereignty such a legally despotic character, as logically follows, as we shall see, from the Austinian view.

It is, also, not difficult to see why it is that this school, so dominant in England, has exerted so little influence in Germany. As Lightwood shows in his work, *The Nature of Positive Law,* not only do the Germans, as a rule, fail to make that clear distinction between law and morality that is made by English lawyers, and contemplate the former only as supplementing and making possible the latter; but also the historical development of their law tends to make the Austinian conception less apparent. In England a strong central government was early established. In Germany this result was not achieved until a comparatively recent date. Hence, the inevitable tendency in the one country to view law as the product of that sovereign power which appeared so omnipotent; and in the other, to see in custom the essential source of law. This view has been also strengthened by the characteristic attitude of the German mind toward political authority. We refer, of course, to the Teutonic particularism, that, starting from a postulate of individual liberty, sees in the State an institution through which personal rights are protected and realized. Hence the tendency to discover in the customs, that obviously owe their creation to the people, the true origin of law; rather than to discover their source in the commands of the State through whose instrumentality they are enforced. "Positive Law," says Savigny, "springs from that general spirit which animates all the members of the Nation, and the unity of the law is revealed necessarily to their consciences and is by no means the effect of chance."[1] The growth of custom he compares to that of language. And, he continues, "Law which lives in the common consciousness of the people is not composed of abstract rules. It exists rather in the actual perception of a legal institute in its organic connection, and the rule appears in its logical form so soon as the need for it is felt; it is then singled out from this connection, and is translated in an artificial manner."[2] In other words, according to Savigny, customary law exists as law independently of the State. When, therefore, it is formally enunciated by the courts or legislature, the function of the State is rather that of realizing and enforcing the law than of creating it. The State thus appears as itself the creator of law only when it establishes by statutory enactment a rule wholly or in part, not founded upon a previously recognized custom.

While the above comments and quotations from Savigny serve to show what has undoubtedly been the dominant attitude of German jurists during the present century, it is to be remarked that within the

---

[1] *System des heutigen römischen Rechtes*, § 7.
[2] *Idem*, § 7.

last few years there has been apparent a tendency to change this, and to turn to a position much more similar to that of the analytical jurists of England. Especially is this apparent in Ihering's *Zweck im Recht*, and Lasson's *System der Rechtsphilosophie*.

In England, on the other hand, the high authority of the Austinian School has been considered as greatly shaken by the historical method introduced into the study of law by Sir Henry Maine. This writer is supposed to have pointed out that there is evidence to show that throughout the greater portion of the world's history, law was created otherwise than according to the Austinian theory; and therefore that if his conception of the source of law be applicable at all, it is applicable only to highly developed States. The following quotation from Maine sufficiently indicates his position. Referring to an Indian despot, he says: "At first sight there could be no more perfect embodiment than Runjeet Singh of sovereignty as conceived by Austin. He was absolutely despotic. Except occasionally on his wild frontier he kept the most perfect order. He could have commanded anything: the smallest disobedience to his commands would have been followed by death or mutilation, and this was perfectly well known to the enormous majority of his subjects. Yet I doubt whether once in all his life he issued a command which Austin would call a law. . . . He had all material of power and he exercised it in various ways. But he never made law." [1]

[1] *Early History of Institutions*, p. 380.

It is to be observed that Maine admits the *verbal* truth of Austin's theory, and adds: "I do not for a moment assert that the existence of such a state of political society falsifies Austin's theory. The maxim by which objections to it are disposed of is, as I have so often said before, that what the sovereign permits, he commands." The position which we shall take, however, is that there is more than a verbal truth in the thesis that all law, as law, emanates from the sovereign; and that when a customary rule is declared by a court of justice to be one which the State will enforce, such rule becomes *specifically* distinct from what it had before been. It might be added, though, that the phrase "what the sovereign permits, he commands," is better expressed as "what the sovereign enforces, he commands."

Probably the strongest argument that has been made in America against the Austinian view is that contained in the opening chapters of Wharton's *Commentaries on American Law*. This author writes as follows: "By whom were existing English statutes winnowed in the colonies of Massachusetts and Pennsylvania, for instance, so as to retain such as suited the temper and met the wants of the people, and to set aside all others? This was not done by the colonial assemblies; had such a process of radical revision been attempted by these assemblies it would have been promptly vetoed by the king in council. It was not done by the British Parliament, though the British Parliament assumed to be the sole supreme legislature by whose laws these colonies were controlled. It was done by popular assent produced by national conscience and national need. It is true that when the colonies became independent sovereigns they passed laws by which the process of selection and rejection thus carried out was approved. But it was never pretended that the process of selection and rejection derived its authority from such legislation. On the contrary, when the colonies became sovereigns, what their court said was, 'this particular English statute was never in force in this State'; in other words, the courts said, 'the law of the land, in this respect, was not imposed by the sovereign on the people, but was adopted by the people and afterwards accepted by the sovereign.' The same may be said of the rulings of our courts as to international and interstate law, and the law regulating Indian tribes."[1]

And again he says, — and this is the strong point made against Austin by lawyers *quâ* lawyers, — "Yet that custom makes the law and not law custom, is shown by the fact just noticed, that when a custom is recognized by the courts as existing, *the recognition operates retrospectively*, the custom being regarded as law before it was judicially recognized."[2]

In considering now these criticisms that are made upon the Austinian position as to the nature of law, it is to be observed that much the greater part of these objections are in fact examples of *ignorantio elenchi*, the confusion arising, as Holland correctly

[1] *Commentaries on American Law*, § 2.   [2] *Idem*, § 15, note.

points out, from the ambiguous sense in which the term "source of law" may be used.[1] Thus this expression may be used either to denote the mode in which, or the person through whom, have been formulated those rules which have acquired the force of law; or, to denote the authority which gives them that force.

Now so far as it is used in the first sense, there is no denial made by the Analytical School that custom is, in very large measure, the source of law. That is to say, that through this medium have arisen the principles of social conduct that have been subsequently embodied in law. Furthermore, it is not asserted that, as an actual fact, the exigencies of public life have not at all times demanded that the sovereign power should found the expression of its will upon these rules. But what this school does maintain, is, that these customary rules do not become law in a strictly legal, or, as Austin would say, positive sense, until they are accepted by the political power and enforced by its might. Force, the power of the State, is thus made the determining principle. As Austin says, "There can be no law without a judicial sanction, and until custom has been adopted as law by courts of justice it is always uncertain whether it will be sustained by that sanction or not."[2] And, again, "The description, completion, and correction of positive morality are as much an end for which political

---

[1] *Elements of Jurisprudence*, 6th ed. p. 49.
[2] *Lectures on Jurisprudence*, II. 561.

government is wanted, as the obtaining by its establishment a more cogent sanction. But the sovereign makes it law, not by the mere description, but by the sanction with which he clothes it."[1]

Now it is obvious that the objections that have been founded on the historical evidences quoted by Wharton and Maine are applicable solely to the question of the origination of the principles embodied in the law, — a question with which the Austinians are not concerned. Thus, when Maine says that the Indian despot never made a law, he can only mean that he never arbitrarily established a general rule of conduct. What he did do, however, was to enforce rules of conduct with the entire might of the State, and thereby, as the Analytical School claims, did elevate such principles into legal rules. It is no answer to say that in the case of many of the earlier monarchies, they were simply tax-collecting empires, and that there was no attempt, or even desire, on the part of their rulers to interfere with the domestic rules that obtained in the various portions of their kingdoms. The point is, that the very least important of the customary rules that did obtain acceptance in those countries by the lowest courts or judicial officers, did thereby obtain a sanction that was ultimately supported by the entire strength of the sovereign political authority. For, in case of resistance on the part of any one to the decree of the judicial officer, founded on the recognition of such rule, it would be neces-

[1] *Lectures on Jurisprudence*, II. 567.

sary to call upon the executive power to enforce it; and, in case of continued resistance (if the rule of law were to be maintained), ultimately to bring into operation the entire force of the State. It is the great advantage of the State, however, that so overwhelmingly superior is its strength, that in all but exceptional cases its actual exercise is made unnecessary.

Again, it is no answer to the assertion that the State is the sole creator of law, to show that no State can maintain its control that does not in general accept as its will those principles of justice and utility that are evolved by the customary habit of its people. That, in other words, the attempt on its part to establish arbitrary rules of conduct not based on the needs and capacities of the people, as evidenced by their customary habits of life, would lead inevitably to revolt and revolution. This would only show that, as a principle of political expediency, (*i.e.* of caution and prudence), a general acceptance of customary rules is necessary.

Finally, it is not a refutation of the position which we have been defending, to point to the fact that a court of justice, in accepting a custom as law, does not declare that *henceforth* such principle shall obtain as law, but holds it to have been the law at the time of the accruing of the cause of action whose merits are then decided.

The position of Holland, who is possibly the best exponent of Austin's system to-day, differs from that of his master upon this point, and is an attempt, it would seem to us, to avoid the objection rather than to answer it. Thus, his reasoning is as follows: " The Courts have, therefore, long ago established as a fundamental principle of law, subject of course in each case to many restrictions and qualifications, that in the absence of a specific rule of written law, regard is to be had in looking for the rule which governs a given set of circumstances, not only to equity and to previous decision, but also to custom. Binding authority has thus been conceded to custom, provided it fulfils certain requirements, the nature of which has also long since been settled, and provided it is not superseded by law of a higher authority. When, therefore, a given set of circumstances is brought into Court, and the Court decides upon them by bringing them within the operation of a custom, the Court appeals to that custom as it might to any other pre-existent law. It does not *proprio motu* then for the first time make that custom a law; it merely decides as a fact that there exists a legal custom, about which there might up to that moment have been some question, as there might about the interpretation of an Act of Parliament. It then applies the custom to the circumstances just as it might have applied an Act of Parliament to them. A good custom or an intelligible Act of Parliament either exists or does not exist objectively, before the case comes into Court; although it is from the decision of the Court in the particular case that a subjective knowledge is first possible for the people of the existence or non-existence of the alleged custom, or that this or that is the meaning of the Act of Parliament." [1]

It would certainly seem to us that Holland admits the very point against which he contends, when he says that the court does not for the first time make a custom a law by its adjudication, but, " merely decides as a fact that there exists a legal custom about which there might up to that moment have been some question, as there might about the interpretation of an Act of Parliament." This would certainly limit the action of the court to that of the interpretating function. And, as one of his critics has properly said, " To say that customs are regarded as laws by virtue of a *tacit* law to that effect, is simply to beg the whole question. It is to say that custom is law in virtue of custom." [2]

As has been indicated, it is maintained by Austin that a custom becomes a law at the time that it is applied by a court and not before, and this would seem to us the only logical position to take. Let it be frankly admitted that judicial legislation is *ex post facto* legislation. But what if it is ? What has this really to do with the question as to the effect of such decisions of the courts upon custom ? It is, to be sure, a general principle of legislation that laws should not be retroactive in their effect, but this is a principle dictated by general considerations of justice, and not of necessity. There is no more inherent dif-

[1] *Elements of Jurisprudence*, 6th ed. pp. 54, 55.
[2] Professor John Dewey in *Pol. Sci. Quar.* March, 1894, p. 47.

ficulty in the State establishing retroactive law, than there is in its creating law that shall be of only prospective application. That this is the case, is seen in the necessity of explicitly providing in our own written constitutions that neither Congress nor the State legislatures shall pass *ex post facto* enactments. In the case of legislatures not thus arbitrarily limited, as, for example, the British Parliament, no judge would hold a retroactive act invalid if passed according to due forms and procedure. Laws established by means of formal statutory enactments, are, as a rule, created without reference to particular cases, and therefore injustice would necessarily result had such enactments a retroactive character. When, however, we come to judicial legislation, we come to a field where this *ex post facto* principle is not recognized, — not recognized because from the very nature of the case no necessity of justice demands it. By the recognition of a custom as law, no arbitrary or novel doctrines of right are established by the court. Principles only are declared as enforcible that have already obtained in practice among the people. Hence no possible injustice is done by declaring such customs then and there to be laws, and at the same time applying them to the causes of action that have previously accrued. There is no need to predicate a tacit law to the effect that such customs shall be law, but simply to admit that judicial legislation is *ex post facto* legislation, and to defend it as such; in fine, to make the action of the court not simply interpretative, but actually creative of law.

Summing up, then, this entire subject, we are justified in defining law in the strict positive or civic sense, as those rules of conduct that control courts of justice in the exercise of their jurisdictions. As distinguished from all other rules of conduct that obtain more or less general recognition in a community of men, they are such as have for their ultimate enforcement the entire power of the State. The scientific value of such a definite connotation of the term "law" is obviously great. By it alone is rendered possible a definite and exact knowledge of the facts to which this department of knowledge relates, and a sound basis afforded upon which to rest the conception of the Sovereignty of the State.[1]

A little reflection shows how indefinite would be the term "law" if applicable to custom and civil rules alike. So long as customary rules retain their purely customary form, that which gives to them force and efficiency for regulation is not the threat of coercion, or the imposition of penalties by a superior power in case of their violation. Their force is solely derived from the pressure of public opinion, of religious sanction, of individual sense of right, or the possibility of personal retalia-

---

[1] Regarding the value of Austin's conception of law and Sovereignty, Mr. Justice Markby (*Elements of Law*, 2d ed. p. 4) speaks as follows: " Austin, by establishing the distinction between law and morals, not only laid the foundation for a science of law, but cleared the conception of law and of sovereignty of a number of pernicious consequences to which, in the hands of his predecessors, it had been supposed to lead. Laws, as Austin has shown, must be legally binding; and yet a law may be unjust. Resistance to authority cannot be a legal right, and yet it may be a virtue."

tion on the part of those persons injured by such violation. Such influences as these are of the most variable character, and personal in the highest degree. Their force depends almost wholly upon the subjective condition of the individual, upon his own peculiar temperament of mind, his sense of justice, his religious reverence, his regard for the traditional, his power of self-restraint, and his sensitiveness to the good-will of the community. Such principles, then, possess no force of their own, no compelling power; obedience to them is secured only by the voluntary consent of the individual, such consent being based upon the dictates of reason, expediency, and right that dwell within his own breast.

When, therefore, it is asked to so broaden the connotation of the term "law" as to include such elements as these, we answer that logical exactness and scientific accuracy demand that a more definite meaning be given to this word. Definitions are valuable only in so far as they give a precision of meaning to words and expressions. Their sole utility consists in the demarkation of a definite field within which the word or phrase is applicable, and it will be apparent that to include within the meaning of law elements that differ so widely as the purely customary principles of which we have been speaking, and the rigid rules of conduct, formally enunciated by the State and enforced by its sovereign right, is to create a signification for the word that cannot be sufficiently definite to serve as a basis upon which to found a formal science of jurisprudence and politics.

What decisive and universally applicable definition shall we give to law, if custom is to share with the State the power of its creation? When shall we know at any one time what is and what is not law? What but confusion must necessarily result from conceiving two co-ordinate law-making authorities, each having the right to create law independently of the other, or to abrogate and overrule each other's creations?

In conclusion of this subject, the reader will see that whereas Austin laid the greatest stress upon the determinateness of the sovereign, because only a determinate body of persons is able to express a corporate demand, or, as he expresses it, " is capable as a body of positive or negative deportment;"[1] we, as will subsequently appear,[2] insist on the distinction between State action and mere social or revolutionary deeds. That is to say, we emphasize the point that sovereign or political action may only be had by regularly constituted governmental organs. The deduction from this, however, as to the location of Sovereignty being necessarily in a determinate body, agrees with Austin. Thus when Austin says that the essential difference between a customary rule and a positive law is that the former " is not a command issued expressly or tacitly, but is merely an opinion or sentiment relating to conduct of a kind which is held or felt by an uncertain body or by an indeterminate party," he is impressed with the

---

[1] *Province of Jurisprudence Determined*, ed. 1861, p. 135.
[2] Chapter on " Location of Sovereignty in the Body Politic."

practical impossibility of such an indeterminate body, as that whence Public Opinion springs, giving voice to a corporate command. We, on the other hand, though agreeing in the result, lay weight upon the logical impossibility of harmonizing such a popular function with the sovereign nature of the State.

In our next chapter we shall see what deductions regarding the nature of the State's Sovereignty are to be drawn from our conception of law as wholly a product of the State's will. In connection with this we shall also consider the legal or non-legal character of constitutional and so-called international law.

CHAPTER IX

THE POWER OF THE STATE: SOVEREIGNTY

THE result of the preceding chapters has been to show that there are in the individual no so-called innate or "natural rights," that is, such rights as exist independently of the State and beyond its control. In so far as the individual has claims upon his fellows to a non-interference upon their part with the free exercise of certain outward acts, such claims have no legal force except as recognized and enforced by the political power. Just as the existence of the State is not due to the will of the individual, so likewise is the validity of none of the State's commands dependent upon their consent. When Blackstone says that, "the law of nature being coeval with mankind, and dictated by God Himself, is of course superior in obligation to any other," and that, "it is binding over all the globe in all countries and at all times; no human laws are of any validity if contrary to this; and such of them as are valid derive all their force and all their authority, mediately or immediately from this original,"[1] he is asserting what we have seen to be incorrect.

If, then, the only rules that possess legal validity are such as have received the sanction of the State,

[1] *Commentaries*, Introduction.

it follows as a logical deduction, that, since no one can be bound by one's own will, the sovereign political power must necessarily be incapable of legal limitation.

"Now it follows from the essential difference of a positive law," says Austin, "and from the nature of sovereignty and independent political society, that the power of a monarch properly so called, or the power of a sovereign number in its collegiate and sovereign capacity, is incapable of *legal* limitation. A monarch or a sovereign number bound by a legal duty were subject to a higher or superior sovereign; that is to say, a monarch or a sovereign number bound by a legal duty were sovereign and not sovereign. Supreme power limited by positive law is a flat contradiction in terms.

"Nor would a political society escape from legal despotism, although the power of the sovereign were bound by legal restraints. The power of the superior sovereign imposing the restraints, or the power of some other sovereign superior to that superior, would still be absolutely free from the fetters of positive law. For, unless the imagined restraints were ultimately imposed by a sovereign not in a state of subjection to a higher or superior sovereign, a series of sovereigns ascending to infinity would govern the imagined community, which is impossible and absurd."[1]

That this reasoning follows as a logical necessity from our definition of law, is without question. It

[1] *Province of Jurisprudence Determined*, ed. 1861, p. 225.

is to be remembered, however, that by the term "sovereign power," we refer to the highest power of the State without reference to the manner in which this power is exercised or in whose hands it rests. When we come to consider the determinateness with which the sovereign power may be located, we shall find it necessary to differ somewhat from Austin.

In every politically organized community, then, there exists a public authority to which, from the legal standpoint, all interests are potentially subject, and therefore liable to regulation and control by the State when this ruling power decides them to be of public interest.

It is true that there are, and have been since the earliest times, certain subjects that it has seemed just and proper should be left to the free exercise of the individual, and it does not seem reasonable to expect that the time will ever come when this opinion as to many of these subjects will be changed. But this is by no means the same thing as saying that these subjects constitute a domain that can never be entered by the State. The present domain of individual liberty is one that, according to present standards of politics, the *Government* is not allowed to enter. From the power of the *State*, however, it cannot be shielded, and, as regards it, its boundary line will ever depend upon political expediency. As Professor Burgess says in his recent work, " The individual is defended in this sphere *against* the Government by the power (*i.e.* the State) that makes and maintains and can destroy the Government; and by that same power, *through* the Government, against encroachments from any other quarter. Against that power itself, however, he has no defence." [1]

Our inquiries, as thus far pursued, have led up to, and in great degree indicated the nature of what is termed the Sovereignty of the State. It here remains to determine, more particularly, the connotation of the term, and to make application of the principles that we shall obtain, to different phases of political life. Thereby we shall ascertain not only the political and juristic character of these types, but demonstrate the correctness of our results by a practical application of them. Especially important in this latter connection will be the examination of the phenomena presented by the union of the States, to which subject we shall devote a separate chapter.

Distinct, however, from the determination of the nature of the sovereign power, is the question of its location in the body politic, — the ascertainment of the person or persons in whose hands its exercise ultimately rests.

Our subject will thus be divided into two parts; the first dealing with the nature of Sovereignty; and the second considering the question of its location. First, then, as to the nature of Sovereignty.

Development of the Theory of Sovereignty. — In beginning the examination of this subject we come

[1] *Political Science and Constitutional Law*, Vol. I. p. 176.

to what is undoubtedly the most important topic to be discussed in political science. As descriptive of the highest power of the State, Sovereignty is the vital principle in the life of the State. The validity of all law is dependent upon it, and all international relations are determined by it. The theoretical basis upon which rested the conflicting claims of the parties to the greatest war of this century, sprang from differing views regarding the nature of Sovereignty, its divisibility, and the tests by which its presence is to be recognized.

In a general way it is convenient to say that Sovereignty is that term which denotes the highest power of the State, and that that person or number of persons, who possesses or possess this power, is or are sovereign. Such a definition as this, however, is of such a general nature as to be scarcely more than an explicative proposition. It is safe to say that there exists no other term in political science, regarding whose signification there exists such confusion and contradiction of thought, and in regard to which such an amount of dogmatism has been preached. What the term "Value" is to the science of political economy, the term "Sovereignty" is to political science.

It was not until the third quarter of the sixteenth century that we find for the first time definitely stated the doctrine that Sovereignty is the essential element of the State.

Bodin defined the State, which he termed the Republic, as follows: " *République est un droit gou-*

vernement de plusieurs mesnages et de ce qui leur est commun avec puissance souveraine." [1]

The sovereign power itself he defined as the "*puissance absolue et perpétuelle d'une république,*" or, in Latin, as the "*summa in cives ac subditos legibusque soluta potestas.*" [2] This power, itself above the law, he thus makes the all-powerful force, by the possession of which the unity of the State is secured, and its existence as an independent body politic maintained. Nor is this power limited in point of time. He says: "*Majestas vero nec a majore potestate nec legibus ullis nec tempore definitur.*" [3] In its sovereign character, the State appears, according to Bodin, in a double aspect. From within, it appears as that force from which all other political powers derive their validity, and in which they may be, if necessary, again absorbed. As objects of this force the citizens are termed subjects (*subditos*). Outwardly, in its relation with other powers, the State appears as independent and free from external legal compulsion of any sort whatever. The logical result of this position was, of course, to render the conception of Sovereignty necessarily territorial in character, that is, as exercisible over a definite portion of the world's surface.

---

[1] *De la République*, I. 1. Upon the significance of Bodin's work, see especially E. Hancke, *Bodin, Eine Studie über den Begriff der Souverainetät*, and Baudrillart, *Jean Bodin et Son Temps*.

[2] *Idem*, I. 8.

[3] *Idem*. Bodin published his work in both French and Latin. The Latin version, however, is rather a revision than a translation of the French, and as such is superior to it.

Finally, Bodin declared Sovereignty to be indivisible, and hence its exercise to be distinguished from its ultimate possession.

These theses, Bodin not only definitely stated, but followed out to many of their logical conclusions. Thus, viewing the State in its internal or domestic aspect, he was led to the negation of so-called limited monarchies, and to a denial of the possibility of conclusively binding constitutional laws in general. Viewed outwardly, he made application of his doctrine of Sovereignty in the interpretation of the relations between vassal States, States paying tribute to others, etc.

The epoch-making character of Bodin's work is seen when we consider the conceptions that had prevailed prior to his time. On the one hand, the old idea of the universality of the Roman Empire, and the alleged supremacy of the Church in matters temporal, had rendered impossible the idea of Sovereignty as including complete State independence; while, on the other, the Feudal System, together with the undisputed acceptance of the doctrines of Natural Law, made equally impossible the idea of the State's power over its own territory as indivisible and beyond all legal limitation.

The Middle Ages had been essentially uncivic. From the ruins of the Roman Empire arose the Feudal System, and for many years no developed types of civic life were to be found in Europe. For centuries society relapsed into earlier and less developed forms of political life. Arts and letters were in large measure forgotten. Greek literature and language became largely unknown, and even the written monuments of the Roman Law were practically lost, only to be rediscovered, or rather reintroduced as a subject of study, in the twelfth century. No such thing as a developed State in a modern sense was known. The Feudal State was scarcely more than a loose bundle of separated groups of men without common aim or organization —scarcely more than an aggregation of individuals, and of almost detached groups of individuals. As Pollock says in his *History of Politics:* "The Mediæval system of Europe was not a system of States in our sense or in the Greek sense. It was a collection of groups held together in the first instance by ties of personal dependence and allegiance, and connected among themselves by personal relations of the same kind on a magnified scale. Lordship and homage from the Emperor down to the humblest feudal tenant, were the links in a chain of steel which saved the world from being dissolved into a chaos of jarring fragments. . . . The old unity of the clan had disappeared, and it was only gradually and slowly, as kingdoms were consolidated by strong rulers, that the newer unity of the nation took its place."

Gradually, however, the centripetal forces overcame the centrifugal. By conquest, by inheritance, by alliance, by marriage, by the weakening of the feudal lords during the crusades and by their own intestine wars, powerful monarchies arose, the rulers of which arrogated to themselves a supremacy over all within their realm. The growth of monarchy was also fictitiously assisted by the old traditions of the Roman Empire, and by the legal doctrines of absolutism laid down in the civil law, which, as said, had been again brought into use in the twelfth century, and had become the foundation of the legal systems of all the European nations. Thus, by degrees, the Germans, in their civic organization, passed from the village and tribe to the nation, without passing through the intermediate city type which had characterized Greece and early Italy.

Thus it was not until the rise of the monarchy of France, and later of the other European nations, that there was presented a political type requiring for its explanation and theoretical justification the enunciation of a theory such as that of Bodin, according to which Sovereignty was indicated as a power not itself subject to the law, but as supreme over the people and as necessary to the State for the maintenance of its national and independent existence.

The manner in which the conception of Sovereignty varied as political conditions varied, may be shown by quoting from the summary of Sir Henry Maine upon this point.[1]

"It is a consideration well worthy to be kept in view," says he, "that during a large part of what we usually term modern history no such conception was entertained as that of '*territorial sovereignty.*' Sovereignty was not associated with dominion over

[1] *Ancient Law,* pp. 99 *et seq.*

a portion or subdivision of the earth. The world had lain for so many centuries under the shadow of Imperial Rome as to have forgotten that distribution of the vast spaces comprised in the empire which had once parcelled them out into a number of independent commonwealths, claiming immunity from extrinsic interference, and pretending to equality of national rights. After the subsidence of the barbarian irruptions, the notion of sovereignty that prevailed seems to have been twofold. On the one hand it assumed the form of what may be called '*tribe*-sovereignty.' The Franks, the Burgundians, the Vandals, the Lombards, and Visigoths were masters, of course, of the territories which they occupied, and to which some of them had given a geographical appellation; and they based no claim of right upon the fact of territorial possession, and indeed attached no importance to it whatever. . . . The King of a whole tribe was King of his people, not of his people's lands. The alternative to this peculiar notion of sovereignty appears to have been — and this is the important point — the idea of universal dominion. . . .

"Territorial sovereignty — the view which connects sovereignty with the possession of a limited portion of the earth's surface — was distinctly an offshoot, though a tardy one, of feudalism. This might have been expected *a priori*, for it was feudalism which for the first time linked personal duties, and by consequence personal rights, to the ownership of land."

Thus we find throughout feudal times, the "suzerain" or "sovereign" considered as the lord paramount of a certain territory, governing all who held land under him. When, by the growth of centralized government and the decay of the power of the feudal nobility, the intermediate links between the common people and their chief rulers were removed, the result was to leave such rulers as sole sovereigns and the people generally in a state of subjection to them.

When, at a later date, the representative character of all rulership gradually gained ground, the attribute of Sovereignty naturally came to be applied to the State as a political entity, and no longer considered as a personal right of rulership based on territorial possession. The change in this conception is indicated by the change of title of the French King after the Revolution from that of *Roi de France* to that of *Roi des français*, thus showing the realm of France was no longer considered as a *patrimonium regis*.

Sir Henry Maine in his *Ancient Law* further points out the influence of international law, as founded by Grotius upon so-called natural law, in promoting the modern conception of Sovereignty. According to the postulates of this newly developing system of international rights, it was claimed: (1) that there was a determinate law of nature binding upon individual States in their relations to one another; (2) that the universal Sovereignty of the Roman Empire which so long had been vaguely held, should be replaced by a conception of Sovereignty that would associate it with each of the independent

States of Europe; (3) that there is a theoretical equality of State irrespective of age, size, or military power; and (4) that as between themselves the various European sovereign rulers are to be deemed not paramount but absolute owners of the State's territory. By this last there is not meant a return to the old idea of *patrimonium regis*, but that in States' transactions with each other this theoretical ownership should be predicated in order that States may deal with each other as individuals, or rather as *persons*.

Returning now from this historical excursion into the development of the concept "Sovereignty," we direct our attention to a consideration of its nature.

The Nature of Sovereignty.— That which first impresses one in a consideration of the attributes of the State, is its possession of omnipotent rulership over all matters that arise between itself and the individuals of which it is composed, and between the individuals themselves. The State is the all-powerful ruling organization of a People. Through its instrumentality alone, directly or indirectly, are finally determined what shall be the rules of conduct that shall obtain in the regulation of all interests that arise from the social and political life of its citizens. Its authority is superior to all other humanly established authorities; and all political powers exercised by other individuals or bodies of individuals are ultimately derived from it. It alone has the power of expressing a command, or of determining the validity of an existing rule with such absolute authority that no recourse is admitted to another power, either in search for the authority upon which such order or command is based, or for the ultimate determination of the wisdom or moral propriety of the actions so ordered. The State is thus supreme not only as giving the ultimate validity to all law, but *as itself determining the scope of its own powers*, and itself deciding what interests shall be subjected to its regulation. In these particulars the State is distinguished from all other persons and public bodies. In contradistinction to the latter, it sets to itself its own rights, and the limits of its own authority. As Jellinek puts it in his work *Gesetz und Verordnung*, "The rights and duties of individuals receive their potency and authority, from grounds set forth in objective law. The State finds the ground for its own rights and duties in itself."[1] Or, as he expresses it in another work, "Obligation through its own will, is the legal characteristic of the State."[2]

To much the same effect is the definition of Gareis: "The ruling State (*Gemeinwesen*) can declare as its interest, and establish as a matter of law (*Rechtsgut*) whatever interest it wills, and can apply whatever means it sees fit for the satisfaction of that interest — this is Sovereignty, an essential characteristic of the State as a ruling public body."[3]

[1] p. 196.
[2] *Die Lehre von den Staatenverbindungen*, p. 34.
[3] *Allgemeines Staatsrecht*, p. 20.

Brie makes the State's "universality of competence" (*Allseitigkeit der Zuständigkeit*) its essential characteristic, and the one attribute by the possession of which the State is distinguished from all other public organizations.[1] But, as Jellinek correctly points out, Sovereignty and *Allseitigkeit der Zuständigkeit* are related to each other as cause and effect. That is to say, unlimited competence follows because, and merely because, the State has this supreme or sovereign power.

We must distinguish, however, between this potentiality of power, as a juristic conception, and the State's actual competence; just as, in international law, the theoretical equality of sovereign States is distinguished from their actual inequality. At any one time the State actually exercises through its governmental organization only those powers which it has drawn to itself by formal adoption. The residue belongs to it only in a potential aspect, and at any one time the amount of this power, and the manner in which it may be actually exercised, depends upon the character and disposition of its citizens; that is to say, upon their willingness to submit to such exercise without insurrection. This ultimate power of the people to condition the exercise of governmental powers will receive consideration in a subsequent chapter.

Sovereignty is something more than a collection of powers. It is something more than a mechanical aggregate of separate and particular capacities. It

---

[1] *Theorie der Staatenverbindungen.*

does, indeed, include and necessitate the possession of certain powers, such as, for example, those of taxation, of contracting treaties, maintaining an armed force, etc.; but its content is not exhausted by an enumeration of these. It is an entity of itself, and represents the highest political power as embodied in the State.

Sovereignty belongs to the State as a person, and represents the supremacy of its will. Sovereignty is thus independent of its particular powers, in the same way that the self-conscious power of volition and determination of the individual human person is distinguished from his various faculties or the aggregate of them. It is the very possession of this sovereign will that gives personality to a politically organized community.

Sovereignty, as thus expressing a supreme will, is necessarily a unity and indivisible, — unity being a necessary predicate of a supreme will. As Rousseau truly says: "Though Power may be divided, Will cannot." The logical impossibility of conceiving of a divided Sovereignty is apparent from the impossibility of predicating in the same body two powers each supreme. The will of the State may find its form of expression through different mouth-pieces, and its activities may be exercised through a variety of organs, but the will itself, as thus variously expressed and performed, is a unity. In every political organization there must be one and only one source, whence all authority ultimately springs.

This leads us to the second view in which the Sovereignty of the State is to be considered: namely, that of the relation of a State to other States. Thus far, we have considered Sovereignty as expressing the supremacy of the State's will over that of all persons and public bodies within its own organization: as binding them all, and being bound by none. Viewing it outwardly, now, in its international aspects, Sovereignty denotes independence, or complete freedom from all external control of a legal character. The State can be legally bound only by its own will. If upon any one point, however insignificant, its own will be not conclusive, but is legally dependent upon the consent of another power, its Sovereignty is destroyed. Theoretically, the State may go to any extent in the delegation of the exercise of its powers to other public bodies, or even to other States; so that, in fact, it may retain under its own direction only the most meagre complement of activities, and yet not impair its Sovereignty. The State's essential unity is not thus destroyed, for in all such cases the other public bodies or States, to which have been delegated the exercise of these powers, act but as the agents of the State in question, and the original State still possesses the legal power, at least, of again drawing to itself the actual exercise of the powers thus granted. Thus, mother countries may concede to colonies the most complete autonomy of government, and reserve to themselves a control that may be of such slight and negative character as to make its exercise of the most rare occurrence; yet as long as such control exists, the Sovereignty of the mother country over its colony is not released, and such colony is to be considered as possessing only administrative autonomy, not political independence. Again, in the so-called Composite State, the individual States may yield to the central government the exercise of almost all their powers, and yet retain their Sovereignty. Or, on the other hand, a State may, without destroying its Sovereignty, yield to particular territorial divisions such amplitude of power as to create of them political bodies endowed with almost all the characteristics of independent States. In all States, indeed, when of any considerable size, efficiency of administration demands that certain powers of local self-government be granted to particular districts.

In all those cases in which, owing to the distribution of governing powers, there is doubt as to the political body in which the Sovereignty rests, the test to be applied is the determination of which authority has, in the last instance, the legal power to determine its own competence as well as that of the others. The relations between different Governments are often so complicated that this point is not easy of determination. Especially is this difficult, where, as sometimes occurs, the fundamental laws determining these relations are expressed in words whose literal interpretation contradicts the actual facts of the case. Thus, for example, in the United States, the individual States are declared by the constitution to be the possessors of sovereign rights, when a careful analysis of the nature of the union shows this to be impossible. We shall return again, in the next chapter, to the questions presented by the so-called Federal State.

This principle of entire legal independence as a consequence of Sovereignty is not contradicted by the existence of a large body of definite international regulations to which all civilized nations render common obedience. Nor is the frequent creation of particular international obligations of more or less permanency by means of treaties and conventions entered into between States. The subjects of international law are sovereign States, and the validity of their promises to each other rest upon no other coercive force than that of morality and public expediency. In no wise do the commands of so-called international law appear as directed by a political superior to a political inferior. Also, in the formulation and ratification of treaties, no power is created superior to that individually possessed by the contracting parties. As to the subject matters to be enforced by them, such parties remain subject only to their own wills, and not to that of a foreign power. As Jellinek briefly puts it "*Der Staatenvertrag bindet, aber er unterwerft nicht.*"[1] *Rebus sic stantibus*, expressed or implied, is a clause in every treaty, and States have ever asserted the right to declare such instruments of no force when by change of conditions their welfare has become so greatly affected or menaced as to overbalance the evil results to be ex-

[1] *Gesetz und Verordnung*, p. 205.

pected, by way of retaliation or otherwise, from the violation of their faith as given in a treaty. Thus says Vattel in his *Law of Nations:* "Though a simple injury or some disadvantage in a treaty be not sufficient to invalidate it, the case is not the same with those inconveniences that would lead to the ruination of the nation. Since, in the formulation of every treaty, the contracting parties must be vested with sufficient powers for the purpose, a treaty pernicious to the State is null, and not at all obligatory, as no conductor of a nation has the power to enter into engagements to do such things as are capable of destroying the State, for whose safety the Government is entrusted to him. The Nation itself, being necessarily obliged to perform every act required for its preservation and safety, cannot enter into engagements contrary to its indispensable obligations." And this is the assertion of the writer, who, possibly more than any other authority on International Principles, emphasizes the obligations of States as moral individuals.

It therefore appears that the force, not only of general international regulations, but of those principles specially created by nations by mutual consent and promise, is no greater than that derived from the continued consent and voluntary acceptance of the legal subjects upon whom the regulations are imposed.

Austin, in his lectures, refused to designate as positive law the rules that control the international relations of States, and in this he was, therefore, logically and scientifically correct. The term "law," when applied to the rules and principles that prevail between independent nations, is misleading because such rules depend for their entire validity upon the forbearance and consent of the parties to whom they apply, and are not and cannot be legally enforced by any common superior. In a command there is the necessary idea of superior and inferior, while in international relations the fundamental postulate is that of the theoretical equality of the parties, however much they may differ in actual strength. Finally, there exist no tribunals wherein these principles may be interpreted and applied to particular cases. The uniformity with which these principles are followed, and the practical necessity under which, at least, the smaller States are to obey them, does not alter the case. The sanction to most of these rules may be, as a matter of fact, very strong and effective, but it is not a legal sanction. Regulations which depend upon the consent of the parties to whom they apply, not only for their interpretation and application, but for their enforcement, certainly partake insufficiently of those qualities which would cause them to be designated, *in sensu strictiore*, laws. International regulations thus resemble in this respect many of the agreements that are daily entered into between individuals, by which moral obligations are incurred, but for the enforcement of which, in case of violation, there are no legal means provided. Of this character, for example, are the verbal promises to pay the debt of another, certain contracts in regard to land not expressed in writing; and, indeed, the countless minor engagements entered into between persons, which cannot be enforced in courts of law, and which yet lay the parties under a moral obligation.

Upon this point, and in fact upon the whole question as to whether custom is law before its acceptance by the State as a rule of conduct to be enforced, a most luminous case is that of *The Queen* v. *Keyn*.[1] In this case, the defendant, an officer commanding a foreign ship, when within two miles of Dover negligently ran his vessel into an English ship and caused the death of a passenger. For this he was tried before an English criminal court and convicted of manslaughter. Upon appeal, the question of jurisdiction was raised, the point being alleged that though writers on so-called international law were substantially agreed that it was the custom of civilized nations to regard the coast water, to a distance greater than that at which the accident occurred from England, as belonging to the territory of the country the coasts of which it washes; yet, that it did not appear that this doctrine had ever been explicitly accepted by any English court or legislature. It therefore remained to be decided whether or not the mere fact of the acknowledged utility, and almost universality of acceptance, of this international principle could give to it sufficient legal force to permit it to be enforced by the English

[1] *L. R.* 2 *Ex. Div.* 63.

courts. The majority of the court held (and correctly as we maintain) that it did not. Thus asks Lord Chief Justice Cockburn, in the opinion rendered: "Can a portion of that which was before high sea have been converted into British territory without any action on the part of the British Government or Legislature — by the mere assertions of writers on public law — or even by the assent of other nations? And when in support of this position, or of the theory of the three-mile zone in general, the statements of the writers on International Law are relied on, the question may well be asked, upon what authority are these statements founded? When and in what manner have the nations, who are to be affected by such a rule, as these writers, following one another, have laid down, signified their assent to it? — to say nothing of the difficulty which might be found in saying to which of these conflicting opinions such assent had been given."[1]

As is to be expected, Maine is unsatisfied with this reasoning. Just as he sees in custom the source of municipal law, so he sees in the consent of nations the creation of true international law. He conceives himself further supported in this view by the proposition laid down in Wharton's *Digest of the International Law of the United States*, according to which "the law of the United States ought not, if it be avoidable, so to be construed as to infringe the common principles and usages of nations, and the general doctrines of international law." Now, to the

[1] Quoted by Maine, *International Law*, p. 43.

writer this would seem to have a diametrically opposite effect, — to invalidate Maine's position rather than to maintain it. "Ought not, if it be avoidable, so to be construed." Here is plainly indicated the power of the United States Congress to enact laws in conflict with international doctrines, and hence what binding force can such rules have over the United States beyond its own consent to them? It is just as the word "ought" indicates, — only a moral duty, or one of political expediency.[1]

In the absence, then, of a common superior, the only rational view in which States are to be regarded in their relations to each other is that of freedom from all possible legal control; and with their mutual interests subject only to such regulations as the considerations of justice and expediency shall dictate. International "rights," strictly speaking, do not exist. Nations are, as individuals, in that state of nature in which Hobbes, Locke, and Rousseau placed primitive man. As Spinoza says: "*duae civitates natura hostes sunt. Homines enim in*

[1] "The expression 'International Law,'" says Stephen, in his *History of Criminal Law*, "is, I think, misleading. . . . When it is applied to principles and rules prevailing between independent nations, the word 'law' conveys a false idea, because the principles and rules referred to are not and cannot be enforced by any common superior upon the nations to the conduct of which they apply. When it is applied to parts of the law of each nation in which other nations are interested, the word 'law' is correct, but the word 'international' is likely to mislead, because though such laws are laws in the fullest sense of the word, and are enforced as such, they are the laws of each individual nation, and are not laws between nation and nation. . . . If Parliament were to pass an act expressly and avowedly opposed to the law of nations, the English courts would administer it in preference to the law of nations, whatever that may be" (pp. 35 *et seq.*).

statu naturali hostes sunt. Qui igitur jus naturae extra civitatem retinent hostes manent."[1] The *jura belli* are the powers of one State to attack or defend itself against another. The *jura pactis* lasts only as long as the agreement, the *fœdus* lasts, and this lasts only as long as the fear or hope which led to its being made continues to be shared by the nations which made it.

No more than so-called international law, does constitutional law place a legal limitation upon the Sovereignty of the State. Not, however, for the same reasons as those advanced by Austin. According to him, constitutional law (designating by that term those rules that define the organization of the State, and the extent and manner of exercise of governmental powers) is not law at all because purporting to control the State, which is, *ex hypothesi*, incapable of legal limitation. That which gives to them force, says Austin, is public opinion regarding their expediency and morality; they are not uttered by the State, nor do they legally control it. In fine, they belong to the class of moral rather than legal rules.

In this Austin is plainly wrong. The position does not follow as a logical necessity from his definition of law. Constitutional provisions do not purport to control the State, but the Government. This vital distinction Austin did not grasp. As we have seen, the State is not limited to its ordinary legislature as a mouth-piece for the expression of

[1] *Tractatus politicus*, III. 13. Cf. Green's *Philosophical Works*, Vol. II. p. 358.

its will. Whether constitutional provisions become established by custom, and are acquiesced in by the political authority, or are formally uttered in constitutional conventions, they express the supreme will of the State. Thus in the United States, though federal constitutional conventions may be but rarely called into existence, they are, when so created, as much organs of the State, as is the Congress that maintains a continued existence; and their utterances are as much expressions of the State's will (and therefore laws) as are the statutory enactments of the ordinary law-making body.

At any one time, the Government of a State is the sovereign organization of that State, and possesses in its entirety all the sovereign powers of the State. Not that any one organ thereof is able to wield the entire power of the State, but that all the organs together possess that power. There is nothing in the essence of the sovereign State to indicate that its Sovereignty may not be given to different organs for its exercise. In the United States, that portion of the sovereign power that may not be exercised by its other organs, is possessed by its constitutional conventions for purposes of constitutional amendment, or by the State Legislatures acting as such. Though the necessity may but rarely, and possibly never, arise for calling these latter organs into activity, their existence is provided for in our scheme of governmental organization, and when there is the necessity for the exercise of that part of the State's power which is given to them, their action will be had. But to speak of a State as not being completely organized in its government, seems as much an absurdity as to say that a man is not completely organized in his physical frame. The Government is the State's organization. By very necessity, the power of every person must be lodged somewhere in its own organs. The State is society politically organized, and there can be no State action or political existence outside of such organization.[1]

The fact is, that Austin's conception of the nature

---

[1] Professor Burgess speaks of a State as not necessarily completely organized in its government.—*Political Science and Constitutional Law.* But it is to be observed that with this writer the terms "Government" and "State" are not distinguished in the same way that they have been in this treatise. With him, the former of these two terms is used to describe the ordinary administrative and legislative organs, while the latter has reference to the body politic as organized in constitutional convention, or otherwise, for the creation of fundamental or constitutional law. Thus, for example, he says of the United States: "With us the government is not the sovereign organization of the State. Back of the government lies the constitution; and back of the constitution the original sovereign state, which ordains the constitution both of government and of liberty." (Vol. I. p. 57.) Of England, he says: "First, the king was the State as well as the government. Then the nobles became the State, and the king became government only. Then the commons became the State, and both king and lords became but parts of the government." (Vol. I. p. 69.) There is, possibly, no logical objection to using these terms in the above manner, and the distinction between constituent and other functions of the political power is of great value in an analysis of governmental duties. At the same time, it appears to us, that to apply the names "State" and "Government" to the body politic when acting in those two capacities, cannot but create confusion. Apart from the inherent difficulty of applying them exactly in this sense to particular cases, there is suggested an antithesis between two classes of functions that differ not as to kind, but only as to the subject matter with which they have to deal. This point will appear more plainly in our next chapter.

of constitutional law was largely determined by the particular conditions under which the powers of his own government were exercised. As a matter of fact a very large portion of the rules according to which the English Government is, and was at Austin's time, habitually exercised, are truly to be considered, as he maintains, not laws at all but customary rules of morality and political expediency. They are, as Dicey says, "Conventions, understandings, habits or practices, which, though they may regulate the conduct of the several members of the sovereign power of the Ministry, or of other officials, are not in reality laws at all since they are not enforced by the courts."[1] Examples of these conventions are the maxims, that the King must consent to any bill passed by the two Houses of Parliament; that the House of Lords may not originate a money bill; that the Ministers must resign office when they cease to command the confidence of the House of Commons, etc.

That which distinguishes these conventions or customs of the constitution from positive law is not so much their lack of actual binding power (for so great is their actual obligatory force as to make the open contravention of many of them as unlikely as if they were actually established in a fundamental instrument of government), but the fact that should they be violated, no greater consequence would be entailed upon the officers so doing, than that of popular blame and unpopularity. There

[1] *Law of the Constitution*, 4th ed. p. 23.

would be no legal action that could be sustained either to enforce the recognition of such violated maxims or to punish their contravention.[1]

Now, in so far as Austin limited the exclusion of constitutional regulations from the domain of law to principles of this class, he was logically correct. But he did more than this. He applied the exclusion without reservation to all provisions that purport to regulate the manner of exercise of the State's power. This was his error.

The freedom of the State from all *legal* limitations upon its competence does not negate the power of a State to set formal limits to the exercise of its own powers, such as are seen in the restrictions placed upon most modern States in their written constitutions. Nor, contrariwise, do the existence of these fundamental restrictions, however severe, contradict the possession of the sovereign power by such States. The creation of these constitutional limitations is due to the fact that, as the necessity for political rights guaranteed to the individual has become recognized, the propriety of fixing with a certain degree of definiteness the powers legally to be exercised by Governments, has been appreciated; and such limits upon governmental activity have been given a fair degree of permanency by means

[1] As shown, however, by Dicey, though these constitutional conventions are not capable of legal enforcement, yet so intimately are they connected with those operations of the English government that are backed by legal sanctions, that it would be practically impossible for a ministry to carry on the administration of public affairs in opposition to them, without bringing itself into almost immediate conflict with positive law. *Op. cit.* Chap. XV.

of self-set restrictions as to the manner in which such limits are to be formally and legally altered. In almost all cases, also, the extra importance of constitutional laws has led statesmen to provide that a more direct expression of the opinion of the people shall be had for their adoption or amendment, than is called for in the case of ordinary laws. Thus, in the governmental schemes of most States, while ordinary laws may be enacted by the representative legislatures; constitutional laws, so-called, require a special vote by the people, or at least the creation of a convention specially convened for the purpose. As thus situated, modern States, though potentially possessed of supreme power, cannot legally draw to themselves additional powers for actual administration except in the formal ways thus provided. Powers otherwise assumed and exercised are revolutionary acts, and, when permanently consented to by the people, amount, *pro tanto*, to the establishment by the people of a new State.

All law is a formal limitation of Sovereignty. Not only constitutional law, but all law, public and private, substantive and adjective, constitutes, while in force, a formal limitation upon the power of the State. Through laws are fixed the rights and the duties of individuals, and the manner in which such rights are to be exercised and enforced. As such, they are all of the same validity and are as binding upon the Government as are constitutional provisions. A public official will be as readily checked by the courts for the exercise of a power that contravenes an ordinary statute, as for an action that transgresses a rule of constitutional law. Constitutional laws differ from other laws only in their subject matter and in the manner in which they are established, amended or repealed. In some countries, as, for example, Germany, Prussia, Italy and England, there are not even these latter distinctions.[1]

[1] As evidencing the extent to which constitutional and ordinary law are assimilated in Germany, we may quote the following from Laband's standard work, *Das Staatsrecht des Deutschen Reiches* (2d ed. I. 546). "There is no will in the State," says he, "superior to that of the sovereign, and it is from this will that both the constitution and laws draw their binding force. The constitution is not a mystical power hovering above the State; but, like every other law, it is an act of its will, subject accordingly to the consequences of changes in the latter. A document may, it is true, prescribe that the constitution may not be altered indirectly (that is to say, by laws affecting its content), that it may be altered only directly, by laws modifying the text itself. But when such a restriction is not established by positive rule, it cannot be derived by implication from the legal character of the constitution and from an essential difference between the constitution and ordinary laws. The doctrine that individual laws ought always to be in harmony with the constitution, and that they must not be incompatible with it, is simply a postulate of legislative practice. It is not a legal axiom. Although it appears desirable that the system of public and private laws established by statute shall not be in contradiction with the text of the constitution, the existence of such a contradiction is possible in fact and admissible in law, just as a divergence between the penal, commercial, or civil code and a subsequent special law is possible." (Cf. Borgeaud, *Adoption and Amendment of Constitutions in Europe and America*, trans. p. 69 *et seq.*, where this passage is quoted and adversely commented upon.) Such a condition as above described by Laband would, of course, be impossible in the United States, where the decision as to the conformity of a given statute with the constitution is vested in an independent judiciary. But in the German Empire, though it is provided that no amendment of the constitution shall be made, if there be fourteen votes opposing in the Federal Council (*Bundesrath*); yet, since it lies only with the legislature or the Emperor to decide when a given statute *does* operate as an amendment of the constitution, it is possible to change that instrument in any way desired by ordinary legislative

It is common, indeed, to speak of constitutional law as of a higher order of law than statutes. But as said, this is true only as concerns subject matter, not as regards validity. Both are equally binding enactment, so long as that body or the Emperor does not see fit to declare such acts to be unconstitutional in character. Thus, as a matter of fact, the German constitution has been several times modified, as Laband says it properly may be done, by special laws in which more than fourteen opposing votes have been registered in the Upper Chamber. What has been here said in reference to the Empire holds true as well in Prussia. In France, likewise, there is no provision guarding against a modification of its constitution by ordinary laws, which, without nominally changing its text, do in fact violate its principles. Thus Dicey, in enumerating the various senses in which the term "unconstitutional law" is used, says: "The expression, as applied to a law passed by a French Parliament, means that the law, *e.g.* extending the length of the President's tenure of office, is opposed to the articles of the constitution. The expression does not necessarily mean that the law in question is void, for it is by no means certain that any French court will refuse to enforce a law because it is unconstitutional. The word would probably, though not of necessity, be, when employed by a Frenchman, a term of censure" (*Law of the Constitution*, 4th ed. Appendix, Note VI.). In a recent very able analysis of the present status of constitutional law in France, the writer says: "The first point to be emphasized is the tendency which now leads the French legislator to render the transformation of the constitutional laws easier by transferring to the domain of ordinary legislation, that is to say, placing within the normal competence of Parliament, matters belonging to the domain of constitutional law." As examples of this tendency are cited the amendment of June 21, 1879, which strikes out from the constitution the provisions relating to the seat of government, and that of Aug. 14, 1884, Article 3, which deprives of their constitutional force Articles 1 to 7 of the Constitutional Laws of February, 1875. (*The Development of the Present Constitution of France*, by Professor R. Saleilles, in the *Annals of the Am. Acad. of Pol. and Soc. Science*, July, 1895.) For an account of the manner in which the present Italian constitution is being constantly modified by statute, see *Annals of the Am. Acad.* VI. 31–57, article by G. Arangio Ruiz.

Another fact worthy of note in reference to German and Prussian law is that it is held by their leading publicists that the essential element in legislation is not the action of the legislative chambers at all,

upon the courts. Because constitutions often set limits to the legal power of legislatures, the enactment by them of laws transcending such limits is declared by the courts to be null and void. But

but the approval of the King in Prussia and of the Federal Council in the Empire. The Chambers simply draft the contents of the proposed law. Its legal character is wholly due to the approval of the executive. Thus says Schulze (*Preussisches Staatsrecht*, 2d ed. I. p. 158): "Everything which is decided or carried out in the State takes place in the name of the King. *He is the personified power of the State.*" And again: "The chambers have no co-ordinate sovereignty, and no *co-imperium*. As individual members and as a whole, they are *subjects* of the King." (*Op. cit.* I. p. 567–8.) "In the acceptance or rejection by the King lies the really decisive act. Only the approval of the King converts a will into a law. . . . It does not correspond with the theory of German constitutional law to speak of the various factors of legislation, still less to designate the positive law-creating power of the King as simply a negative veto. The King is not only one of the factors in legislation, *he is the law giver himself.*" (*Op. cit.* II. p. 21–22. Cf. *The Constitution of Prussia, Translated and Supplied with an Introduction and Notes* by J. H. Robinson, published as supplement to the *Annals of the Am. Acad.* Vol. V. No. 2, in which the above citations from Schulze are quoted.) Likewise says Laband in reference to imperial law: "The sovereignty of the State does not enter into the determination of the content of law, but only into the sanction which gives to the law its value. The sanction alone is an act of legislation in the legal sense of the word" (*Das Staatsrecht des Deutschen Reiches*, 2d ed. Vol. I. p. 517, quoted by Borgeaud, *op. cit.* p. 70). To much the same effect as the above is the view of the Austrian publicist, Jellinek. "*Nicht die kammern im Vereine mit dem Monarchen, sondern der Monarch allein nimmt die entscheidende legislatorische Thätigkeit vor,*" says he. "*Die Zustimmung der kammern zum gesetzesbefehle ist Bedingung, nicht Ursache desselben.*" (*Gesetz und Verordnung*, p. 317.)

Reasoning the same as above is likewise applicable to English law, notwithstanding the apparent weakness of the Crown in that country and the actual overwhelming power of the "Commons." In theory, at least, all British law owes its existence to the will of the Throne, and Queen Victoria possesses to-day, in a strict juristic sense, the same plenitude of legislative power that William the Conqueror exercised. Professor Hearn, in his work on *The Government of England*, is perhaps the one among English writers who most strongly empha-

when so acting, the courts do not thereby recognize a conflict of laws in which an inferior law yields to the higher validity of a superior one. That which they do, is simply to say that the statute in question, though enacted in the usual form, is not

sizes this point. "We hear constantly of the royal veto," says he, "of its absolute character, and of the danger that its revival might produce. It is assumed that the power of legislation resides in the council; and that the sovereign has merely a negative control on its deliberation, which power, however, he is bound not to exercise. Such a doctrine is altogether inconsistent with a right understanding of our constitution. The very use of the term 'Veto' suggests a false analogy. There is nothing in common between the refusal of our King to add to or alter the law, and the power of a Roman tribune to prevent in a particular instance the application of an existing law. Every act of Parliament bears in its very front the work of its original. It is 'enacted by the Queen's Most Excellent Majesty.' It is in the Crown, and not in the body which law assigns as the assistants and advisers of the Crown, that our constitution places this right. It is the King, as the old Year Book asserts, that 'makes the law by the assent of the peers, etc., and not the peers and the commune.' The power of legislation resides in Queen Victoria no less than it resided in William the Norman; but the conditions under which that power is exercised are indeed very different" (p. 51. Cf. Jellinek, *Gesetz und Verordnung*, Pt. I. Ch. I.).

As regards legislation in the United States, it need scarcely be said that all of the departments of its government trace their origin to the same source; and, in so far as they divide among them the law-making power, are co-ordinate organs for the exercise of the sovereign power. Thus the final approval affixed by the President to the acts of Congress is essentially a legislative act, but is not a more vital element in the law-creating process than is the approval of the Chambers. That is to say, the law, as finally established, embodies the joint will of the President and Congress, and not that of one alone. As regards his function of approving or disapproving of acts of Congress, the President is to that extent as much a part of the legislative organ as is any Representative or Senator. The case is not changed even in those cases in which laws are passed over the presidential veto. His will is overcome, but not excluded from the legislative act any more than the will of any member of the legislative body itself may be said to be so treated, when his vote is with that of the minority.

law at all, and never was law, because its subject matter did not lie within the legal competence of the legislature enacting it. As Cooley says in his *Principles of Constitutional Law,* "Such enactment is in strictness no law, because it establishes no rule: it is merely a futile attempt to establish a law."[1] Strictly speaking, then, the term "unconstitutional law" is a *contradictio in adjecto.*

Carrying this point still further, it will be seen that this distinction as to degree of validity is not to be drawn between law and ordinance. As ordinarily understood, an ordinance signifies a command of limited application, not necessarily permanent, and usually issued as an administrative direction by a department of Government. If legally issued, however, that is, if within the legal competence of the authority uttering it, these ordinances are of equal legal validity with the more general and formal mandates of the State.

To repeat, then, the limitations upon State action set by law are obviously merely formal in character. They are self-set by the State, and the same power that has decreed them still has the power to alter or abolish them, though this alteration or abolishment must be done in the formal and legal way. An unalterable law is a legal impossibility.

In other words, it must ever be the case that even the most fundamental provisions contained in written and formally adopted instruments of government are capable of alteration. To this assertion it may be

[1] *Student's Edition,* p. 24.

responded that there may be, and in fact are, instances of written constitutions that contain no grant of amending power. Such, for example, is the present constitution of Italy. In such cases we must say that it is to be considered as tacitly understood, that amendment may be made either by the ordinary legislative method, or by that same power by which the constitution was originally adopted. Where public demand has wrung written instruments of government from autocratic rulers, it is but natural that, in the absence of specific provisions for amendment, this power should be construed as residing in the legislative body which partakes of a popularly representative character. Thus, this has been the interpretation that has been accepted by Italian jurists. But, from the legal standpoint, it would seem that the more logical solution of the problem would be to say that this amending power is reserved by the monarch. Where the origin of the constitution is due to a grant from the ruler, it would seem that the same competence that enables him to make such a grant would enable him to alter its provisions at will.

But there may be alleged the possibility of a more extreme case than the one we have been considering; namely, that of a constitution containing the express provision that it shall be unalterable for all time. How is amendment to be legally secured in such a case as this? Here we are obviously thrown back upon the party or parties by whom, and the manner in which, the constitution was itself adopted.

We must examine the nature of this original act of establishment. In those cases where this has been in the nature of a concession or grant by a monarch previously unrestricted in the exercise of his power, it is clear, as we have already said, that a modification may be brought about by an exercise of the legal power of such ruler. There would be no more difficulty in a monarch so doing, than there is in an ordinary legislature repealing one of its own acts that it has previously declared to be unalterable and irrepealable.

It is very common to speak of the written constitutions of Europe that have been promulgated by monarchs in obedience to popular demand, as compacts between the Peoples and their respective sovereigns. But this is juristically incorrect. However expressed, and whatever may have been the actual conditions that have necessitated the establishment of these instruments, they do not have a contractual character. The two parties do not stand upon an equal footing. The authority of the Prince always predominates. It is his will that is contained in the constitutions, however much that will may actually have been influenced by the political exigency of popular demand.

When, however, we come to the case of a constitution adopted by a People in a revolutionary manner, that is, without the consent or legal action of the political authority under which such People had been previously living, we have a problem to which there is not such an obvious answer. We need first of all to inquire how such a constitution itself obtained a legal character in the beginning; or, in fact, how the constitution of any State, whether written or unwritten, acquires a legal force. If a people act in an illegal or revolutionary manner in the erection of a constitution, how do its provisions obtain a legal force; or, if action be again called for, for purposes of amendment, how are the People to act in a legal manner?

In answering this question, we must anticipate somewhat a discussion that is shortly to follow regarding the distinction between *de facto* and *de jure* governments. It will there appear that the terms *de facto* and *de jure*, as applicable to governments, are purely relative. That is to say, their force depends upon the standpoint from which the given government is viewed. When a revolutionary government is termed illegal, it is such only as viewed from the standpoint of that political power from which its adherents have forcibly removed themselves. Viewed, however, from the standpoint of those who favor the establishment of such a political power, it possesses a legal character. Its adherents claim that a new State has been established and that their action is legally justified by such State. In other words, Sovereignty, upon which all legality depends, is itself a question of fact, and not of law. If, now, it be asked by what means were established the organs by which the constitution was framed in such a case as we have stated, and whence the authority of such organs to declare the manner in which such instrument is to be considered as adopted and as valid,—to this it must be responded that the act was a purely popular one. The State, as has been said, is in all cases essentially popular in origin, resting upon a sentiment of unity. Its establishment is not a juristic act. Synchronous with the creation of a political power, some sort of governmental organization is, by necessity, established. Now, this original primitive organization, spontaneously evolved, as it were, from a popular source, we must consider as due to an act of the State organized for the time being upon a completely democratic basis. Therefore, all States, at the time of their first inception, necessarily have a popular form of governmental organization, and from this popular governing body is derived the authority of particular persons or bodies of persons to frame definite and more permanent principles of government, and to declare the conditions according to which such principles shall be considered as legally adopted.

Hence, we must conclude, that in those cases in which there is the explicit assertion that the constitution shall not be altered, amendment is to be secured in the manner in which the constitution itself was originally adopted; and, if the constitution have a revolutionary basis, and there is a denial in it of any right of amendment, this residual portion of Sovereignty resides in the people acting as a democratic organ of Government. It is to be emphasized, however, that, any provisions for the amendment of a constitution once established, the action of the sovereign State is henceforth formally limited thereby. That is to say, its subsequent action must be in conformity with such provisions, and, if they become irksome, they must first be amended or repealed in the formal manner provided. The State cannot, in other words, exercise any of its powers in other than a legal manner. The State's will can be expressed only in the form of law, and an illegal act is not an act of the State. The State may, indeed, so surround the assumption of this or that function with legal restrictions that when the exercise of it becomes necessary, revolutionary, and therefore illegal, methods become an easier means of obtaining them than constitutional ones. But when such action is had, and is permanently acquiesced in by the People, it must be juristically held that the old State has been destroyed and a new State with new and additional governmental powers established.

It may seem that we have followed to unnecessary length this hypothetical case, — one so opposed to all ideas of political expediency as to make its occurrence scarcely possible in this age at least, — but it has been necessary to do this in order to carry out to its logical proof the fundamentally important position that the State is not and cannot be itself controlled (except formally) by constitutional law. Somewhere within its power must lie the legal competence to express a will that is sovereign and therefore without limitation.

Another way of stating the fact that the State is not subject to legal limitation is the assertion that it cannot by law deprive itself beyond recall of any portion of its Sovereignty.

Distinct from the question of the power of the State to alienate its Sovereignty to another political body, is that of its ability to decree its own dissolution. Upon this point says Dicey, in the work already cited, "The impossibility of placing a limit on the exercise of Sovereignty does not in any way prohibit, either logically or in matter of fact, the abdication of Sovereignty. This is worth observation because a strange dogma is sometimes put forward, that a sovereign power, such as the Parliament of the United Kingdom, can never by its own act divest itself of Sovereignty. This position is, however, clearly untenable. An autocrat, such as the Russian Czar, can undoubtedly abdicate; but Sovereignty, or the possession of a supreme power in a state, whether it be in the hands of a Czar or of a Parliament, is always one and the same quality. If the Czar can abdicate, so can Parliament. To argue or imply that because Sovereignty is not limitable (which is true) it cannot be surrendered (which is palpably untrue) involves the confusion of two distinct ideas. It is like arguing that because no man can, while he lives, give up, do what he will, his freedom of volition, so no man can commit suicide. A sovereign power can divest itself of authority in two ways, and (it is submitted) in two ways only. It may simply put an end to its own existence.

Parliament could extinguish itself by legally dissolving itself and leaving no means whereby a subsequent Parliament could be legally summoned. A sovereign again may transfer sovereign authority to another person or body of persons." [1]

To this argument we give our full approval, though, for the sake of perfect explicitness, it will be well, perhaps, again to call attention to the distinction that is to be made between Sovereignty itself and the person or body of persons through whom it is legally exercised. Where there is, in fact, a legal transfer of the power of exercising Sovereignty from one body to another, such an act is the surrendering of power by a particular governing body, but it is not a parting with Sovereignty by the State. Hence it is, as Dicey says, not to be compared with the power of the State to decree its own dissolution, nor to be supported by analogy with the control that man has over the continued existence of his own life, though without the power, while living, to limit his own volitional powers. The State is therefore no more able to transfer its Sovereignty, that is, its very life and personality, than a man has the power to transfer *his* life or personality.

But we are not yet done with the objections that are made to the position that we have assumed in this chapter. Criticism has been made to the assertion that no State, however willing, can surrender its own Sovereignty, or, if we may use the expression, grant away a territorial portion of it, on the ground that

[1] *Law of the Constitution*, 4th ed., p. 65, note.

it would lead to the *reductio ad absurdum* that Athens and Rome must still be regarded as sovereign and the United States as yet subject to England.[1] But this is by no means the logical result. The United Colonies in America acquired Sovereignty when they organized themselves as an independent community. Their Sovereignty did not date from the signing of the treaty with England, but, if any exact date can be placed to it, from the signing of the Declaration of Independence.[2] It is true that in the treaty of Paris and Versailles, in 1783, England for the first time conceded this independence; but the mere fact that this was done by a treaty shows that the United States was already a State. England but formally acquiesced in and recognized a state of affairs that had already become an established fact. From the English standpoint, the action of the colonies in revolting was undeniably an illegal act, and it was not made a legal one by her recognition of our independence. On the other hand we did not need the acknowledgment of England in order to assume the character of a sovereign nation. Before that, we had entered the family of nations, and had been recognized by them as a member. When, for

---

[1] "The Nature of the Federal State," by E. V. Robinson, in *Annals of Am. Acad. of Pol. and Soc. Sci.*, May, 1894.

[2] In *McIlvaine v. Coxe's Lessee*, 4 Cr. 212, the Supreme Court of the United States say, "That the several States which compose this Union, so far at least as regards their municipal regulations, became entitled, from the time when they declared themselves independent, to all the rights and powers of sovereign states, and that they did not derive them from concessions made by the British King. The treaty of peace contains a recognition of their independence, not a grant of it."

example, in 1778, France entered into a treaty of alliance and commerce with us, she did so upon the express declaration that "the people of these colonies were in the public possession of their independence."

To take another example: How did Germany obtain her Sovereignty over the provinces of Alsace and Lorraine, ceded to her at the end of the Franco-Prussian War? We answer that it was by virtue of actual annexation by Germany, and submission on the part of their inhabitants to such annexation; not by virtue of the treaty of Versailles in which the transfer was acquiesced in by France. The fact may be that the inhabitants of these provinces never actively desired this transference of allegiance, and even at the present day would gladly return to France, but this does not affect the Sovereignty of the German Empire over them. When it is said that that which gives birth to the Nation and State is the feeling of unity that exists in the People, it is meant that, taking them as a whole, this sentiment is sufficiently strong to keep them united and make them obedient to the ruling authorities that be; that the General Will shall support the State, not that each and every particular inhabitant or group of inhabitants shall freely accept the State's authority as just and proper. In fact, disaffection on the part of the people may extend, without destroying the Sovereignty of the State, to any point short of that which will occasion and support successful revolution.

States de facto and Governments de facto and de jure. — A State is not amenable to the qualification of *de jure* or *non de jure,* because it is not a creature of law. Such terms are applicable only to government bodies. As we have already several times said, a juristic origin cannot be ascribed to the State. An organized community of men either constitute or do not constitute a State, according to whether there is or is not to be discovered therein a supreme will acting upon all persons or other bodies within its limits.[1]

This point may seem sufficiently obvious, but it will scarcely be a waste of space to quote from Green a paragraph in which it is philosophically demonstrated with complete clearness. "But whether or no," says he, "in any qualified sense of 'sovereign' or '*jus*,' a sovereign that is not so '*de jure*' is possible, once understand by 'sovereign' the determinate person or persons with whom the ultimate law-imposing and law-enforcing power resides, and by '*jus*,' law, it is then obviously a contradiction to speak of a sovereign '*de jure*' as distinguished from one '*de facto*.' The power of the ultimate imponent of law cannot be derived from, or limited by, law. The

---

[1] Thus Hurd states the problem as to the character of the national government established in 1789, as depending upon "Whether each or any one of the thirteen original States ever, at any moment after their ceasing to be dependent as colonies, had exhibited force and will as sustaining, severally, the powers belonging to every sovereign nation, or State, in that sense; or — Whether it was only by a common force and will exerted by them as one integral nation or State that they had claimed and sustained those powers." *The Union-State,* p. 11.

sovereign may, no doubt, by a legislative act of its own, lay down rules as to the mode in which its power shall be exercised, but if it is sovereign in the sense supposed, it must always be open to it to alter these rules. There can be no illegality in its doing so. In short, in whatever sense '*jus*' is derived from the sovereign, in that sense no sovereign can hold his power '*de jure*.' So Spinoza held that '*imperium*' was '*de jure*' indeed, but '*de jure naturali*' ('*jus naturale*' = natural power), which is the same as '*de jure divino*'; only powers exercised in subordination to '*imperium*' are '*de jure civili*.' So Hobbes said that there could be no 'unjust law.' A law was not a law unless enacted by a sovereign, and 'the just' being that to which the sovereign obliges, the sovereign could not enact the unjust, though it might enact the inequitable and the pernicious, the 'inequitable' presumably meaning that which conflicts with the law of nature, the 'pernicious' that which tends to weaken individuals or society."[1]

The terms *de jure* and *non de jure* are, however, applicable to Governments.

All bodies claiming political authority, possess or not a *de jure* character according to whether or not they are established, represent, and are guided by the will of the State into which the individuals, over whom their claim to authority extends, are organized. Thus, given a certain State, no persons or bodies may exercise legal functions except those included

[1] *Philosophical Works*, Vol. II. p. 412.

within the formal limits that the laws provide. All powers otherwise exercised are not State powers; and, of course, those exercising them do not, *ad hoc*, constitute parts of its government. At the same time, from the standpoint of those who have openly cast off their allegiance to an existing State, and claim to have organized themselves into a new State,— from their standpoint,— such governmental authorities as they have established, have a *de jure* character, and the old governmental machinery can only be considered by them as maintaining a *de facto* existence. Thus Rousseau considered all the governments of his time as having only a *de facto* and not a *de jure* existence from the fact of their not being founded upon the one legitimate basis of popular sovereignty as he understood it. In the same way the government of Cromwell, from the Royalist standpoint, never obtained a *de jure* character; any more than the present French Government is held as such by Orleanists and Legitimists.

In the rules that regulate international relations, however, there is used the term *de facto* State, and it often becomes a very important point to determine whether the conditions in particular instances are such as authorize the recognition of given organizations by the family of Nations, as maintaining a *de facto* existence as independent political bodies. This arises from the fact that the rules of international procedure require that, in contests between States, certain international rights shall be recognized. It, therefore, frequently becomes necessary to determine whether or not such contesting bodies shall be entitled to these rights. The circumstance under which this question most frequently arises is in the case of revolutions or rebellions, in which certain communities of men have openly separated themselves from their former political bonds and are claiming an independent political existence. When these seceding communities have obtained for themselves a certain degree of stability and prospect of ultimate success, it becomes necessary for other Nations to determine whether or not, in their relations with them, they will recognize them as independent States; that is, as *Subjects* of so-called international law. The recognition by a neutral power of the government of a revolting people as a State *de facto,* is a proper *casus belli* for the power claiming dominion over such revolting country, if such recognition precedes the exhibition by the newly formed government of an ability to maintain its independence. In our late Civil War, when English sentiment seemed so strongly to incline towards the Southern cause, there was the gravest apprehension felt as to the attitude that would be taken by the British Government in this connection. It is true that the United States recognized the Confederate Government, *sub modo* from principles of humanity, as a State, to be treated with for the exchange and humane treatment of prisoners, and saw fit, among other belligerent rights, to exercise the right of declaring a blockade of the Southern ports, instead of interdicting commerce through these ports by municipal regulation.

Furthermore, our courts have repeatedly held in particular instances since the war that the Confederate Governments possessed a *de facto* existence for domestic purposes. But this has been done from principles of justice and humanity, and not because the Federal Government ever recognized in the seceding States a *status* as an independent Nation, and entitled as such to full international rights. Certainly there never was a time at which we would not have considered it equivalent to a declaration of war on the part of the foreign Nation that should have recognized them as such.

The fact that the insurgent States were able to establish a government that had the power of exercising coercive authority for several years over a large portion of the Southern territory, was not sufficient to give to them the status of *de facto* States. This was because at no one time did they exercise the supreme authority without active contest on the part of the United States, nor did they ever prove themselves able to maintain a permanent control. Thus the Confederate States were distinguished from the *de facto* government of England under Cromwell, under which, for a while, the regularly constituted powers were expelled from the seat of power, and the Commonwealth's own public officers put in their places, so as to represent in fact the Sovereignty of the Nation. As say the Supreme Court of the United States, " The Confederate Government was not of this kind. It never represented the Nation; it never expelled the public authorities from the country; it never entered into any treaties, nor was it ever recognized as that of an independent power. It collected an immense military force and temporarily expelled the authorities of the United States from the territory over which it exercised an usurped dominion; but in that expulsion the United States never acquiesced; on the contrary they immediately resorted to similar force to regain possession of that territory and re-establish their authority, and they continued to use such force until they succeeded." [1]

The conclusion follows from all that we have said, that Sovereignty being inalienable, a new State can take its origin only by the entire withdrawal of the people organized under it, from the civic bonds in which they have been living, and the establishment then, by them, of a new body politic. Not until the old State has been destroyed, either peaceably or by force, can the new State take its rise. For it is obvious that a People cannot live under two sovereign powers at the same time; that is, under both the old and the new. Nor, can the new State draw its vitality directly from the old; for, as we have seen, the transference of Sovereignty is impossible.

Whenever there is established a new government, whose powers are obtained through constitutional

---

[1] *Williams* v. *Bruffy*, 6 Otto 176. See also *Smith* v. *Stewart*, 21 La. Annual 67, and cases there cited. For a *resumé* of the whole topic, see *The American and English Encyclopædia of Law*, article "Government."

means, no new State is created, however much its powers may differ from those exercised under the old regime. There is only an amendment of the constitution of the old State. It may thus happen that in one case constitutional amendments may be so important and radical as to change entirely the governmental organization of a State; and in another instance a new State may be established by revolutionary means, whose powers and organization may differ only in the slightest degree from those of the old State. But the essentially different juristic natures of the two actions are not to be confounded. *It is not the amount of change, but the manner in which such change is effected, that determines whether or not a new body politic is created.*

That which gives life to the State, and maintains its vitality, is the feeling of unity that binds together the People. It is indeed possible, and, in fact, is very generally the case in modern times, that in the establishment of a new State in the place of a formerly existing one, the old political forms and governmental machinery are utilized by the People in attaining the purposes of their new political life. Furthermore, it is entirely possible that the establishment of the new State may be declared by the People in assemblies and through organs that have existed as a part of the machinery of the State that is destroyed; but in so acting, it is the People that act, and not the old State through whose mechanical organization they may have operated. In the United States, one of the means provided for the ratification of constitutional amendments is the approval of three-fourths of the State legislatures. When so acting, however, these legislatures, though primarily the law-making organs of the individual Commonwealths, represent the whole people, and act as agents of the central power.

CHAPTER X

THE NATURE OF THE COMPOSITE STATE

THE facts that seem especially to contradict the principles that have been above evolved in reference to the subject of Sovereignty, are those presented by types of Composite, or so-called Federal States. In these political forms appear to be, and by many publicists are recognized to be, examples of States with divided or limited Sovereignty, of non-sovereign States, and of States created by the joint action of other States. So important in the modern world has become this federal type of State life, that it is worth our while to consider at some little length the problems in political theory to which it gives rise. Just as in the Middle Ages the tendency was towards feudalism, and in the fifteenth and sixteenth centuries towards absolutism, so at the present time the movement seems towards Federalism. In Europe we see the federal empire of Germany, the dual empire of Austria-Hungary, the dual kingdom of Norway and Sweden, the Swiss Federation, and the more or less close unions between the various nationalities of the Balkan Peninsula and the other powers. In South America are to be seen the Brazilian and other Federations; in North America, Mexico, and the Dominion of Canada, with their essentially federal features, and, above all, our own federal Union. The drift towards federalism is also strongly exhibited in the English government of Australasia. Already several of her provinces have joined in federal bonds, and a movement towards an imperial federation of all the English possessions is believed by many to be steadily gaining ground. The strength of the federal movement in general depends upon the means that it affords for satisfying the demands of local or national particularism, and, at the same time, for obtaining unity of political action between Peoples allied by economic, historical, or ethnic interests.

So difficult of classification and interpretation have become many of the phenomena connected with these federal forms, that many writers have been wont to escape from their perplexity by considering this type of political life as *sui generis,* and as such to be interpreted by laws other than those that apply to ordinary forms. Such a conclusion as this is, however, an obviously fatal objection to any system of political philosophy. If a philosophical system be correct, its laws must be universally applicable, and this is as true in the field of political phenomena, as it is in other domains of fact. It is incumbent upon us, therefore, to apply the principles which we have evolved to the federal form of State life, as well as to other forms, and thereby to demonstrate that the apparent incongruities which the former exhibits are apparent rather than real. The success with which this undertaking is accomplished will determine in a large measure the correctness of the conclusions which we have drawn.

The problem of properly classifying and designating the various unions into which the States of the world have at different times entered, is one that has especially attracted the attention of German publicists. The most important work in this field is that of Jellinek, entitled *Die Lehre von den Staatenverbindungen*, which we have already had occasion to cite. Other works are those of Brie,[1] Westerkamp[2] and Waitz.[3] This subject is also of course considered by all writers dealing particularly with the public law of the German Empire. The work of Laband[4] is especially valuable in this respect. Those American writers who have dealt with the constitutional character of their own States, have generally limited themselves to a consideration of the differences between a "Federal State" and a "Confederacy."[5]

Jellinek, in his classification of unions, makes the first division into *Unorganized* and *Organized Unions*.

---

[1] *Theorie der Staatenverbindungen.*

[2] *Staatenbund und Bundesstaat.*

[3] *Das Wesen des Bundesstaat*, contained in his *Grundzüge der Politik*.

[4] *Das Staatsrecht des Deutschen Reiches.*

[5] Professor A. B. Hart has a monograph entitled, "An Introduction to the Study of Federal Government" (*Harvard Univ. Historical Monographs, No.* 2) which is rich in bibliographical matter. The work is, however, descriptive and comparative, rather than theoretical. It might also be said that the work of the English historian Freeman entitled *Federal Government*, is limited to an historical examination of the Grecian types.

These names serve to indicate the distinction that is made between the two classes. In the first class are included instances in which more or less permanent relations between States have been entered into for the regulation of certain mutual interests, but in which no central organization has been created. Such common action as is necessary in these unions is had through one or all of the governmental organs of the individual States. Of course there is not created in any of such cases what would be called a composite State, even by those publicists who use the term "non-sovereign State." Within this category fall such types as "Alliances" for offence or defence, and for the guarantee of particular rights; as, for example, perpetual neutrality of particular territories, etc. Within this class Jellinek also places that type which he terms the *Staatenstaat*, or that form of union in which there is a superior and an inferior State or States, the latter receiving the orders from the former as from a foreign power, and the citizens of the inferior States owing allegiance only to their own State. The most conspicuous historical examples of this type have been the feudal States of the Middle Ages and the old German Empire. Of this nature are also the relations between the Ottoman Porte and some of his Christian Provinces; as well as the relation between our own State and some of the Indian tribes. Of this order is also the relation of Egypt and Turkey, of Japan and some of the Javanese principalities, and of Nicaragua and the Mosquito Indians. All of the above unions Jellinek designates as unorganized unions of a juristic character (*Nichtorganisirte Verbindungen mit juristischen Charakter*).

We may properly ask ourselves, however, whether these "Alliances" constitute in any proper sense of the word, unions of States. Every international treaty provides for the regulation of certain interests in common, or according to conditions mutually agreed upon. In the above mentioned instances there is not the first beginning made or step taken toward the fusion of the contracting States. Certainly, at any rate, they cannot be designated as unions of a juristic character, for, as our previous analysis has shown, treaty relations are not of this character.[1]

Coming now to "Organized Unions" we find established in them, as their name imports, permanent central organs. They admit of segregation into four classes, as follows: (1) International Administrative Unions, (2) The Realunion, (3) The Staatenbund (Confederacy), (4) The Bundesstaat (Federal State).

Examples of the first sub-class are combinations of States for the common regulation of particular interests wherein permanent administrative authorities are created. Of this kind are the commissions for the regulation of navigation upon the rivers Po and Danube, and the international Postal and Telegraph Unions. There is the same objection to considering these as types of unions of States, that

---

[1] Upon this point, compare Gareis, *Allgemeines Staatsrecht*, pp. 103–5.

we have made to the whole of the first class of unorganized unions above considered.

By the term "*Realunion*" is indicated by German publicists that composite type of State life in which there is an intimate and lasting union entered into between two or more States, according to which there is a common ruler, but a preservation of the territorial divisions, and a recognition and protection of the constitutional rights of each of the uniting States. Thus, it is "that form which arises when two or more independent States unite for common protection, according to which one and the same physical person appears as the representative of the States' authority, and according to which no legal means is provided for extending this union to other functions."[1] In other words the essential element of the *Realunion* is that it is constitutionally provided that the representative of the Sovereignty of the two or more States (*Repräsentationshoheit*) shall be in one and the same physical person. That is, that this connection shall obtain irrespective of who the prescribed qualifications happen to determine this common ruler shall be. The most conspicuous examples of this form of union are those exhibited by Austria and Hungary, and Denmark and Sweden.

A type very much resembling the *Realunion*, and often confused with it, is what is termed the *Personalunion*. There is, however, a clear distinction between them. In the first there exists a permanent

---

[1] Jellinek, *Die Lehre von den Staatenverbindungen*, p. 215. See also Gareis, *Allgemeines Staatsrecht*, pp. 105–6.

provision that the two States shall be commonly represented by a single sovereign. In the latter, community of ruler is accidental, and is occasioned by one sovereign becoming invested by descent or other casual circumstance with two or more rulerships. In such cases the union of course lasts only during the reigns of such monarchs. Of this character were the relations for a time between England and Hanover, Denmark and Schleswig-Holstein, Prussia and Neurenburg; and such is the relation that now exists between Holland and Luxemburg. In these cases the ruler is to be considered as possessing as many political personalities as there are States under his rule. It is thus proper to consider each of the members of a *Personalunion* as well as of the *Realunion* as having its own ruling head. The Sovereignty of each of the individual States is preserved.[1] They are connected with each other by no juristic relations, and are thus but species of *Staatenbunde;* which type we will consider more particularly.

The two main types of the composite State are the Confederacy (*Staatenbund*) and the Federal State (*Bundesstaat*), and a critical examination of the nature of these two forms will serve to bring out all the general principles that are applicable in de-

---

[1] Thus says Jellinek (*op. cit.* p. 212), "*Die Personalunion ensteht durch Momente, welche keine Willeneinigung der Staaten voraussetzen und zur Folge haben, die Realunion hingegen beruht auf dem übereinstimmenden, geeinigten Willen der Staaten, welche die Fülle der Staatsgewalt, die Entscheidung über die wichtigsten Angelegenheiten der Staaten Einer natürlichen Persönlichkeit zuweisen.*"

termining the juristic form of all kinds of political unions. The necessity of this examination is amply testified to by the great diversity that exists in the views held by different publicists upon the various points involved. Thus, Waitz, Bluntschli, Ruttiman,[1] de Tocqueville, and in general American writers, maintain the doctrine of divided Sovereignty in a Federal State. As regards the nature of our own union, Wheaton and Halleck and other writers declare that the international Sovereignty of the individual State is destroyed, but domestic Sovereignty retained, though it is apparent that in taking this view a conception of Sovereignty is taken that makes of it a mere collection of powers so loosely related that they may be separated without loss of real Sovereignty to the possessor of any part. According to Twiss, the members of our union though not "independent" are yet "all sovereign States."[2] According to Calhoun and his school, they are completely sovereign; while by the opponents of that school, they are held as entirely devoid of this character. As opposed to complete Sovereignty either of the individual States or of the national Government, Brownson holds that, "while the Sovereignty is and must be in the States, it is in the States united and not in the States severally."[3] "The organic

[1] *Das Nordamerikanische Bundesstaat verglichen mit dem politischen Einrichtungen der Schweiz*, I. Theil 549. See also opinions of the U. S. Supreme Court in 5 How. 504 and 588; 21 How. 506; 13 Wall. 397; 92 U. S. 512; and Cooley, *Principles of Constitutional Law*, p. 21.
[2] *The Law of Nations Considered as Independent Political Communities*, Vol. I. § 23
[3] *The American Republic*, p. 221.

American people do not exist as a consolidated people or State; they exist only as organized into distinct but inseparable States."[1] Bliss, in his work, comes flatly forth with the assertion that a division of the exercise of power is at the same time a division of Sovereignty. "I only insist," says he, "that in a true federal State upon any definition that can make it attach to a people or State, sovereignty does not exist in unity, — it is divided, and in part transferred."[2]

Surely, where there is such a lack of agreement as above indicated between writers upon a point of such importance as this, it will be well worth our while to consider with some degree of care the conclusions to which the speculations in which we have thus far indulged, will lead us.

We shall find that the determination of the sovereign or non-sovereign character of any political body rests upon the following principles which we have already stated, viz. : —

1. That Sovereignty signifies the exclusive power of the State to determine its own rights and attributes.

2. That Sovereignty, being the supreme will of the State, is indivisible and inalienable.

3. That all law is expressive of the will of the State, and is in essence a command directed by a political superior to a political inferior, — from a sovereign to a subject.

---

[1] *The American Republic*, p. 245.   [2] *Of Sovereignty*, p. 115.

4. That treaties do not possess a legal nature, and are therefore not creative of law.

5. That that which creates and gives life and personality to the State is the feeling of unity on the part of the people that finds realization in the establishment of the body politic. That, therefore, it is impossible to ascribe to the State a conventional origin, or one arising from a compact between the individuals composing it. That it is not the joint will of contracting parties, but the higher will of the State itself which gives ultimate validity to all political action.

6. That, as a consequence from the above, a State cannot be created through the joint action of two or more States. This is nothing more than to say that political Sovereignty cannot rest upon a treaty, — a treaty being the only way in which two or more independent nationalities can enter into permanent mutual relations. The reasoning of Calhoun is irresistible that by a treaty it is impossible to create a political power superior to that of the contracting parties. The same power that enables States to contract, gives to them the power to withdraw when they see fit. Granting Calhoun's premise that the constitution of the United States is a creation of the individual States, his doctrine regarding the nature of our federal union follows as a necessary logical conclusion. As he truly says, "that a State as a part to the constitutional compact, has a right to secede acting in the same capacity in which it ratified the Constitution, cannot, with any show of reason, be

denied by any one who regards the Constitution as a compact. This results necessarily from the nature of the compact where the parties to it are sovereign, and of course have no higher authority to which to appeal." [1]

The impossibility of one State transferring its Sovereignty to another, we have already shown. How, then, can a new State be created by the joint action of other States? Though we may not acquiesce in all of Brownson's views, we may accept his reasoning upon this point, when he says, " An independent State, a nation, may, with or without its consent, lose its Sovereignty, but only by being merged in, or subjected to, another. Independent sovereign States cannot, by convention or mutual agreement, form themselves into a single sovereign State or nation. The compact or agreement is made by the sovereign States, and binds by virtue of the sovereign power of each of the contracting parties. To destroy that sovereign power would be to annul the compact, and render void the agreement. The agreement can be valid and binding only on condition that each of the contracting parties retains the Sovereignty that rendered it competent to enter into the compact; and States that retain severally their Sovereignty do not form a single State or nation. The States in convention cannot become a new and single sovereign State, unless they lose their several Sovereignty and merge it in the new Sovereignty; but this they cannot do by agreement, because the moment the parties

---

[1] *Works of Calhoun*, Vol. I. p. 300.

to the agreement cease to be sovereign, the agreement on which alone depends the new sovereign State is vacated in like manner as a contract is vacated by the death of the parties: — The convention either of sovereign States or of sovereign individuals, with the best will in the world, can form only a compact or agreement between sovereigns; and an agreement or compact, whatever its terms or conditions, is only an alliance, a league, or a confederation, which no one can pretend is a sovereign State or republic." [1]

Applying these principles to those cases in which there appear to be two or more States organized under a common government as regards the exercise of certain of their functions, that which first becomes evident is that the so-called "Federal-State" is a misnomer, if it be meant by that name to describe a State formed by a federation of States. Strictly speaking, the only correct manner in which the term may be used, and as it will be employed in this treatise, is to designate a State in which a very considerable degree of administrative autonomy is given to the several districts into which the State's territory is divided: not a political type in which there are *imperia in imperio*. Strictly speaking, there can be no such thing as a federal State. The State is by nature a unity, and is characterized by the possession of a sovereign political will that is of necessity a unity. Therefore, all those unions, in which individual members still possess their

[1] *The American Republic*, Chap. IX.

Sovereignty and maintain a continued existence as States, must be founded upon treaty relations, for in no other way can sovereign States enter into mutual relations with each other. In such cases, then, there is created no federal State. A central Government may indeed be created, but its acts look for their validity to the authority of the individual States, and, when performed, must be considered as the separate acts of each of the States. Thus when a treaty is formed, accepted and ratified by a so-called confederate or composite State, it must be considered as though such a treaty had been separately made by each of the respective States in the union. In Norway and Sweden and in Austro-Hungary we have instances of two States united under a common King, who is, however, to be juristically considered as two persons, and, when serving in such dual capacity, his acts are to be treated as the separate acts of each of the kingdoms he represents.

On the other hand, in those unions where the individual members have lost the power of themselves finally determining their own competence (this power being possessed by the central power), the individual members are no longer possessed of the sovereign power; and, as thus deficient, are no longer to be termed States in the true sense of the word. The Union is thus the only real State, and its members, not being States at all, the term "Federal State" is not strictly applicable.

There is thus no middle ground. Sovereignty is indivisible, and either the central power is sovereign and the individual members not, or *vice versa*. In this refusal to designate as States those political bodies that do not possess the sovereign power, and thus to consider the expression "non-sovereign State" a *contradictio in adjecto*, the author is supported by the recent writings of Professor Burgess and, impliedly, Professor Goodnow.[1]

Commenting upon Laband's *Staatsrecht des Deutschen Reiches*, wherein the opposing view is taken, Professor Burgess says: —

"The learned author betrays much anxiety to preserve to the separate States the character of real states, while he denies to them the possession of any sovereign power. The jurist comes again to the front, and rescues the State from the category of organizations having only derived powers by the proposition that the distinguishing characteristic of the state in general is not sovereignty, but only the power to command and compel obedience to its commands from the free subjects of the state. It seems to me that his distinction will not hold. If this power to command and to compel obedience be underived and independent, then it is sovereignty pure and simple. If, on the other hand, it be in any sense derivative, then the criterion of distinction which Dr. Laband sets up between the relation of the states to the union and that of the municipal divisions of the state to the state largely breaks down, since these municipal divisions have also the power to command and compel obedience to their commands from the free subjects of the state, and in their case this is clearly a vested power. If sovereignty in the federal system be exclusively in the union, then it seems to me that this makes the union the only real state, and that the only distinction which remains between the separate states and the municipalities lies in the fact that

[1] *Comparative Constitutional Law.*

while the municipalities derive their authority from the states in a positive and definite manner, the states derive their power from the union in a permissive and general manner. To be completely scientific, then, in our nomenclature and emancipate ourselves completely from the power of customary phrases, we should give the name *state* only to the union and find some other term to designate its members. In America we have already the suitable title, '*commonwealth.*'"[1]

The propriety of terming certain non-sovereign political bodies States, probably finds its best argument from the pen of the eminent Austrian publicist, whom we have already so often cited, Dr. Georg Jellinek. To maintain this position, however, Jellinek is required to take a position that certainly renders indistinct the line of demarkation between "States," and such other political bodies, as administrative districts. It will be remembered that he has already distinguished the State by its juristic quality of setting to itself its own legal rights. In order now to detect this distinguishing quality in non-sovereign bodies, he says, "It is not essential to the conception of one's own right, that it should have arisen in the person of its possessor; furthermore, it is not necessary that it should be such as cannot be again withdrawn against its own will. . . . The essence of one's own right consists neither in its originality nor in the impossibility of its being withdrawn. Its specific characteristic is solely and entirely that the one to whom it belongs is legally unanswerable for its

[1] *Pol. Sci. Quar.* III. No. 1, p. 128.

exercise. By 'one's own right' is meant a right that is subject to no legal control." [1]

It is the possession of this independence of action as to certain matters, continues Jellinek, that distinguishes the non-sovereign State on the one hand from the purely administrative body, which possesses it as to none, and, on the other hand, from the sovereign State, which possesses it as to all. In the non-sovereign State he holds that an independent will may sometimes be expressed, while in the administrative unit, its functions are exhausted in the execution of the will of another. But discretionary powers are often, and, in most cases, necessarily, given to administrative organs, and in the exercise of such discretion, it is difficult to see why an independent will (according to Jellinek's definition of one's own will) is not as much exerted as when the so-called non-sovereign State employs any of its powers. As a matter of fact, however, we hold the statement to be paradoxical that the essence of one's own will consists neither in its having risen in the person by whom it is exercised, nor in the impossibility of its being withdrawn at the will of another. It would seem, then, that in distinguishing between the non-sovereign State and the administrative body, Jellinek can only mean that, in the one case, the sovereign State can only prevent the non-sovereign State from exercising powers not constitutionally granted it, and if it be desired to alter those powers can only do so by formal constitutional amendment; while in the other

[1] *Die Lehre von Staatenverbindungen*, pp. 41-2.

case, the acts of the minor body may be annulled by ordinary statute or executive action on the part of the sovereign body. That this is, at most, only a formal distinction, our discussion of the essential likeness between ordinary and constitutional law must have made plain. In both cases the legal competence of the inferior is determined by the will of the superior body, though a greater degree of formality surrounds the alteration of such competence in the one case, than in the other.

If it were true that in the operation of a sovereign upon a non-sovereign body, the sovereign body had only the power of preventing the non-sovereign body from exceeding its constitutional powers, there might be some warrant for claiming an essential distinction between such a non-sovereign political body and a mere administrative district. But, as a matter of fact, the sovereign State always and necessarily possesses, in addition to this negative and prohibitive power, the ability to alter at will the legal competence of the subordinate body, even to the extent of utterly destroying it. As Jellinek himself says in another and later work, "The Sovereignty of the superior State as contrasted with the non-sovereign State, appears in three ways: first, in a negative control by it of the activities of the latter; second, in the power of the sovereign State to use the non-sovereign State for its own ends, be it as the direct object of its will or as a relatively independent member of a federal union; thirdly, that the sovereign State has at all times the right to draw to itself in a constitutional manner the highest rights belonging to the non-sovereign State. The existence of the non-sovereign State as a State is therefore itself determined by the sovereign will of the supreme State. The sovereign State can exploit the non-sovereign State, to an extent to which no formal *a priori* legal limit can be set." [1]

Professor Wilson, who accepts Jellinek's reasoning upon this point, says, "In the federal State, self-determination with respect to their law as a whole, has been lost by the member States. They cannot extend, they cannot even determine, their own powers conclusively without appeal to the federal authorities." But, he continues, "They are still States because their powers are original and inherent, not derivative; because their political rights are not also legal duties; and because they can apply to their commands the full imperative sanctions of law. But their sphere is limited by the presiding and sovereign powers of a State superordinated to them, the extent of whose authority is determined under constitutional forms and guarantees, by itself." [2]

"Their powers are original," he says. But are they? If the States have their status as political bodies only in the Union, as Lincoln says, in what sense can their powers be said to be original, except in a historical sense, as related to the time at

---

[1] *Gesetz und Verordnung,* p. 203.
[2] *An Old Master and Other Essays,* chapter on "Political Sovereignty," pp. 93–1.

which they were independent States, if ever they were? In the juristic sense, the legal competence of the members of the composite State is derived from the federal constitution.[1] Secondly, Professor Wilson says, they are States, "because their political rights are not also legal duties." If I understand this, it is meant that to a very great extent the exercise, or non-exercise, or the manner of exercise of their powers is left to their own discretion. But is not this true as well, to a considerable extent at least, of such bodies as cities and counties, which all would concede to be merely administrative units? Finally, says he, these non-sovereign bodies are States because, " they can apply the full imperative sanctions of law." In other words, that all rules of conduct promulgated by them within their legal competence are valid as laws. But this is no less true of all administrative bodies.

The conclusion, then, seems irresistible that, from a juristic standpoint, no fundamental distinction can be drawn between non-sovereign members of the union and their administrative units. What difference there is, aside from historical associations, is one of degree; that is, as to scope of powers and the ease with which the superordinated power may alter this competence.

Moreover, as a matter of fact, in several of our Commonwealths, various of their urban districts are

---

[1] In what sense, it may be asked, can those present members of our Union, which have been admitted since 1789, be said to have possessed "original" powers?

protected in their administrative competences by provisions in the constitutions of their respective Commonwealths. This is true in more than twenty States.[1]

But do we, for this reason, consider such protected districts any less purely administrative units, or to be distinguished in specific character from other less favored towns and counties? Did not Patrick Henry himself declare to his constituents at the time of the "Virginia and Kentucky Resolutions" that Virginia had put forth a false doctrine, and compare her position in the Union with that of the County of Charlotte in the Commonwealth of Virginia, and ask whether a county had the right to dispute the authority of Commonwealth law?

It is fully recognized by the writer of this treatise that, when it is possible, the use of terms in scientific treatises should conform as nearly as possible to that given them in common use. In thus refusing to dignify by the name of "State" any political bodies not possessed of the sovereign power, he is aware that he is running counter to what general use has dictated. At the same time, if any department of speculative inquiry is to make progress, it is essential that its terms be reduced to the utmost exactness and definiteness, and this cannot be done by accepting in all cases popular definitions. In

[1] Commenting upon this fact, Professor Burgess says: "This is a most serious question. It demonstrates the fact that the government of the Commonwealth has ceased to be, in many respects, the *natural* local government." Article "The American Commonwealth," in *Pol. Sci. Quar.* Vol. I. No. 1.

the case in question he believes the inconvenience to be felt by narrowing the common meaning of the term "State" is more than compensated for by the increased definiteness thereby obtained. The use of the looser meaning obscures the analysis of political forms, and renders indistinct the line of demarkation between the State and administrative bodies—a distinction that it is of the greatest importance to make as clear as possible, and to make which, indeed, has been one of the chief purposes of this chapter.

But even were we to accept the position of Jellinek and others who take the same view, the term "State," as they define it, cannot be so applied as to harmonize in all cases with the loose use made of it in popular speech. Jellinek, while maintaining the propriety of terming as States the individual members of the so-called Federal State, is yet forced to maintain that the Dominion of Canada cannot properly be so designated; and this, notwithstanding the comparatively slight control exercised by England over its action,—a control that does not compare in amount and importance with that exercised by the general government of the United States over the so-called individual States. A definition that leads to such a conclusion as this cannot, therefore, be said to possess even the advantage of comporting with popular usage. The "Home Rule" bill proposed by Gladstone in 1886, had it become a law, would have given to Ireland a wider scope of powers than that at present exercised by the members of our Union. But it can scarcely be maintained that under such a regime Ireland would have been entitled to be termed a "State." It is very true that to ourselves the stricter use of the word "State" seems at first particularly strange, but this is due to the historical connections that centre around our individual "Commonwealths" (as Burgess would call them). This disinclination to refuse to them the dignity of the title they have so long enjoyed, will only disappear with the advance of that sense of national unity that has made such strides since the late war. It is a characteristic of all phenomena of life, for names to continue in use long after they have been rendered meaningless by the change in character of the objects to which they relate; just as in England, the Queen is still termed "Queen by the grace of God," although the idea of a divine right of rulers originally signified by this phrase, has long since disappeared; and the "Treasury Board" has long been a "Board" in name only.

But words cannot change legal facts, and in a scientific discussion they must be held to their strict meaning.

Summarizing, then, the conclusions that we have thus far reached regarding the nature of the composite State, we may state them as follows: In the Federal State a true central State is created, the several units are legally and constitutionally united, and Sovereignty — the power of ultimately determining its own legal competence — resides in the federal body. In the Confederacy, on the other hand, the individual States retain their character as States, and their relations to each other are of an international or treaty character. Consequently, no central State is created, and Sovereignty lies wholly within such individual political units. What union there is in the Confederacy, is the creation of the wills of the individual States. In a Federal State, on the other hand, its foundation rests in itself. It is created by the people as a whole, and the so-called individual States, or, as we prefer to term them, "Commonwealths," are creations of its will. This is true whatever may have been the historical steps by which the Federal State has been created. From this standpoint, then, we are to consider the citizens of a Federal State as first divesting themselves of their old State Sovereignties, and then, as a People, establishing a national Federal State. These two volitional acts may be synchronous and made apparent by a single outward act, viz., the establishment of a federal control, but they are distinct acts from a political standpoint. The apparent continued existence in the Federal State of what were formerly independent political bodies, is not real. Such bodies politic are destroyed when their citizens transfer their allegiance to the central power. They are recreated as Commonwealths by the federal constitution. They are thus creations of the Federal State, and, as Lincoln said in his first message to Congress, "The States have their status in the Union and they have no other legal status.

The Union is older than any of the States, and in fact created them as States."[1]

Thus, if we take the position that a national State was created by the American people in 1789, we must consider them to have become a united People before that time and to have destroyed their former individual States when they established the present Federal State. This being so, the fact that the constitution was adopted by conventions convening in what had formerly been the several States, must be interpreted as meaning merely that a united People saw fit, for the sake of convenience and expediency, to utilize existing governmental machinery and territorial divisions for the formal adoption of its new

---

[1] Bearing upon this point, as well as upon the comparison which we have before made of our individual Commonwealths with their own subdivisions, may be cited the following quotation from an address by Lincoln to the Legislature at Indianapolis, February 12, 1861. "In what consists the special sacredness of a State? I speak not of the position assigned to a State in the Union by the Constitution; for that, by the bond, we all recognize. That position, however, a State cannot carry out of the Union with it. I speak of that assumed primary right of a State to rule all which is *less* than itself, and ruin all which is larger than itself. If a State and a county in a given case should be equal in extent and territory, and equal in number of inhabitants, in what, as a matter of principle, is the State better than the county? Would an exchange of *names* be an exchange of *rights* upon principle? On what rightful principle may a State, being no more than one-fiftieth part of the nation in soil and population, break up the nation, and then coerce a proportionately larger subdivision of itself in the most arbitrary way? What mysterious right to play tyrant is conferred on a district or county, with its people, by merely calling it a State?" From what has been said in this chapter it would follow that ascription of "limited sovereignty" to the members of our Union by American courts and Congress is, strictly speaking, incorrect. A more proper phrase would be that of "limited legal competence."

constitution. And that therefore such conventions were, in fact, Federal and not State organs.

Austin, in his lectures on the *Province of Jurisprudence Determined*, has some remarks upon the nature of the so-called non-sovereign State as well as upon the distinctions we have just been making, that will well bear quotation. "Now I think it will appear on analysis," says he, "that every government deemed imperfectly supreme is really in one or another of the three following predicaments. It is perfectly subject to that other government in relation to which it is deemed imperfectly supreme: Or it is perfectly independent of the other, and therefore is of itself a truly sovereign government: Or in its own community it is jointly sovereign with the other, and is therefore a constituent member of a government supreme and independent. And if every government deemed imperfectly supreme be really in one or another of the three foregoing predicaments, there is no such political mongrel as a government sovereign and subject.— 1. The political powers of the government deemed imperfectly supreme, may be exercised entirely and habitually at the pleasure and bidding of the other. On which supposition, its so-called half sovereignty is merely nominal and illusive. It is perfectly subject to the other government, though that its perfect subjection may be imperfect in extent. For example: Although, in its own name, and as of its own discretion, it makes war or peace, its power of making either is merely nominal and illusive, if the power be exercised habitually at the bidding of the other government. — 2. The political powers exercised by the other government over the political society deemed imperfectly independent, may be exercised through the permission, or through the authority, of the government deemed imperfectly supreme. On which supposition, the government deemed imperfectly supreme is of itself a truly sovereign government: those powers being legal rights over its own subjects, which it grants expressly or tacitly to another sovereign government. . . . — 3. The political powers of the government deemed imperfectly supreme, may not be exercised entirely and habitually at the pleasure and bidding of the other: but yet its independence of the other may not be so complete, that the political powers exercised by the other over the political society deemed imperfectly independent, are merely exercised through its permission or authority. . . . But on the supposition which I have now stated and exemplified, the sovereignty of the society deemed imperfectly independent resides in the government deemed imperfectly supreme together with the other government: and, consequently, the government deemed imperfectly supreme is properly a constituent member of a government supreme and independent. The supreme government of the society deemed imperfectly independent, is one of the infinite forms of supreme government by a number, which result from the infinite modes wherein the sovereign number may share the sovereign powers." [1]

[1] pp. 211–13.

"A composite (federal) state, and a system of confederated states, are broadly distinguished by the following difference. In the case of a composite state, the several united societies are one independent society, or are severally subject to one sovereign body; which, through its minister, the general government, and through its members and ministers the several united governments, is habitually and generally obeyed in each of the united societies, and also in the larger society arising from the union of all. In the case of a system of confederate states, the several compacted societies are not one society, and are not subject to a common sovereign: or (changing the phrase) each of the several societies is an independent and political society, and each of their several governments is properly sovereign or supreme. Though the aggregate of the several governments was the framer of the federal compact, and may subsequently pass resolutions concerning the entire confederacy, neither the terms of that compact, nor such subsequent resolutions, are enforced in any of the societies by the authority of that aggregate body. To each of the confederated governments, these terms and resolutions are merely articles of agreement which it spontaneously adopts; and they owe their legal effect, in its own political society, to laws and other commands which it makes or fashions upon them, and which, of its own authority, it addresses to its own subjects. In short, a system of confederated states is not essentially different from a number of independent governments connected by an ordinary alliance. And where independent governments are connected by an ordinary alliance, none of the allied governments is subject to the allied governments considered as an aggregate body: though each of the allied governments adopts the terms of the alliance, and commonly enforces those terms, by laws and commands of its own, in its own independent community. Indeed, a system of confederated states, and a number of independent governments connected by an ordinary alliance, cannot be distinguished precisely through general or abstract expressions. So long as we abide in general expressions, we can only affirm generally and vaguely, that the compact of the former is intended to be permanent, whilst the alliance of the latter is commonly intended to be temporary: and that the ends or purposes which are embraced by the compact, are commonly more numerous, and are commonly more complicated, than those which the alliance contemplates." [1]

In a Federal or Composite State the right of secession on the part of the individual Commonwealths is of course excluded. The Commonwealths have their sole political status in the union, and can therefore have none outside of it. This doctrine has been repeatedly affirmed by the Supreme Court of the United States, it being held by that body that the seceding Southern Commonwealths never were legally out of the Union, and hence that no legal validity could be attached to any of the acts of their

[1] *The Province of Jurisprudence Determined*, ed. 1861, pp. 223-4.

legislatures that were in any wise opposed to their obligations to the federal constitution.

The analysis of the Federal State as thus far conducted enables us, by way of negative criticism, to point out the invalidity of the following *criteria* that had been variously applied in distinguishing the *Staatenbund* and *Bundesstaat*.

First, the distinction does not lie in the amount of powers actually vested in the central government, as compared with those retained by the individual Commonwealths. As long as the governments of the individual members of the union are considered but as parts of the central government, no essential distinction can arise regarding the distribution and actual exercise of its powers. Sovereignty consists not so much in the direct exercise of functions, as in the power potentially possessed to draw to one's self those particular powers that may be seen fit. Federal States may be conceived in which but very few functions are centrally exercised; and, on the other hand, Confederacies imagined, in which the powers of the central government are most ample. But in neither case is the political character of the union determined thereby.

Secondly, the distinction between these two political types does not consist in the fact that in the Federal State the operation of federal law is, in all cases, directly upon individuals, while in the Confederacy, the acts of the central power apply to the Commonwealths as such, and through them to their citizens. It is true that the Federal State must not be dependent upon the acquiescence of the individual Commonwealths for the execution of its laws; but it is entirely possible that the Federal State may, in some instances, operate through the individual Commonwealths as such.

Also, *vice versa*, in the Confederation, law may operate in some instances directly upon the individual. Thus while we have been accustomed to distinguish our present Union from that maintained under the Articles of Confederation upon this ground, as a matter of fact, this rule does not hold good in all cases. As Madison points out in the *Federalist*,[1] "In some instances, as has been shown, the powers of the new government will act on the states in their collective characters. In some instances also, those of the existing government act immediately on individuals. In cases of capture; of piracy; of the post-office; of coins, weights and measures; of trade with the Indians; of claims under grants of land, by different states; and above all, in the case of trials by courts-martial in the army and navy, by which death may be inflicted without the intervention of a jury, or even of a civil magistrate; in all these cases the powers of the confederation operate immediately on the persons and interests of individual citizens."

In fact, then, the exact means through which laws are executed does not so much matter. The essential point is whose will is embodied in

[1] No. 40. Cf. Westerkamp, *Staatenbund und Bundesstaat*.

them? Political expediency of course demands that the greater and more important functions of the federal government should be performed through its own organs, rather than through those political bodies in which there rest historical traditions of complete Sovereignty and national autonomy, and a jealousy of over-control by the central power. If the Federal State trust too much to such particular organs, there is always the danger of its commands being less faithfully performed than they would be by its own agents. This was of course the consideration that caused the United States to create its own courts and marshals and other officers for the determination and execution of matters of federal or interstate interest. In cases where there is even a remote danger of rebellion on the part of the Commonwealths, the necessity is proportionately enhanced, that the central power should keep well within its own hands not only the formulation but the execution of its own orders. The same principles of course require that in Confederacies, where there is danger that the central power may usurp the Sovereignty, the States should limit to the smallest amount the functions actually exercised by their common and central organs.

Thirdly, the absence of a requirement for unanimous consent of the Commonwealths for purposes of amendment of the instrument of union is not decisive as to the non-confederate character of such union. For example, the constitution of the Confederate States of 1861–65, though avowedly creating but a *Staatenbund*, did not require such unanimity. In this case the express provision that each State was to continue individually sovereign, and with the right at any time to withdraw from the union, saved such union from being a federal one. Without this express sovereign provision, the power of a fraction of the individual Commonwealths to amend the constitution, against the will of the remaining fraction would necessarily have resulted in creating a *Bundesstaat*. For under such a condition it would be theoretically possible at any time for any particular Commonwealth to be subjected to a legal control against its own will, — a condition of course incompatible with its Sovereignty.[1]

On the other hand, also, where there is this requirement of unanimity of vote for purposes of constitutional amendment, a Confederacy is not necessarily created, any more than the absence of such a provision denotes the existence of a Federal State. To be sure, under such a condition, no individual Commonwealth can be further deprived of any of its powers without its own consent; yet, on the other hand, they may not legally be able to escape from the obligations already imposed upon

[1] "Granting the correctness of the theory that the several States were once political sovereignties, and that each surrendered a portion of its inherent powers to the general government, such surrender would go no further than the express provisions of the constitution; as to all other matters not reached by that instrument, their sovereignty would remain intact. By this theory, then, it is entirely impossible that three-fourths of the States can compel the remaining one-fourth to give up a further portion of their attributes contrary to their will." Pomeroy, *Constitutional Law*, § 111.

them by the constitution, or to withdraw from the union. Where there is not this power on the part of a Commonwealth of avoiding obligations already created, the Sovereignty must be held to rest with the general government. The fact that the unanimous vote of the Commonwealths (*i.e.* majority of the people grouped in Commonwealths) is necessary, means only that the federal government has made the act of altering its actual competence extremely difficult. In other words, no one individual Commonwealth has the power to alter its actual competence, and hence it is not sovereign. The central government alone has the power of constitutional amendment, though it be a power subject to extreme formal limitation. But the fact that it is so formally limited does not mean that the power does not exist, any more than it is claimed that the Polish assembly had not the legislative power because of the existence of the *liberum veto*. Practically, of course, in any State of developing civilization, such a condition as this, in which the individual Commonwealth has not the power of secession, and, at the same time, the central power cannot change its governmental powers except under conditions that in the great majority of cases could not be obtained would soon prove unworkable, and would precipitate a revolution, either by way of secession on the part of the individual Commonwealths, or by an unconstitutional extension of central powers.

Fourthly, and finally, the distinction between a Federal and a Confederate State is not one of enumerated or unenumerated powers. It is not a question, as has been already said, of the amount of powers actually exercised at any one time by the central government. Even Westerkamp, who holds the distinction between these two forms to be a quantitative rather than a qualitative one, does not place any weight upon this feature.[1]

The final test in all cases is, as has been so many times said, as to the power or lack of power of the individual State or Commonwealth to determine the extent of its own obligations under the articles of union, and, in the last resort, if their view be not acquiesced in by the general government, to withdraw from the union. Where it is constitutionally provided that in case of alleged conflict between federal and commonwealth or State law, such conflict shall be considered by a federal tribunal whose decrees are enforceable by the federal executive, then, in such case, a *Bundesstaat* certainly exists. If, on the other hand, it be held that a dissatisfied State has the right of secession, there is, of course, only a provisional right of federal enforcement, namely, provisional upon the consent of the State to remain in the union.

The doctrine of nullification, which grants to the individual members of the union the right to refuse obedience to any general law that it deems inconsistent with the articles of union, is of course applicable only to a Confederacy. But even there it cannot be termed a "right" of nullification. Each

[1] *Staatenbund und Bundesstaat*, p. 45.

member of the union being completely sovereign, may govern its action by its own will, and no other member may legally say nay. But it is inconceivable that the assertion of such a power on the part of a particular State would not lead to disruption of the union. For it can scarcely be imagined that the other members would consent to the avoidance by such State of the execution of a part of the general law, while they held themselves bound to it. Such a condition of affairs would in fact result *ipso facto* in a destruction of the union to that extent, its sole purpose being but to secure a concert of action in matters of general interest. It would indeed be a just *causus belli* against the State so refusing obedience to the agreement in which it bound itself to common action. Jefferson, the author of the Kentucky Resolutions, himself asserted the propriety of even a confederate government coercing a State when he wrote to Cartwright advising the Congress of the old Confederacy to send a frigate and compel a State to pay its *quota* of taxes.

United States. — In our own country, to such an extent are Commonwealth agencies employed for the performance of governmental duties, and even for the purposes of amendment of the federal constitution, that it has not been plain to what extent these organs act merely as agents of the central power, and to what extent as independent bodies politic.

The outcome of the Civil War has forever determined the question of the nature of our Union as a matter of fact, but the greatest diversity of opinion still prevails regarding which side, as a point of constitutional law, was in the right in this contest.

Our fundamental instrument of government, not itself containing a solution of the problem, arguments upon this question have been largely governed by what have been conceived to have been the nature of the historical steps that led to the adoption of the Constitution. Upon the one side, the endeavor has been to prove that the individual Commonwealths never were independent States before the creation of the national government, and, therefore, could not have contracted as States; or if they were independent sovereignties, that the ratification of our present instrument of government was not secured by their consent as such, but by the People of all thirteen acting as a unit. Upon the other side, the contradictories of these propositions have been maintained.

It is well agreed that the present Union is not an outgrowth of the union established under the old Articles of Confederation. Those articles undoubtedly created nothing more than a Confederacy. The States still retained their individual Sovereignty. No powers of Sovereignty were vested in the central government. When the convention, that was called to revise these Articles, proposed a new scheme of Union, that was to take effect upon ratification of only nine colonies, it exceeded the powers with which it was endowed. And when the people accepted this instrument by such a partial vote, it was not an amendment or revision of its "Articles," for such articles could be amended only by a unanimous vote. It was the establishment of an entirely new Union. Whether or not this new union created a Confederacy or Federal State, turns upon a point that does not admit of historical verification.

Since the Articles of Confederation created only a *Staatenbund*, under them the thirteen colonies were, or became, sovereign and independent States. From this standpoint, therefore, it is immaterial what their character had been before that time. To maintain the federal view, then, it is necessary to show that at the time of the adoption of the new constitution such a sentiment of unity existed among the colonies as may fairly be said to have welded them into a single Nation, and that therefore the people, though ratifying in state conventions, yet ratified as members of a whole, and merely used then existing state divisions and agencies from motives of convenience; that in so doing they committed a revolutionary act towards their several States; and that thereby such States were destroyed, and were recreated as Commonwealths by the new constitution, and, as such, endowed with only a partial and delegated competence of political action.

To maintain the States' Rights theory upon historical grounds, it is necessary to hold the reverse of this; that the people when ratifying the constitution, did so as citizens of thirteen independent Sovereignties; and that the conventions in which they so ratified were essentially state organs. The contention that thus separates these two parties is one that obviously does not admit of final determination upon historical grounds. Historical evidence abounds showing both the existence of feelings of political unity and of the lack of it, and it is inherently impossible to so balance these opposing evidences as to obtain a demonstrably certain result.

Coming now to internal proof, to the interpretation of the instrument of union itself, we do not find the question much clearer. So general and indefinite are some of its statements, that either "States' Rights" or federal deductions may be fairly drawn.

The people of the United States are spoken of as the adopting parties, but no decisive clue is given as to whether this means the people of the United States as a unit, or as divided into thirteen independent sovereignties. It is provided that: " This constitution and the laws of the United States which shall be made in pursuance thereof; and all treaties made, or which shall be made, under the authority of the United States, shall be the supreme law of the land; and the judges in every State shall be bound thereby, anything in the constitution or laws of any State to the contrary notwithstanding." On the other hand it is decreed that, " The ratification of the convention of nine States shall be sufficient for the establishment of this convention *between* the States so ratifying." This latter, taken by itself, would certainly give a contractual aspect to the Union. "What was the political character of Rhode Island, after the adoption of the present constitution, but before its entrance into the Union," the States' Rights advocate will ask? "Certainly it was no part of the English possessions, nor did it even belong to the old Confederacy which had then ceased to exist. Surely it must then have been sovereign." To which the Federalist will ask in return, "What is to be considered the status of those members of our Union subsequently created as Commonwealths from the Territories? What possible claim of Sovereignty can they allege ever to have possessed?"

Without going further into these questions that have been so often and so fully discussed by our jurists, it seems sufficient to say that we can no more obtain a final and conclusive answer to the question regarding the character of the Union entered into by the American People in 1789, from the mere wording of our fundamental instrument of government, than we can from purely historical data. It is, in fact, entirely probable that this indefiniteness of expression in the constitution was deliberately adopted. The needs of the time demanded the establishment of a Union of a certain degree of strength and coherence; and, on the other hand, commonwealth particularism was so strong as to make impossible of adoption an instrument that should definitely declare the Sovereignty to be in the central body, and which should deny to the individual members the right of withdrawal at will. It is quite rational to believe that in order to avoid the two horns of this dilemma, the statesmen of that period purposely declined to take an unequivocal position.

This is the view taken by Professor A. W. Small, in his essay *The Beginnings of American Nationality,* in which he says: "The people of the United States simply dodged the responsibility of formulating their will upon the distinct subject of national Sovereignty until the legislation of the sword began in 1861." President F. A. Walker, in a recent paper, takes the same ground.[1]

But it is not to be concluded from this that our political character long remained, or still remains, in this indeterminate condition. Even granting that the constitution at the time of its adoption created, and was intended to create, a Confederacy, the growth of a national feeling and the interpretation of that instrument by Congress and by the Supreme Court of the United States (an interpretation that was acquiesced in by the people), soon placed beyond all doubt the character of the Union.

One of the very first laws passed by the Federal Congress was the Judiciary Act creating the inferior federal courts and outlining federal jurisdictions. The 25th Section of this act provided for a final review of all cases decided in the highest courts of the several Commonwealths, in which were drawn into question the relative competences of the Union

---

[1] *The Growth of American Nationality (Forum,* June, 1895). "The issue was one," says he, "which, if not purposely *made* doubtful, was purposely *left* doubtful, because any attempt to force the issue at that time; to resolve the difficulties of the situation; to define the relations of the States to the general Government, away back to their source; to raise the question of coercion, should one State seek to secede from the others, would have meant nothing more or less than the immediate and complete failure of any scheme of union."

and of the Commonwealths, and in which the decisions were adverse to the federal power. This one act, together with its acceptance by the people and by the Supreme Court, was, it seems to us, almost decisive of what was henceforth to be the character of the United States government. Thus was claimed and exercised by the central power the right of determining, in the last instance, the construction of its instrument of government. It is no wonder that Calhoun and his school so strongly inveighed against the propriety and constitutionality of this section.

This appellate power as exercised by the United States Supreme Court determined conclusively that there remained in the several Commonwealths no legal power of refusing obedience to, or in any way nullifying the effect of, a federal law that has been decided to be constitutional by the federal tribunal; nor right of enforcing laws of their own that have been declared by the same tribunal to be in excess of their legislative competence. The claim was still made, however, by the States' Rights party — a claim that in 1861 they attempted to put into actual operation, — that the individual members of the Union had the right to withdraw from the Union, without the consent of the rest, in case they felt their interests too greatly prejudiced by longer remaining in the Union. The outcome of the Civil War finally decided that it was the dominant will of the People that the constitution was to be so construed as to render this claim of right of secession unwarranted; and, as said, *post bellum* decisions of the Supreme Court have repeatedly held that the Southern Commonwealths never were out of the Union and never legally could be.

These facts determine the present federal character of our Union. In the process of constitutional amendment, the several Commonwealths cannot be considered, therefore, as playing more than formal parts as agents of the National State. This reasoning does not, of course, attempt to fix the exact date of the birth of the National State, and in fact, as has been previously shown, it is impossible to determine historically the exact moment of creation of any State, Composite or Unitary.

Granting that it was intended to create a Confederacy in 1789, the fact is that the constitution was so indefinitely worded that it could be interpreted as creating a National State without doing too much violence to the meaning of its words. The People were thus enabled, through Congress and the Supreme Court, gradually to satisfy their feelings of political unity without a resort to those open revolutionary means which would have been necessary had the constitution been more definitely worded. If we grant, however, that a correct legal interpretation of the constitution would determine that not only was a Confederacy originally intended, but actually provided for; then, however peaceably and gradually the change to a Federal State was effected, — a change that was not disclosed until the crisis of civil war, — such a change must necessarily be considered revolutionary in character, and, in contradiction to this, it would not do to point to the manner in which this

T

transition has been clothed in apparent legal form. If, on the other hand, it be said that a Federal Union existed from the beginning, there is of course no difficulty in maintaining its continued existence.

Argument such as the above is in complete consonance with the principles laid down in this treatise, and renders useless for our purposes any further consideration of the character of the historical steps that led to the adoption of our instrument of union in 1789. Sovereignty is an attribute that has to be proved, not as a matter of law, but of fact, but not as such a fact as may be demonstrated by the historical evidence ordinarily adduced to explain the character of the constituent act of 1789. Sovereignty expresses the supreme will of a People, and this will is exhibited in outward political acts. But all acts, even though supported by the entire force of a community, and based upon its desires, are not necessarily expressions of the sovereign political will. Though Sovereignty may not itself be proved as a matter of law, the existence of legitimate organs and legitimate powers for the expression of its will must be so demonstrated. Acts, if they would be considered as of the State, must be performed in accordance with the formal provisions of law, constitutional or ordinary. In other words Sovereignty is not to be identified with popular will, nor the power of the State with mere force. This point we hope to make plain in the next chapter. Thus when Hurd maintains,[1] that the original thirteen

[1] *The Union State.*

colonies never were severally sovereign after their separation from England, and before their union in 1789, for the reason that each of them severally lacked the power to maintain an autonomous existence, he is confusing the two conceptions of Sovereignty as a legal power, and force, as a mere physical fact. Even his assertion that contemporary records show the existence of a sentiment of national unity, and a general desire for concert in action, does not help the thesis. For, whatever this will may have been, unless there were provided organs through which its commands might be legally expressed, a sovereign national power can not be alleged to have been established.

CHAPTER XI

LOCATION OF SOVEREIGNTY IN THE BODY POLITIC

Historical Retrospect. — Since very early times there has been constantly present in political life, the question of the extent to which the people at large should select their own rulers and determine the manner in which their public affairs should be administered. In a very general, and, as we shall see, incorrect manner, this problem has been treated as one concerning the location of Sovereignty in the body politic.

We may say that the first recognition of the right of citizens to a sphere of activity in which they should be protected from arbitrary interference on the part of Government is to be found in Roman Law. Though it is true that the Romans adopted the principle that *quidquid principi placuit legis habet vigorem*, yet it is to be remembered that they postulated that the original source of such political power is in the People, and that the powers of the governing are derived from a grant by them. This grant, however, they held to be an *alienation* and not a revocable *delegation*.

In our sketch of the history of the contract theory we have seen the direction taken by political theory in connection with the long-continued dispute between the Empire and the Papacy. In this dispute as to the basal prerogative of the State, — whether directly divine or human, — it might have been expected that the doctrine of Popular Sovereignty would be fully discussed. As a matter of fact, however, though distinctly stated, and by the end of the thirteenth century accepted by all parties alike, as originally in force, this doctrine received for many years but very slight development. And for this reason. As yet the dispute was merely one between Church and temporal rulers. The limits to the exercise of the political power itself were not yet questioned. The time was not ripe for the people themselves to contest this point. Absolutism, whether ecclesiastical or temporal, was not seriously attacked.

Gradually, however, new conditions were introduced that rendered the continued existence of such a state of affairs impossible. Closely following the growth of kingly power, and the decay of the feudal barons, came the enfranchisement of the communes, and the rise of commercial towns with forms of free municipal government. The growth of the liberties of these urban centres was favored by the kings as a check against the barons, and the burghers thus became a political element of importance in the State. Following the Crusades came a revival of classical learning, an enlightenment of manners, a development of arts and industries, and an increased knowledge of, and commerce with, all parts of the known world. Everything tended to the widening of the intellectual horizon of Europe.

The art of printing with movable blocks of type was invented, thereby furnishing the means for the diffusion of knowledge beyond all limit that had been previously dreamed of. Schools and universities arose, theology and law being the chief studies pursued. With the fall of the Eastern Empire came an influx of foreigners into Western Europe, bringing with them their arts and sciences. The Arabs and the Jews contributed from their great learning to the increasing enlightenment of Europe. Finally, in the sixteenth century came the Protestant Reformation declaring the freedom of conscience, the right of individual thinking, the emancipation from the bonds of ecclesiastical despotism and from the traditions of the past, and the propriety of freedom in speculation and inquiry.

Political science felt the immediate influence of this development. Hotman,[1] Languet,[2] Buchanan,[3] Althusius,[4] and others, constituting a school of writers, termed the *Monarchomachi*,[5] refused to view the royal power as unlimited and illimitable, and openly declared the modern doctrine of Popular Sovereignty.[6] "Who will dare say," wrote Althu-

[1] *Franco-Gallia, sive tractatus de regimine regnum Galliae.*
[2] *Vindiciae contra tyrannos.*
[3] *De jure regni apud Scotus.*
[4] *Politica methodice digesta.*
[5] Upon the views of the *Monarchomachi*, see especially Gierke, *Johannes Althusius u. die Entwicklung der naturrechtlichen Staatstheorien;* and Rudolph Treumann, *Die Monarchomachen.*
[6] An additional significance attached to the theory of popular sovereignty in connection with the contests between Pope and Council as to whether the council represented the whole clergy, and in this capacity was superior to the Pope, or whether it acted in an inde-

sius, "that the people are able to transfer to any one their Sovereignty? Sovereignty is the power indivisible, incommunicable, and imprescriptible to any authority. . . . Bodin is deceived in attributing Sovereignty to the kings or nobles; it is the right of society entire."

Thus the development of the idea of Popular Sovereignty became intimately bound up with one view of the contract theory; and its subsequent development in this connection, we have already outlined in our treatment of that phase of political speculation. Beginning with the outbreak of the French Revolution, the subsequent history of Europe is largely a record of the manner in which it has been attempted to put the theory in actual practice.

The Location of Sovereignty. — The inquiry concerning the location of the sovereign power in the body politic is, as has been said, distinct from the question whether this or that organization is endowed with this attribute. Admitting the possession of Sovereignty in a body politic, we have now to discover the person or persons in whose hands its exercise ultimately rests. It might appear at first blush that this were a question whose solution would be dependent upon an analysis of the governmental organization under examination, and, as such, would fall within the peculiar province of constitutional law, rather than of political philosophy. But such is not

pendent capacity and was of less authority than he. Marsilius and Occam, in their application of the theory to this point intimated that even the laity properly participated in this popular ecclesiastical Sovereignty.

the case. As a matter of fact, the question is a much deeper one than this, and for its answer requires the inquiry to be pursued far beyond the regions of mere constitutional analysis, and demands a closer consideration than we have yet made of the essential relations that exist between a People and the State in which they are politically organized.

Remembering that by Sovereignty is designated the supreme will of the State, and that that person, or body of persons, is the sovereign, in whose hands rests the power, in the last resort, to impose his or its will *in a legal manner* upon the whole body of persons that constitute the State, — remembering this, we may say that the one question to be determined is, whether it be possible to locate this power in the hands of a definite person or body of persons, constituting a particular part of the body politic; or, whether the possession of such power is predicable only of the whole people. That this is, in fact, the only question which we need to discuss in this chapter is shown by the following reasoning.

If the sovereign power may be located in the hands of a definite individual, or body of individuals, other than the whole people, the remaining portion of the investigation would demand nothing more than an analysis of the constitution of each particular State in order to discover such person or persons. Such a study would obviously not fall within the scope of this treatise. If, on the other hand, it be determined that the search for the sovereign power leads ultimately and inevitably to the entire people, then the form of government is immaterial, and no further analysis is necessary.

The belief in the view that in every political community Sovereignty is discoverable in some definite person or body of persons, constitutes one of the chief tenets of the Analytical School of Jurisprudence. We repeat Austin's famous definition of Sovereignty: "If a determinate human superior receive habitual obedience from the bulk of a given society, that *determinate* superior is sovereign in that society, and the society, including the superior, is a society political and independent."

In accordance with this definition Austin proceeds to maintain that there is such a determinate sovereign discoverable in every political and independent society, and that such a determinate sovereign is, indeed, a *conditio sine qua non* to a State's existence as such. Furthermore, as we have already seen, he defines all law as proceeding directly, or indirectly, from this sovereign; and, as a logical result therefrom, deduces the freedom of such a sovereign from all legal limitations. "Sovereignty or supreme power," he says, "is incapable of legal limitation, whether it reside in an individual or in a number of individuals."

In a preceding chapter we have demonstrated the legally absolute character of the State. We shall here consider more particularly the manner in which this complete legal competence is practically restricted. The arguments brought forth by such writers as Clark,[1] Lightwood,[2] Bliss,[3] Jameson,[4] Lowell,[5] and others, in attempted refutation of Austin's position, are almost wholly directed to the demonstration that, as a matter of fact, there never existed a monarch, however despotic in power, who possessed the actual power of absolutely controlling all branches of the laws by which his subjects were governed. As a proof of this, is cited the fact that in the most extreme cases of absolutism, the power of altering or abolishing existing law has extended but very little beyond the field of public law. As Professor Bliss says, "The ruler may succeed in revolutionizing public law, although success in that, without large private co-operation, is scarcely known; yet the power to thus change the body of private law can hardly be conceived. We have no example in history. Alterations have been made; and these, if radical, and without corresponding change of opinion, will excite commotion, although affecting but a single title. But to sweep away a whole system and substitute a new one,— one foreign to the habits of the subject, one that runs counter to his prejudices and passions, one from its very novelty supposed to endanger his rights, — would be almost as impossible as to change the order of the seasons."[6]

The fact is, as must be apparent to all, that there are limits to the endurance of any People, however patient, unenlightened, and submissive, and

---

[1] *Practical Jurisprudence: A Comment on Austin.*
[2] *The Nature of Positive Law.*   [3] *Of Sovereignty.*
[4] *Political Science Quarterly*, Vol. V. No. 2.
[5] *Essays on Government.*   [6] *Of Sovereignty*, p. 48.

when oppressed beyond this limit they will prefer the evils of open resistance to those of submission; and if this oppression be carried so far as to excite the opposition of the entire people, or a large portion of them, the ruling powers will be overthrown. These are facts that are necessarily recognized by every ruler. As Hume well says, "As force is always on the side of the governed, the governors have nothing to support them but opinion. It is therefore on opinion only that government is founded, and this maxim extends to the most despotic military governments as well as to the most free and most popular."[1]

In fact, Austin himself expressly and repeatedly affirms that the legal sovereign is actually controlled in the exercise of power by the wishes of the community. In his very definition he says, "If a determinate human superior not in a habit of obedience to a like superior receive *habitual* obedience," etc., the word "habitual" thus indicating the possibility of the sovereign will being opposed. Again he says, "If perfect or complete independence be of the essence of sovereign power, there is not in fact the human power to which it will apply. Every government, let it be ever so powerful, renders occasional obedience to the commands of other governments. And every government defers habitually to the opinions and sentiments of its sovereign subjects."[2] And, also, "To an indefinite though limited extent,

[1] *Collected Essays*, Pt. I. No. 4.
[2] *Lectures on Jurisprudence*, ed. 1867, Vol. I. p. 242.

the monarch is superior to the governed, his power being commonly sufficient to secure compliance with his will. But the governed, collectively or in mass, are also the superior of the monarch, who is checked in the abuse of his might by fear of exciting their anger and of arousing to active resistance the might which slumbers in the multitude." [1]

These are but other ways of expressing the truth that in no government can there be found an actual power greater than that to be found in the nation. That the whole is greater than any of its parts.

States differ in their governmental organizations, as to the amount of political power placed in the hands of their agents, and the manner of exercise of such power, but the *quantum* of their power is ever the same. They are despotic or popular, according to the ease with which their constitutions permit of a legal expression and execution of the wishes of the people in regard to the administration of their public affairs. Popular government is thus synonymous with sensitiveness of the ruling powers to public opinion. In modern times this sensitiveness has been secured in a large measure by popular representation, by extension of the suffrage, by local self-government, and by such devices as the *Referendum* in Switzerland, by the "appeal to the country" by a defeated Ministry in England, and by frequent elections in America.

[1] *The Province of Jurisprudence Determined*, p. 14 (ed. 1861). See also *idem*, note to p. 192, and p. 272. Professor Dewey, in the *Political Science Quarterly* for March, 1894, shows the tendency of Maine and others to treat Austin's system as if it ignored this ultimate conditioning power of popular approval.

If, now, we admit that the power of the people ultimately conditions the actions of those who govern them, have we reached the end of our inquiry? By no means. First of all, the definite connotation of the term "People" is to be fixed. If by this term we refer to the sum of the individuals composing the State, we have "the State resolved into its atoms, and supreme power ascribed to the unorganized mass or to the majority of these individuals. This extreme radical opinion contradicts the very essence of the State, which is the basis of Sovereignty." [1]

If, however, by the People we refer to them as united and politically organized, we have made no advance in locating Sovereignty; we have only repeated the proposition that Sovereignty is a necessary ingredient of the State; for a people politically organized is the State. Neither can we say that the term "People" in this connection refers to those citizens actually voting, nor to the majority of such; nor, much less, to the representatives whom they elect. This will not do. To be sure, those citizens, who have the privilege of voting, possess the easiest means of exerting their influence over the conduct of the State, but it is not upon their consent alone that the powers of the government are supported. Even where manhood suffrage prevails, the electorate composes, as a rule, not a fifth part of the population, and it can hardly be said that the wishes of the remaining four-fifths do not

[1] Bluntschli, *Theory of the State*, trans., 2d ed., p. 497.

need to be reckoned upon in determining political action. In the case of a revolution, it is never the electors alone who are able to give to it success. Back of them, and adding to their strength, they must have the assistance, or at least the passive acquiescence, of the great bulk of the community. Even in the exercise of their rights of suffrage, the electors are to be considered as selecting men and measures, not according to their own wish alone, but according to the desires of the entire community.

If, then, we would speak of the Sovereignty of the people, we can mean nothing more than the Sovereignty of Public Opinion, — that power which Lieber defines as "the sense and sentiment of the community, necessarily irresistible, showing its power everywhere," and the power which "gives sense to the letter and life of the law; without which the written law is a mere husk."[1] Sovereignty is thus, as Professor Woodrow Wilson forcibly puts it, reduced to a "catalogue of influences."[2]

Surely, if this be the correct conclusion, it is an unsatisfactory one from the juristic standpoint, however comforting it may be to the adherents of popular government. The highest attribute of the State — its Sovereignty — is thus upon analysis discovered to be a power definite only as to its actual omnipotence, and with no precise organs of expression. Furthermore, the political action of the State in almost all cases can only be in more or less approximate

[1] *Political Ethics*, Chap. 65.
[2] *An Old Master and Other Essays*, p. 78.

conformity to its will, even in the most popular of governments; and its influence is felt, for the most part, in only a negative manner, its supreme might being positively evinced only when demonstrating its ability to oppose or destroy existing political conditions that have become obnoxious to it. If this be the nature of Sovereignty, it would seem to possess but few qualities that would stamp it as a legal conception.

But we do not need to take this view. The entire trouble is, that those who assume this position are led astray in their search for the ultimate location of Sovereignty, and settle upon a power that indeed *conditions political action, but is not itself of a legal or civil nature.* Public Opinion, with no governmental organs through which its power may be enforced, is certainly not, strictly speaking, a civil power. The mere fact, as above stated, that political action rarely conforms exactly with, and is often in direct opposition to its desires, would seem to be sufficient proof that it cannot be identified with the State's will. It is of course a force that must be reckoned with by statesmen in determining political policies, and thus *conditions* the direction and manner in which the power of the State shall be exercised, but is not itself of the State. Sovereignty is a political term and designates political power, and true political power can be exercised by society only in its politically organized capacity; that is, through its established political agencies.

Rousseau would say, however, that the sovereign

General Will has the popular assembly in which every citizen may participate, as an organ through which its command may be expressed. If, however, it were practically possible in any but extremely small States, for such a body to be convened, there would even then be no certainty that the commands of such body would exactly represent the General Will. There is ever the danger of such assembly being controlled by factions for selfish ends. Rousseau himself recognizes this. "If the people being sufficiently informed," he says, "deliberates, and citizens have no communication with each other, — from a great number of small differences will result the General Will, and the conclusion will always be good. But when they divide into factions and partial associations at the expense of the whole, the will of each of these associations becomes general with regard to its members, and individual with regard to the State; it may then be said that there are not as many voters as men, but only as many as there are associations. The differences become less numerous and give a less general result. Finally, when one of these associations is so large as to surpass all the others, you no longer have the sum of small differences, but a single difference; then there is no longer a General Will, and the opinion which prevails is only an individual opinion."[1] In other words, says Rousseau, given a society of men, the members of which are not only generally enlightened and honest, but active in their own political interests,

[1] *The Social Contract*, Bk. II. Chap. III.

and free from factional associations,—given such an ideal community, then, and only then, is there any certainty of obtaining an expression of the General Will, even in an assembly in which every citizen is a member. In fine, we must conclude that the "General Will," or "Public Opinion," or "Popular Sovereignty," or whatever it may be called, cannot be said to possess any one organ or number of organs through which its wishes may obtain valid, authoritative, and accurate expression.

All that we have actually proved as embraced in the idea of the so-called "Sovereignty of the People," is their "right," or rather "might," of revolution,—a might that follows from their unorganized mass, rather than from their organized strength. But, whether revolutionary right or revolutionary might, in neither case do there appear legal qualities. Legal rights and legal obligations are only created and imposed by virtue of positive law, and such law exists only as an utterance of a political body. By the mere fact of a people putting themselves in a revolutionary attitude toward their government; that is, attempting the enforcement of their demands in ways other than those provided by law, they are placed outside of the State so far as such acts are concerned. However proper their conduct from a *moral* standpoint, from a *legal* standpoint they are then acting not as a body politic, but as a mob. They have, in fact, expressly repudiated State agencies. This, then, cannot be an act of Sovereignty, for Sovereignty, as expressly defined and conceded by all, is of the State and is possessed by a political community, and not by an uncivic aggregate of men. Until a people become politically organized there is no Sovereignty.[1]

[1] Thus says Bluntschli in his *Staatswörterbuch:* "*Es giebt keine Souveränetät der Gesellsschaft. Keine Souveränetät vor oder über dem Staate. Die Souveränetät als ein staatlicher zunächst ein staatrechtlicher Begriff ist durch die Existenz und durch die Verfassung des Staates bedingt.*"

To the same effect says Cooley (*Constitutional Limitations*, 3d ed. p. 598): "The voice of the people in their sovereign capacity can only be of legal force when expressed at the times and under the conditions which they themselves have prescribed and pointed out by the constitution, . . . and if by any portion of the people, however large, an attempt should be made to interfere with the regular working of the agencies of government at any other time, or in any other mode than as allowed by existing law, either constitutional or statutory, it would be revolutionary."

According to Judge Jameson, Sovereignty resides in a society only as a body politic; "in the corporate unit resulting from the organization of many into one, and not in the individuals constituting such unit, nor in any number of them as such, nor even in all of them, except as organized into a body politic *and acting as such*" (*The Constitutional Convention*, § 21). However, though assuming this correct position, he proceeds to declare that Sovereignty may be exercised in an extra-governmental or revolutionary manner. Its characteristic as a *legal* power is thus explicitly abandoned. "Sovereignty," says he, "manifests itself in two ways: first, *indirectly* through individuals acting as agents or representatives of the sovereign, and constituting the civil government; and, secondly, *directly* by organic movements of the political society itself, without the ministry of agents; the movements referred to exhibiting themselves either in those social agitations, of which the resultant is known as *public opinion*, that *vis a tergo* in all free commonwealths, by which the machinery of government is put and kept in orderly motion; or in manifestations of *original power* by which political or social changes are achieved irregularly, under the operation of forces wielded by the body politic itself immediately." (*Idem*, § 23. Citation is made to Lieber's *Political Ethics*, Vol. I. p. 256.) But what the tests are by which "organic movements" of society are to be distinguished; how Sovereignty, as necessarily inhering in a social body only as a political body, and exercised *as such*, can likewise be discovered in mere opin-

If it be necessary to make this point still more conclusive, the circumstance may be pointed out that in all cases the actions of the States are, as a matter of fact, largely determined and limited by the claims of other States, and thus their independence practically governed by influences identical in character with these exercised by the public opinion of their own citizens. The legal, or rather non-legal, nature of both are the same. No greater validity can be predicated of the one than of the other, yet even Lieber or Jameson would not hold that Sovereignty rests not with the individual States, but in the Community of States.

Professor Ritchie, in an article upon this subject,[1] distinguishes between this power of the people exercised by public opinion, which he terms "the ultimate political Sovereignty," and the highest political power of the State as exercised through its legally established organs, which he designates as "legal Sovereignty." It is undoubtedly correct thus to make this distinction if it be seen fit, but to the writer it seems unfortunate that the same term, "Sovereignty," should be applied to two forces so radically different, even though distinguishing adjectives be prefixed. Is it not better to term such

ion or in "irregular" acts for the achievement of social as well as political changes; what valuable distinction there is between revolutionary and legal conduct — a distinction emphasized throughout the work; — these are questions that Judge Jameson does not attempt to answer. Cf. his article entitled "National Sovereignty," in the *Pol. Sci. Quar.*, Vol. V. p. 193.

[1] *Annals of the American Academy of Pol. and Social Science*, January, 1891.

force simply "Public Opinion" or "General Will," and to limit the word "Sovereignty" to its purely legal application?

In thus distinguishing between Sovereignty and General Will or Public Opinion, between legal absolutism of the State and its powers as absolutely limited by political exigencies, we are, in fact, but stating a result that correlates with the position which we assumed in regard to the relation of custom to law. That is to say, we have denied to the people a capacity for legal action irrespective of State organs. As we have said, it is the essential office of representative or public government to make possible an approximately correct formulation of Public Opinion, and to secure political action in conformity thereto.[1] But this is not to place the legal power of Sovereignty in the community as such.

In conclusion, then, Sovereignty, though in a legal sense absolute, is to be considered in reference to the institutions, the character of the people governed, and other objective conditions. While force is and always must be an incident of Sovereignty, the highest ideal of statesmanship is to render the actual exercise of such force as seldom necessary as possible, and the extent to which this aim is attained will depend largely upon the

---

[1] See the remarks of Dicey (*Law of the Constitution*, pp. 73-76), according to which the function of representative government is to produce a coincidence between what he terms the "external limits" to Sovereignty, arising from the possibility of resistance on the part of the people, and the "internal limits," depending upon the wishes of those who wield the sovereign power.

degree in which state action corresponds with the desires of Public Opinion or the General Will. As says the philosopher whom we have already had occasion several times to quote, " If once the coercive power which must always be an incident of Sovereignty becomes the characteristic thing about it in its relation to the people governed, this must indicate one of two things; either that the general interest in the maintenance of equal rights has lost its hold upon the people, or that the sovereignty no longer adequately fulfils the function of maintaining such rights, and thus has lost the support derived from the general sense of interest in supporting it. . . . It is certain that when the idea of coercive force is that predominantly associated with the law-imposing or law-enforcing power, either a disruption of the State or a change in the sources of Sovereignty must sooner or later take place."[1]

It may now be asked whether we have not come back to the position of Austin as regards the location of Sovereignty in a definite portion of the body politic. Not exactly. Austin, with all his logical accuracy and preciseness of definition, did not fully distinguish between the legal sovereign or sovereigns, and those who, by their suffrages or other less direct influences, give to such legal depositaries of Sovereignty their powers, and maintain them in their possession. The position taken in this treatise is that those persons or bodies are the sovereigns who have the legal power of expressing the will of

[1] Green, *Philosophical Works*, Vol. II. p. 410.

the State. Behind these persons we do not as publicists or jurists need to look. When we have located these authoritative, volitional organs of the State, we, *quâ* lawyers, do not need to search further. We leave to the sociologist or practical politician the examination of the nature and force of Public Opinion.

Austin, however, though ever avowing the determinateness of its location, goes back of the law-making bodies, to the electorates, in his search for the original abiding ground of the sovereign power of making and unmaking laws. By so doing he abandons the position which he has placed himself upon of viewing and defining laws only from the standpoint of their legal validity, and without reference to the ultimate forces that condition them.

Following this method, Austin discovers the Sovereignty in Great Britain to be in the King, Lords, and Commons. But by "Commons" he is not satisfied to mean the lower branch of Parliament, but designates thereby the electors of the lower house. "Speaking accurately," says he, "the members of the commons' house are merely trustees for the body by which they are elected and appointed; and consequently the Sovereignty always resides in the Kings and the peers, with the electoral body of the commons."[1] Here, as Professor Ritchie has pointed out, he no longer speaks as a lawyer. "For a lawyer *quâ* lawyer a law is good law though it were passed by a Parliament which had abolished the Septennial

[1] *The Province of Jurisprudence Determined*, ed. 1861, p. 201.

Act and had gone on sitting as long as the Long Parliament, quite as much as if the law were passed by a newly summoned Parliament of the elected part of which an overwhelming majority had been returned expressly pledged to vote for this very law. With the wishes or feelings of the electors the lawyer as lawyer has nothing whatever to do, however much they may affect him as a politician or as a reasonable man."[1] To the same effect is the dictum of Professor Dicey, that nothing is more certain than that no English judge ever conceded, or under the present constitution can concede, that Parliament is in any legal sense a trustee for the electors: a dictum that is conclusively verified by the power of Parliament shown in the Septennial Act to lengthen its own existence without any reference whatever to the voters by whom its then members had been elected for a much shorter period.[2]

[1] *Annals of the Am. Acad. of Pol. and Soc. Science*, January, 1891, p. 302.

[2] *Law of the Constitution*, 4th ed. pp. 69-71. We may profitably quote the following paragraphs as showing not only this point, but as illustrating the distinction, that we have above emphasized in this chapter, between Sovereignty as a purely legal conception, and as denoting the ultimate conditioning force of public opinion. "It should, however, be carefully noted," says Dicey, "that the term 'Sovereignty,' as long as it is accurately employed in the sense in which Austin sometimes uses it, is a merely legal conception, and means simply the power of law-making, unrestricted by any legal limit. If the term 'Sovereignty' be thus used, the sovereign power under the English constitution is clearly 'Parliament.' But the word 'Sovereignty' is sometimes employed in a political, rather than in a strictly legal sense. That body is 'politically' sovereign or supreme in a State the will of which is ultimately obeyed by the citizens of the State. In this sense of the word, the electors of Great Britain may be said to be, together with the Crown and the Lords, or perhaps, in strict accu-

In like manner, Austin does not discover legal Sovereignty in the United States, in the legislative bodies of the individual Commonwealths, or in the federal Congress, or in both combined. He sees the legal competence of these bodies apparently limited by written constitutions, and therefore places Sovereignty in the electorates that select the bodies by which these written instruments may be amended.

"I believe," says he, "that the Sovereignty of each of the States, and also of the larger State arising from the federal union, resides in the States' governments as forming an aggregate body: meaning by a State's government, not its ordinary legislature, but the body of its citizens which appoint its ordinary legislature, and which the union apart is properly sovereign therein."[1] The same criticism is here applicable to Austin that was applied to his location of Sovereignty in the English electorate. These positions of Austin are therefore unsatisfactory, not only from the strictly juristic standpoint, but they do not accord with the view of those who by Sovereignty refer to the ultimate force of Public Opinion, — of the General Will; for those

racy, independently of the King and the Peers, the body in which sovereign power is vested. . . . But this is a political and not a legal fact. The electors can in the long run always enforce their will. But the courts will take no notice of the will of the electors. The judges know nothing about any will of the people except in so far as that will is expressed by an Act of Parliament, and would never suffer the validity of a statute to be questioned on the ground of its being passed or being kept alive in opposition to the wishes of the electors."

[1] *The Province of Jurisprudence Determined*, ed. 1861, p. 222.

who take this latter view (and very correctly from their standpoint) make the electorate but an organ of the whole body of citizens, by whom it is influenced and controlled in many ways.

Professor Dewey, in an article already cited,[1] makes also the criticism that this electorate is not even determinate. His argument is as follows: If the electorate be the sovereign, then each voter is a sharer in the Sovereignty. But what of the voters who prove to be in the minority? "If we say he (*i.e.* one of the minority) did share in Sovereignty because he had a right to vote, we say Sovereignty may be exercised apart from the utterance of commands, indeed, even in opposing the fundamental command. But if we say that, since not participating in the expression of the supreme command, he is not sovereign, the question arises by what right he voted at all."

This reasoning appears to us very insufficient, and is, in fact, just as applicable to a legislative body as to a popular gathering. What of the members of the minority in the English Parliament? The fact is, that when Austin or any other writer refers to an electorate as exercising Sovereignty, he, or they, refer to such an electorate as a collective body of which each member possesses an indivisible portion of the Sovereignty of the whole. That is, that the citizen shares in the Sovereignty not as an individual but as a member of the whole. Each citizen holds, as law-

[1] "Austin's Theory of Sovereignty," *Political Science Quarterly*, March, 1894.

yers say, *per tout* only, and not *per my*, as Professor Dewey would seem to think. Rousseau makes this distinction very plain by expressly distinguishing between the "will of all" and the "General Will."[1] The distinction between Sovereignty as a juristic conception and the ultimate conditioning power of popular opinion, was, however, one that was never reached by Rousseau, who completely identifies Sovereignty with the "General Will." It is in consequence of this assumption, that, in searching for the manner in which this sovereign power may be legally exercised, he is forced to hold that "laws being but authentic acts of the General Will, the sovereign cannot act except when the People is assembled."[2] And again, that "Sovereignty cannot be represented for the same reason that it cannot be alienated; it consists essentially of the General Will, and the will cannot be represented; it is the same or it is different; there is no mean. The deputies of the people then are not, and cannot be its representatives, they are only its commissioners; they can conclude nothing definitely. Any law which the people in person has not ratified is null; it is not a law."[3] Thus the position is taken that all authority exercised other than by warrant of the general assembly of the people is illegal, and a government thus acting has only a *de facto* and not a *de jure* existence — a position according to which there was not at the time of Rousseau's writing,

---

[1] *The Social Contract*, Bk. II. Chap. III.
[2] *Idem*, Bk. III. Chap. XII. [3] *Idem*, Bk. III. Chap. XV.

nor has there been since, a State in Europe in which rebellion would have been an illegal act.

Comparing these views with those held by Hobbes and Locke, we find that according to the former of these writers a sovereign organ, be it a monarch or a popular assembly, is made practically identical with the sovereign State itself, and as such incapable of legal limitation. Thus in all truthfulness the absolute ruler might say that *L'état, c'est moi.* The agent is identified with the principal, government is confused with the State, the machine absorbs that power that moves it. Apart, however, from this confusion between State and Government Hobbes developed a substantially correct theory of law and Sovereignty, though he needlessly based it upon an illogical fiction.

Locke, though founding his system on the same fictional contract, came much nearer the comprehension of the true nature of government, in his declaration of its limited delegated character, and the essentially representative capacity of all political agents. It would seem also at times that he perceived the distinction between the actual ultimate power of the people to condition political action, and the legal or sovereign action of the State. "And thus," he declares, "the community may be said in this respect to be always the supreme power but not as considered under any form of government, because *this power of the people can never take place till the government be dissolved.*"[1] But his precon-

[1] *Two Treatises on Civil Government*, II. § 149. Italics my own.

ceived ideas of natural rights and of Sovereignty as resting upon a contract makes him speak in general of this ultimate right of the people as something more than a mere moral right, and as a power founded upon mere might. For the same reason, he does not always sufficiently recognize that the State may be so organized as to permit sovereign action greatly opposed to public will and to public interest, and yet strictly constitutional and legal. Thus, in considering what is to be done in case an executive to whom has been entrusted the power of calling together the legislative branch, should refuse to exercise such power, to the detriment of the people, — such action he describes as "contrary to the trust put in him that does so," and as "a state of war with the people who have a right to reinstate their legislative in the exercise of their power."[1]

Here the theory of a contract between governed and governing again crops out. But just as in our discussion of the origin of the State we demonstrated the invalidity of the contract theory, so likewise is it necessary to refuse to characterize as such the relation between the people and their rulers. Governmental agents exercise a power delegated or granted to them by the State, and not one created by a joining of their wills with those of the subjects. The only will concerned is that of the State. Public officials are, in other words, agents of the State, not of the People. They have no relation to the People as such, and therefore there can be no breach of

[1] *Two Treatises of Government*, II. § 155.

contract with them in whatever manner they may exercise their power. If they exceed their legal competence, or are in any way guilty of non-feasance or malfeasance of office, they are punishable only by the State. Therefore, any action of theirs, however oppressive, does not, as Locke would say, *ipso facto* deprive them of political power, and place them in a state of war with their former subjects. Such action is not even illegal if within their competence, and is as fully valid as would be the most beneficent measure. If *ultra vires*, however, the action is of course illegal and not an act of the State, but of the official as a private individual, and one for which he is personally responsible. But such illegality extends only to the particular act itself. It has no influence over the general public or sovereign *status* of such official. Rousseau is thus perfectly correct in denying that government is established by a contract.

The assertion that "governments are instituted among men, deriving their just powers from the consent of the governed," as it appears in our Declaration of Independence, and in substantially similar form in most of the constitutions of our Commonwealths, and as constantly repeated by our publicists and declared by our courts, has no other meaning than that the conduct of public officials should be as nearly as possible in accordance with the wishes of the governed; not that the legal validity of governmental action is determined according to such a standard. That standard is determined by the existing prescribed forms for determining the will of the State.

The value of *constitutional* government is not that it places Sovereignty in the hands of the people, but that it prescribes definite ways in which this sovereign power shall be exercised by the State. The value of *popular* government is that it provides the means through which the wishes of the people may be known and felt, and that thus the conduct of a State may be brought into conformity thereto.

Constitutional government thus protects the citizen from arbitrary action on the part of the State: popular government secures to him the probability that his wishes and interests will be considered therein.

Understanding now by Sovereignty a power which is capable of exercise only through existing governmental agencies, it necessarily follows that this supreme power is exhibited whenever the will of the State is expressed. In fact, it is almost correct to say that the sovereign will is the State, that the State exists only as a supreme controlling will, and that its life is only displayed in the declaration of binding commands, the enforcement of which is left to mere executive agents. These executive agents, while acting as such, have no will of their own, and are but implements for the performance of that will which gives to them a political and legal authority.

This, then, locates the exercise of Sovereignty in the law-making bodies. By whomsoever, or whatsoever body, therefore, the will of the State is expressed, and law created, there we have Sovereignty exercised. If we distinguish between executive, judicial and legislative departments of the State, it is in this last-named department that the exercise of Sovereignty rests. As Locke correctly maintains, " In all cases whilst the government subsists, the legislative is the supreme power. For what can give laws to another must needs be superior to him, and since the legislative is no otherwise legislative of the society but by the right it has to make laws for all its parts, and every member of the society, prescribing rules to their actions, and giving power of execution where they are transgressed, the legislative must needs be supreme, and all other powers in any members or parts of the society derived from and subordinate to it." [1]

The only point that we must remember is that the term " legislative " must not be so narrowly construed, as to limit its application to those bodies by which formal statutory enactments are made. In so far as the chief executive of the State has the ordinance power, he may express the sovereign will and therefore exercise Sovereignty. As we know, this power was, in former times, very extensive in England, and still persists to a considerable degree in all modern States. The entire constitutional history of England is in fact but little more than a record of the manner in which this royal power of law-making has been curtailed, and the legislative power of Parliament taken its place.

[1] *Two Treatises of Government*, II. § 150.

Again, constitutional conventions, in so far as they have the direct power of creating constitutional law, exercise this sovereign power. Finally, in so far as courts are the organs of the State for the creation of law, they express the will of the State and hence exercise Sovereignty. In so far, however, as their work is merely interpretative of existing law, they of course do not exercise this power. It is true that, strictly speaking, judges are not supposed to exercise any function other than the interpretative one, but as a matter of fact, as we have already seen, they do necessarily go beyond this and actually create law.

Now it may be said that courts are able to do this only by the acquiescence of the legislative body, which may negative by statute the principles which they have declared; and hence that they act but as agents of the legislature proper. In the same way, it may also be said that the ordinary legislature exercises its powers only by right of constitutional law, and that, therefore, it, in turn, but voices the will of those that establish this fundamental law. This is certainly true, and therefore in any given State it may be said, in one sense, that that organ possesses the final sovereign power, which creates those laws that organize the State, and distributes its powers among its several governmental agents. In a measure we have already discussed this point in our consideration of the nature of constitutional provisions as compared with that of other forms of law. In a country like England, such a supreme body would be the Parliament, but in those countries where government rests upon written instruments, it would, according to this view, be with those organs that have the power to modify such instruments. But in reference to this position it may be said, in the first place, that such organs may be brought into action only at long intervals, or conceivably never, if society remains in a sufficiently stationary condition.[1] Therefore, according to such a view, we would be obliged to consider this, the very essence of the State, its life and its highest power, as continuously latent. In the second place, the question properly arises, as to the source of the power of these organs thus to create constitutional laws, and, in order to answer this, we are brought back, as we have already seen, to the original creation of the State, and to the establishment of its first government.

The fact is, however, that when as jurists or publicists we seek for the location of the sovereign power in the body politic, we are concerned with the State as it then is and as actually organized. In pursuit, therefore, of this aim we have only to find that organ or those organs that may express the State's will. The problem does not involve the question of the ultimate source whence has been obtained by these organs the volitional power that they exercise. That is a question which we have already attempted to explain in our consideration of

---

[1] For example, the present constitution of Belgium, though provided with an amending clause, was not altered for more than fifty years.

the origin of the State and of its right to be. Our task here is, as jurists, to find what person or persons here and now have the power of giving expression to rules of conduct that will be, if necessary, coercively enforced by the political power. The only truly sovereign act, therefore, that may be performed by the People, as such, is the original creative act by which, at the very inception of the State's life, they are to be conceived as justifying the existence and the powers of those organs that provided for its more permanent organization. The State once equipped with governmental machinery, political Sovereignty may henceforth be exercised only through the means that it provides.

As we have already said, the electorate is to be distinguished from the People. There are instances in which this former body may act as an organ of the State for the exercise of its Sovereignty. This happens whenever there exists a provision according to which law may be created by a *referendum* or other method of *plebiscite*. When so called upon for its vote, the Electorate is to be considered as *ad hoc* a legislative body. Of course, in those cases where a vote of the people is had merely for the purpose of better discovering what the public sentiment is upon a given proposal, and without the power of such a vote itself to give a legal validity or non-validity to the proposal, we do not have the electorate exercising the law-making power. Nor can we consider the electors as exercising such power in the selection of public officials.

That is but a popular method of appointment, and appointment to office is purely an executive act. That only is a legislative act which creates legal rights, and determines what shall be the legal competences of public officials when appointed.

Thus in general we do not regard the purely executive branches of the government as exercising Sovereignty, because they are not organs of volition. Their activities are limited simply to the enforcement of the sovereign will when declared. Likewise, as said, the activities of judicial tribunals are excepted from sovereign acts, in so far as they are concerned simply with the interpretation and application of existing laws.

To repeat, then, in conclusion; all organs through which are expressed the volitions of the State, be they parliaments, courts, constitutional assemblies, or electorates, are to be considered as exercising sovereign power, and as constituting in the aggregate the depository in which the State's Sovereignty is located.

Professor Woodrow Wilson, in the essay already quoted, places the exercise of Sovereignty in the legislative body, but limits this term to the formal law-making organ of the government, as, for example, the Congress in the United States. Thus as he forcibly and correctly says: "Sovereignty is the daily operative power of framing and giving efficacy to laws. It is the originative, directive, governing power. It lives; it plans; it executes. It is the organic organization by the State of its law and policy; and the sovereign power is the highest originative organ of the State. It is none the less sovereign because it must be observant of the preferences of those whom it governs. The obedience of the subject has always limited the power of the sovereign." The subsequent text shows, however, that the term "law-making body" is to be strictly construed, and that even in the case of constitutional law adopted by popular vote, the People, when so voting, are not giving voice to a sovereign will. In fact, as Professor Wilson holds in the next paragraph, written constitutional law is not really the utterance of a sovereign at all, but "covenants of a community" and "only very formal statements of standards to which the people, upon whom government depends for support, will hold those who exercise the sovereign power."[1] The inference from this would of course be that so-called constitutional law is not, strictly speaking, law, for it cannot be law if not an utterance of the sovereign will, or if it partake of a contractual character.

In substance, Professor Wilson's view is substantially the same as that of Locke, who, as shown by the quotations which we have made in this and previous chapters, maintains both the contractual nature of fundamental law and the sovereign character of the formal legislative body in a *de facto* government.

[1] *An Old Master and Other Essays,* p. 88.

CHAPTER XII

THE AIMS OF THE STATE

THE discussion thus far had concerning the conditions that necessitate the establishment of some sort of public control over the individual, has, at the same time, indicated in a general way the purposes for which the State exists. Legally, as we have seen, the State is omnipotent; but how much of this legal potentiality shall be actualized obviously depends upon the aims that are sought to be realized.

In determining the aims of the State, it is plain that we shall have to make a distinction between what may be termed the true or highest conceivable purposes that may be subserved by the State's existence, and the aims of a given State that are practically obtainable under given objective conditions of civilization. In a treatise of such a nature as is the present one, it is evident that a consideration of the facts and principles connected with this second branch of the inquiry cannot be considered. Such a study would belong rather to a work upon practical politics. Our inquiry will therefore be concerned rather with the aim of the State in general; that is, with the question of the character of the functions for the performance of which the State is essentially and peculiarly adapted, and the aims which, according to our conception of the highest good of humanity, it seems desirable should be obtained. It is to be remembered, however, that this conception is one that must necessarily be based upon the study of present and past social conditions and tendencies. Therefore, just as our view differs from those views that have been held in former periods of history (or which under the then conditions of society could rationally have been held), so too, in the years to come, such may be the nature of developed conditions of life (the character of which, our limited faculty of prevision prevents us from discovering) that our conception of what is either desirable or attainable will be so altered that the ideal aim of the State will be otherwise formulated than as here stated.

Essential Functions of the State. — The fact that the exercise of a power by a State is, *pro tanto*, a limitation of the freedom of action of the individual, necessarily brings the interests of the two into frequent opposition, and, in each particular instance, the question resolves itself into the proper balancing of them.

It is admitted by all that the State should possess powers sufficiently extensive for the maintenance of its own continued existence against foreign interference, to provide the means whereby its national life may be preserved and developed, and to maintain internal order, including the protection of life, liberty, and property. These have been designated the essential functions of the State, and are such as must be possessed by a State, whatever its form.

The particularity with which it is necessary that the control of the State should be exercised in regard to these essential matters, and especially in regard to those that have to do with the definition and protection of private rights, is largely determined by the character of the people governed, and by their state of civilization.

The primary purpose of the State is undoubtedly that of keeping the peace between individuals, and, in the first stages of barbarism, this, together with that of offence and defence against other tribes, is almost its sole aim. As Bagehot has pointed out, in his *Physics and Politics,* in these early times the quantity of government is much more important than its quality. That which is wanted is a comprehensive rule that shall bind men together and make them act in accordance with some definite rule of conduct. " What this rule is does not matter so much. A good rule is better than a bad one, but any rule is better than none." Thus this urgent necessity for a public control of some sort or other leaves but little room for the freedom of the individual, — a freedom which, indeed, the individual has not yet learned to desire, or properly to exercise should he possess it. The variety of the powers that are exercised in this stage by the ruling authority is not, in actual practice, so great; but the rules that define the scope and manner of exercise of this authority are so general and indefinite in character that in almost no direction does the individual possess any guarantee against State molestation.

As civilization advances, however, not only does the orderly habit of the people increase, but their moral qualities become more developed. The distinction between right and wrong becomes more clearly recognized, and principles of justice are more frequently followed without reference to the sanction of the State. The feeling of self-dependence arises, the desire for a certain latitude of action uncontrolled by the powers of the State comes into being, and thus, by degrees, the arbitrary and extensive control of the State becomes irksome. Thus arises a struggle between authority and liberty — a struggle that has continued and will probably continue throughout all history.

This struggle, it is to be remarked, is of a twofold nature: First, to secure to the individual a certain field in which he shall be free to act as he will, without interference either by the political power or by private individuals. Secondly, to establish general rules according to which the functions that are given to government shall be exercised; that is, to substitute for the arbitrary and uncertain action of government a more or less certain and uniform regulation of public affairs. Neither one of these aims is necessarily bound up in the other. Each is separately obtainable. We thus distinguish between political freedom and individual freedom. The former refers to the extent to which the people participate generally in the management of the State, or at least dictate the manner in which its powers shall be exercised. The latter has to do with the extent to which private rights of life, liberty and property are secured.

Thus, for example, under the Roman Empire there was little political freedom, while individual rights were, as a rule, ample and well protected. On the other hand, a much higher degree of political freedom existed among the early Teutonic tribes, with a far smaller protection to private rights. It is thus possible, also, that in the most popular of governments, individual rights may not be well respected. Some go to the extent of asserting, indeed, that under such a rule they are not as well respected as they are under monarchial forms of control. As examples of this fact they cite the various Irish Land Acts of the British Parliament of recent years, by which rights of landlords have been violated and certain amounts of their rents arbitrarily confiscated. Thus the Arrears of Rent Act of 1882 provides in certain cases for the payment of one-half of the arrears of rent by a land commission whereby the other half is extinguished. Other acts interfere generally with the right of contract, and remove from the parties interested the power of arranging terms, and vest it in the government. In our own country the large amount of the State legislation directed to the regulation of labor and to the promotion of morality is pointed to, which, it is asserted, is of this nature. It scarcely need be said that this legislation is not to be considered as *per se* inadvisable, any more than it is to be absolutely maintained that economic and political exigencies have not demanded English legislation regarding "landlordism" in Ireland. The only point here made, is concerning the character of such legislation as regards the general insecurity of individual rights.

From the nature of the case, there are no precise limits that can be placed to the extent to which a popularly organized government may go in the diminution of individual freedom; and we may find it necessary to say a few words further upon this subject in the concluding chapter, in which we shall consider the alleged inherent tendency of democracy to establish a "tyranny of the majority." In a general way we may say, however, that it is the aim of constitutional government to obtain political freedom, and, at the same time, by the restrictions placed upon the power of government, especially by those contained in the so-called "bills of rights," to protect individual liberty.

The boundary line between the two principles of civic liberty and of authority has varied with social conditions. When authority has trenched upon the domain claimed for liberty, the people have been oppressed, and despotism has been the result. When freedom of the individual has exceeded its proper limits, license has been the result, and the stability of the State has been endangered. Nations have thus ever oscillated between governmental oppression and individual license, and the great political problem of all ages has been to determine the proper boundary line between the two: to give to the people all the liberty that they are capable of enjoying, without destroying the stability and the efficiency of the State.

While it is thus seen that in a sense "liberty" and "authority" are contradictory terms, as comprehending domains of activities that are mutually exclusive, and, therefore, that the extension of the one is the corresponding limitation of the other; at the same time, the distinction that we have made between political and individual freedom indicates that they are in fact to a considerable extent relative. That is, that it is only through the existence of a certain amount of public authority, that any personal freedom of action or liberty is secured. As Rousseau says, "What man loses by the social contract is his natural liberty and an unlimited right to anything that tempts him which he can obtain; what he gains is civil liberty and the ownership of all he possesses. . . . We must distinguish the natural liberty, which has no limits but the strength of the individual, from civil liberty, which is limited by the general will; and possession which is only the effect of the force and right of the first occupant, from the ownership which is founded only upon a positive title." [1]

Without any authority whatever, the State ceases to exist, and there is then no means whereby the sanctions of law may be enforced. In fact, no legal code of conduct can be said to exist. It is only when the

[1] *The Social Contract*, Bk. I. Chap. VIII.

State lays down and enforces general rules of conduct, that the individual is protected in the exercise of that freedom of action which is left to him. Public laws are necessarily of a general character, and within the limits that they set, a field of activity is created within which the freedom of the individual is protected. Thus, laws regulating the holding and transference of property defend the people in the possession of their wealth and its use and consumption. General laws regulating contract, provide the individual with a protection under which he may enter into contractual relations with his neighbors, with the assurance of having his rights protected. Penal laws, and their enforcement, protect both the life and the property of the person, without which freedom would be either impossible or worthless. The sum of the rights thus secured to men through the State, constitutes their civic freedom, and all that can be demanded from the individualistic standpoint is that the governmental authority be exercised in as general a manner, and to as small an extent, as is compatible with the capacity of the people for the proper exercise of the freedom of action that is thereby reserved to them.

But this is just the point. Upon what general principles is the line to be drawn between public control for the public good, and individual freedom for individual good?

The question has often been raised whether the State is only a means to an end or an end in itself. Either position may be taken according to the standpoint from which the State is viewed. Considered from the purely individualistic standpoint the State is nothing more than a means to an end, namely, the instrumentality through which the highest possible development of humanity is obtained. But, viewed as having an existence apart from the individual, and as related to its citizens, who have no existence as citizens, except as members of the body politic, the State is of course an end in itself. This distinction between members of a community considered as individuals and as citizens we have already mentioned. Bluntschli is therefore right when he says, " On the one hand it (the State) is a means for the advantage of the individuals who compose it. From another point of view it has an end in itself, and for its sake the individuals are subordinate, and bound to serve it. . . . Just as the nation (*Volk*) is something more than the sum of persons belonging to it, so the national welfare is not the same as the sum of individual welfares. It is true that a close relationship exists between the two, and that they usually rise and fall together. If the individual welfare of the majority is diminished, that of the State is usually suffering from serious evils. But the lines and direction of the two are not always parallel. Sometimes they cross each other, and sometimes they are altogether separate. Every now and then the State is compelled, either for its own preservation, or in the interest of future generations, to make heavy demands from its present members, and to impose weighty burdens upon them. It sometimes happens, also, that the needs of individual welfare call for extraordinary aid and support from the State which thus incurs serious obligations."[1]

The relation between individual and general interest not being capable of precise statement, men differ in their opinions not only as to the practical possibility of obtaining certain results through governmental action, but as to the desirableness of such action, even when such results are practically obtainable. We may roughly divide the views upon this question into four classes : (1) the anarchistic, (2) the individualistic or *laissez faire*, (3) the common welfare, (4) the socialistic and communistic.

Anarchistic. — The anarchistic view illustrates the logical extreme of individualism, according to which all government is considered not only essentially an evil, but an unnecessary evil. As defined by Mr. Huxley, anarchy is that form of society "in which the rule of each individual by himself is the only government the legitimacy of which is recognized. . . . Which abolishes collective government, and trusts to the struggle for existence modified by such ethical and intellectual considerations as may be freely recognized by the individual, for the *modus vivendi* in which freedom remains intact, except so far as it may be voluntarily limited."[2]

The argument of those who hold this extreme negative view as to the proper province — or rather as to the no province at all — of the State, is, that reason

---

[1] *Theory of the State*, trans., 2d ed., pp. 307, 308.

[2] "Government: Anarchy or Regimentation," *Collected Essays*, Vol. I. pp. 393 and 419.

will urge the orderly minded majority to combine against the disorderly disposed minority to secure justice and order. Thus, for instance, they say, that citizens, — or rather individuals, for there would be no citizens in the absence of a State, — will voluntarily unite to secure general improvements such as roads, sanitation, illumination and the like, and to protect themselves against threatened violation of their lives and property. In this way mutual action will be secured by clubs or associations voluntarily formed. All such regulation the anarchist says is legitimate as based upon purely voluntary action. But to this assertion we must demur. We may properly ask, how about the minority who are coerced by the action of such associations? Certainly they are coerced, and to them it is none the less compulsion because proceeding from such a so-called voluntary source, rather than from a more permanent and general political power. In either case it is the application of an outside force binding their wills or actions to a conformity with its desires. Again we may ask, what conditions, and who, are to determine when, and for what purposes, the majority are thus to unite; and to what extent shall their coercion extend? Can there be placed any other rational limit to this compulsion than that dictated by the will of the party that is most powerful, — most powerful either on account of superiority of numbers or wealth, or other influences? A society may, in fact, be easily imagined based upon this so-called voluntary or anarchistic principle, in which the actual freedom of its members is reduced to an absolute minimum, by means of the varieties of control exercised over them by these smaller groups, clubs, safety committees, etc. Thus Mr. Donisthorpe (himself an extreme individualist) says, "Whether we adopt despotism or democracy, socialism or anarchy, we are always brought back to this unanswerable question, what are the limits of group actions in relation to its units?"[1]

As a system of rational politics, then, anarchism is without a logical basis. While it denies the right or utility of political action in general, it opens the way to the introduction of a compulsion that is not to be distinguished from it in essence, and which is, in addition, arbitrary and incapable of limitation or regulation according to precise principles.

Individualistic. — According to the individualistic school, the importance of the so-called private rights of property, life and liberty is greatly emphasized, and the proper province of the State held to be limited solely to the protection of them. The coercive power of the State according to this view is regarded as a necessary evil, being required only because of the weakness and imperfectness of man's moral nature. Hence, it is held that, with a developing sense of order and morality, the State's importance will diminish, until, when the millennium shall arrive, its absolute vanishing-point will be reached.

[1] Mackey (Ed.), *A Plea for Liberty*, Chap. "The Limits of Individual Liberty."

At this point individualism merges into anarchism pure and simple, and the two views are thus distinguishable only by the fact that, while the anarchist would depend upon such occasional coercion as voluntary association would provide, until this moral perfection of man is attained, the individualist advocates the exercise, until then, of police powers by a regularly constituted State.

Conspicuous among those holding this view regarding the limited province of the State's activity, and of the possibility of its ultimate disappearance, is Mr. Herbert Spencer. Thus in his *Social Statics* he says: "Have we not shown that government is essentially immoral? . . . Does not it exist because crime exists, and must government not cease when crime ceases, for very lack of objects on which to perform its functions?" Again he says: "It is a mistake to consider that government must last forever. . . . It is not essential but incidental. As amongst Bushmen we find a State antecedent to government, so may there be one in which it shall have become extinct."

Janet apparently takes the same view of the essential purpose of the State. In his *Histoire de la Science Politique* he says: "Imaginez en effet une politique parfaite, un gouvernement parfait, des lois parfaites, vous supposez par là même des hommes parfaits. Mais alors la politique ne serait plus autre chose que le gouvernement libre de chaque homme par soi-même: en d'autres termes, elle cesserait d'être. Et cependant, c'est là sa fin et son idéal.

L'objet du gouvernement est de préparer insensiblement les hommes à cet état parfait de société, où les lois et le gouvernement lui-même deviendraient inutiles."[1]

Hume too, in his essay entitled *Of the Original Contract,* would seem to have held this view. "Were all men possessed of so inflexible a regard to justice, that of themselves they would totally abstain from the properties of others," says he, "they had forever remained in a state of absolute liberty, without subjection to any magistrate or political society." The assertion of M. Jules Simon, "The State ought to render itself useless and to prepare for its own decease," would indicate also the same view.[2]

It is to be observed, that in thus limiting the State to the exercise of police functions, the position is taken that "what one sane adult is legally compelled to render to others should be merely the negative service of non-interference, except so far as he has voluntarily undertaken to render positive services."[3] The point to be emphasized in this position, if strictly adhered to, is that the utilitarian basis, as applicable to each particular proposed action of

---

[1] Vol. I. p. c.

[2] "As for discussions about any one ideal form of government," says Professor Freeman (*Hist. Essays,* 4th Series, p. 353), "they are simply idle. The ideal form of government is no government at all. The existence of government in any shape is a sign of man's imperfection." "Government, like dress, is the badge of lost innocence," says Paine, in his *Common Sense.* "The palaces of kings are built upon the ruins of the bowers of Paradise."

[3] Sidgwick, *The Elements of Politics,* p. 38.

the State, is disallowed. The province of government is to be summed up in legal coercion merely; that is, the prevention of worse coercion by private individuals. The claim that the State may go further than this and perform positive duties, and compel performance of actions on the part of individuals on the ground that some apparent beneficial social result may be obtained, is denied.

The view of Humboldt is possibly the clearest statement of this doctrine. "The aim of the State should be," says he, "the development of the powers of all its single citizens in their perfect individuality; that it must therefore pursue no other object than that which they cannot pursue of themselves, viz., security." This he gives as the abstract or general rule that should govern the political power in the exercise of its function. As he subsequently says, this rule cannot be universally applied, but when it is infringed, it should be because of imperative *necessity* and not in obedience to the apparent dictates of utility.[1]

As regards this purely individualistic idea, it may be stated in the first place, that it is one that has never yet been strictly followed by any party of men, and is, in fact, an ideal impossible of attainment. Spencer's famous law of justice or equal freedom, according to which "every man shall be free to do that which he will, provided he does not infringe the equal freedom of any other man,"[2] if rigidly

---

[1] *Ideen zu einem Versuch die Grenzen der Wirksamkeit des Staats zu bestimmen*.

[2] *Social Statics*, abridged and revised, p. 55; *Justice*, p. 46.

applied can only mean the total disruption of all social control. It would compel either an almost total abstinence from action by every individual, or introduce a veritable war of all against all.[1]

In the analysis of governmental functions that Professor Sidgwick has given us in his recent work, *The Elements of Politics*, he shows that individualists themselves go beyond their avowed aim, and, instead of making personal freedom the sole purpose of governmental interference, do, as a matter of fact, accept the utilitarian basis for the State's action. Thus, for a single example: "The individualistic minimum of governmental interference is commonly stated to include protection of property as well as of person; and it is obvious that an individualist is bound to prevent any interference by one man with the property of another — either by actually excluding him from the use of what he owns, or otherwise impairing its utility to him — if we suppose private property already instituted: since, in fact, the institution of private property *means* the prohibition of such interference. But we have yet to determine the prior question why and how far the institution of private property can be included in the general principle of Individualism. And if we take freedom — in the ordinary sense — as an ultimate end, without any regard to utility, this inclusion seems to me very

---

[1] Cf. on this point, Ritchie, *Natural Rights*, pp. 142-7, and article by L. F. Ward, in *Annals of the Am. Acad. of Pol. and Soc. Sci.*, Vol. IV. No. 4, pp. 101-5, entitled "Political Ethics of Spencer."

disputable; it would seem that the end would be most completely realized by preventing A from thwarting B's actual use of material things, without going so far as to support B in the exclusion of other men from the enjoyment of things that he has once used."[1] In like manner it can be shown that in a governmental regulation of personal security, and the enforcement of contracts, utilitarian elements are necessarily included.

We may leave then as impracticable, if not impossible, that doctrine of pure individualism which justifies State coercion only to prevent individual coercion; and turn to the consideration of that modified individualistic doctrine, which, admitting the utilitarian principle involved in the maintenance of private rights, yet limits strictly the application of this principle to these particular subjects, and thus denies the general propriety of the State's requiring positive services from the individual, other than those freely contracted for.

If, now, this individualistic minimum is to be maintained, it can only be upon the ground that, from the very nature of the State, and from the necessary character and effect of its action, the best utilitarian results to mankind are thereby to be obtained. For, upon what other logical grounds can it be held improper for society to avail itself of an instrument of its own creation. We are of course not concerned here with the alleged support given to this view by the doctrine of Natural Rights.

[1] *The Elements of Politics*, p. 45.

The insufficiency of that doctrine we have already shown.

Even were historical proof obtainable (as Spencer seems to think there is) to show that wherever, in the past, the State has departed from its essential field of activity, its efforts have been, as a rule, attended by mischievous results, this would not be a conclusive demonstration of the correctness of the individualistic view. That a State has erred in judgment in the past is not absolute proof that it will err again in the future. It may be that such failures have been due to imperfect governmental organizations, to the demands of class interests, or to the lack of adequate information, — all of which evils are now removed or removable. If the individualistic rule is to obtain as a general rule of State action, — as one that will render improper the application of utilitarian consideration to each particular instance, — it must be founded upon an inherent characteristic of all State action that renders it unsuited for the performance of any but police functions, and that even as to these, their performance is called for only on account of imperfect social conditions that may ultimately be corrected.

Analyzing now the essential postulates upon which the individualistic doctrine rests, we find them to be, in effect, the following: —

First, that self-interest is a universal principle in human nature.

Secondly, that each individual, in the long run, knows his own interests best, and, in the absence of arbitrary restrictions, is sure to follow them.

Thirdly, that in absence of external restraint, free competition can and does exist; and

Fourthly, that such free competition always develops the highest human possibilities, by enabling each individual to do that for which he is best fitted, by eliminating unfit elements, and thus most surely advancing the welfare of all.

We need not especially consider the first principle, viz., that of self-interest, as it would lead us into an unnecessary ethical discussion of the relations between egoism and altruism that would be foreign to the purposes of this work.

As regards however the second postulate, that the individual will best know his own interests, or that he will follow them when known, we enter an emphatic denial. Nothing is more obvious than, as for example, in the matters of compulsory education, sanitation and the like, that it is the very persons upon whom coercion is needed who are least qualified to judge concerning the value of the conduct that such compulsion demands. This ignorance is seen in the attitude often displayed by the working classes against the introduction of machinery, and may be pointed out in numberless other directions.

The third postulate, as to the necessary existence of free competition in the absence of external restraint by the State, is also not necessarily true. Genuine competition is possible only where the contesting parties possess comparative equality of strength. Where there is not this equality a contest means not competition, with any of the resulting benefits that the fourth postulate predicates, but simply a destruction of the weaker party. It is thus possible that in many instances the interference of the State, by rendering conditions more equal, may actually promote competition rather than destroy it. Furthermore, as Professor H. C. Adams has shown in his excellent monograph, *The State in Relation to Industrial Action*, law may often serve not so much to check competition as to raise its moral plane. Proof of this is to be seen in the results following from factory legislation and the regulation of the employment of women and children.

Finally, we turn to the fourth and last postulate, that the ultimate effect of free competition, where possible, is beneficial. The consideration of this assertion brings us to the question of the applicability of the so-called evolutionary laws of "struggle for existence" and "survival of the fittest," to social and political man.

The fact that the operation of this principle of struggle for existence is the principal means through which nature secures the development and evolution of her species, leads the individualistic school of thinkers to maintain the necessity for allowing free scope to the operation of this same law when applied to human society. So universal and powerful do they consider the operation of this force, and so certainly do they regard its ultimate effect to be the improvement of the human race, that the fatalistic position is taken of maintaining it to be useless and even dangerous to attempt to control, assist or oppose in any way its workings. For this reason, they assume the attitude of extreme *laissez faire*, and discourage all organized effort on the part of society, or of the State, to assist in the regulation and improvement of the industrial life of its people. Thus says Mr. Spencer in his essay entitled *The Man versus The State:* "Society, in its corporate capacity, cannot without immediate or remote disaster interfere with the play of these opposed principles under which a species has reached such fitness for its mode of life as it possesses, and under which it maintains that fitness."

In accordance with this position this philosopher bewails the interference of the State in the regulation of factory labor, employment of women and of children, and the limitation of hours of labor in certain employments. He considers unwise the assumption by the State of the right to enforce sanitary regulations, as, for instance, those of drainage and of preventing the spread of contagious diseases; and he even reprobates the monopolization by the State of the sole right of coining money. All of these matters he thinks should be left to the regulative law of competition.

The most thorough-going criticism of this Spencerian doctrine is that of Professor Lester F. Ward, contained in his recent work which we have already had occasion several times to cite, *The Psychic Factors of Civilization*, and in an article contributed by him to the *Annals of the American Academy of Political and Social Science*. So satisfactorily has this writer laid bare the inaccuracies and insufficiencies of this doctrine that in the following paragraphs it is necessary to do little more than reproduce his arguments.[1]

It is to be observed that with Spencer and his followers the ultimate beneficence of the natural law of competition is everywhere lauded. "Pervading all natures," says Spencer, "we may see at work a stern discipline which is a little cruel that it may be very kind."[2] All activities of government beyond mere police powers tamper with this beneficent law and are against the order of nature.

Now the first point that impresses one in the operation of this law of nature, is its extravagance as manifested in all the lower domains of life. Thousands and even millions of progeny are produced in order that, in this competition, the survival of a single individual may be secured. "It thus appears," says Professor Ward, "that in biology, while nothing takes place which does not secure some advantage, however slight, the amount of energy expended in gaining this advantage bears no fixed proportion to the value of the result. Nature acts on the assumption that her resources are inexhaustible, and while she never buys a wholly useless article she usually pays an extravagant price for it. The expressions 'natural selection' and 'survival of the fittest' both contain the significant implication that the bulk of things are not selected, and that

---

[1] Reference should also be made to the able essay by Professor Ritchie, entitled *Darwinism and Politics*.
[2] *The Man versus The State*.

only the select few who prove fit survive, while all else perish. The first member of the biologic law of economy may be characterized by the term 'practical.' The second may in like manner be characterized by the term 'prodigal.' Nature is therefore at once the most practical and the most prodigal of all economists; practical in that she never makes anything which has not the elements of utility, prodigal in that she spares no expense in accomplishing even the smallest results." [1]

The operation of such a principle as this in human society is manifestly abhorrent, and the fact is that it has never been allowed to operate undisturbed. "Competition . . . not only involves the enormous waste which has been described, but it prevents the maximum development, since the best that can be attained under its influence is by far inferior to that which is easily attained by the artificial, *i.e.* the rational and intelligent, removal of that influence."

"Hard as it seems for modern philosophers to understand this, it was one of the first truths that dawned upon the human intellect. Consciously or unconsciously it was felt from the very outset that the mission of mind was to grapple with the law of competition and as far as possible to resist and defeat it. This iron law of nature, as it may be appropriately called (Ricardo's 'iron law of wages' is only one manifestation of it), was everywhere found to lie athwart the path of human progress, and the whole upward struggle of rational man,

[1] *The Psychic Factors of Civilization*, p. 251.

whether physical, social or moral, has been with this tyranny of nature — the law of competition. And in so far as he has progressed at all beyond the purely animal stage he has done so through triumphing little by little over this law and gaining somewhat the mastery in this struggle. In the physical world he has accomplished this so far as he has been able through invention, from which have resulted the arts and material civilization. Every implement or utensil, every mechanical device, every object of design, skill, and labor, every artificial thing that serves a human purpose, is a triumph of mind over the physical forces of nature in ceaseless and aimless competition. The cultivation and improvement of economic plants and the domestication of useful animals involve the direct control of biologic forces and the exemption of these forms of life from the operation of the great organic law which dwarfs their native powers of development. All human institutions,— religion, government, law, marriage, custom, — together with innumerable other modes of regulating social, industrial, and commercial life, are, broadly viewed, only so many ways of meeting and checkmating the principle of competition as it manifests itself in society. And finally, the ethical code and the moral law of enlightened man are nothing else than the means adopted by reason, intelligence, and refined sensibility for suppressing and crushing out the animal nature of man — for chaining the competitive egoism that all men have inherited from their animal ancestors."

"The simple truth is that everything that is done at the behest of the intellectual faculty is *per se* and of necessity purely artificial in the only sense that the word has. The whole difference between civilization and other forms of natural progress is that it is a product of art."[1]

To the same effect is the pertinent query of Professor Ritchie. "Where are we to find a line between 'natural' and 'artificial,'" he asks, "if all the phenomena of society are, as the evolutionist is bound to hold, subject to the same laws of nature? If we are content to remove only some artificial restrictions, on what principle can we justify ourselves? If we were to remove every artificial restriction that hampers the struggle for existence, are we not going back to Rousseau's 'State of Nature,' the primitive uncivilized condition of mankind?"[2]

Not only is the brute struggle for existence too wasteful, but it does not necessarily lead to the survival of the fittest in the highest sense of that word. It is not always remembered that evolution

---

[1] *The Psychic Factors of Civilization*, p. 261. "Men in society are undoubtedly subject to the cosmic process," says Huxley, in his remarkable Romanes lecture entitled *Evolution and Ethics*. "As among other animals, multiplication goes on without cessation, and involves severe competition for the means of support. . . . But the influence of the cosmic process on the evolution of society is the greater the more rudimentary its civilization. Social process means a checking of the cosmic process at every step, and the substitution for it of another, which may be called the ethical process; the end of which is not the survival of those who may happen to be the fittest in respect of the whole of the conditions which exist, but of those who are ethically the best."

[2] *Darwinism and Politics*.

is not necessarily progress. As Huxley somewhere says, "the creature that survives a free fight only demonstrates his superior fitness for coping with free fighters—and not any other kind of superiority." And as he further says in his recent Romanes lecture upon *Evolution and Ethics:* "In cosmic nature what is fittest depends upon the conditions. . . . If our hemisphere were to cool again, the survival of the fittest might bring about in the vegetable kingdom a population of more and more stunted and humbler and humbler organisms, until the fittest that survived might be nothing but lichens, diatoms, and such microscopic organisms as those which give red snow its colour; while if it became hotter the splendid valley of the Thames and Isis might be unhabitable by any animated beings save those that flourish in a tropical jungle. They, as the fittest, the best adapted to the changed conditions, would survive."[1]

Furthermore, as Ritchie points out, the struggle goes on not merely between individual and individual, but between race and race, and while the race fittest to survive may survive, "it does not follow that the individuals thereby preserved will be the fittest, either in the sense of being those who in a struggle between individual and individual would have survived, or in the sense of being those whom we should regard as the finest specimens of their kind."

In fine, the entire distinction that is to be made

[1] *Collected Essays,* Vol. IX. p. 80.

between mankind and brute creation is contained in the fact that while the animal is transformed by its environment, man transforms the environment, — that the slow and expensive method of structural development by means of the biologic law, is supplanted by the intellectual capacity of man to transform and adapt his environment to his needs, and thus to secure an improvement higher than the mere biological law could obtain, and without its painful and prodigal methods.

The fact is, that when we reach man, the competitive biologic law holds good and is beneficent rather in its psychic than in its physiological aspects, while with Spencer and his followers, the physiological features are emphasized and the psychic elements almost ignored.

The conclusion that we draw from the foregoing reasoning is the *prima facie* propriety of man using all his efforts, and availing himself of all possible agencies for restricting the effects of the competitive law when its operation is seen to be harmful. In accordance, then, with the preceding we may formulate the following general law which should, and of necessity will, govern societies of men so long as reason and intelligence hold their sway.

"First, where the Darwinian law in its application to social man is too cruel or wasteful, or works in any way to destroy those who from the broad and highest standpoint of race improvement are best fitted to survive, to that extent the law is to be checked or regulated if possible by the organized effort of society. Secondly, where the law does not so operate as to eliminate those essentially unfit to survive, the impeding cause is to be removed and the operation of the law rendered possible."[1]

A consideration of the various economic and social problems that surround us will show that in the solution of almost all of them is involved the direct application of this law which we have laid down. All that class of questions relating to the State regulation of labor, factory acts, child and women work, Sunday laws, prohibition of sweating, anti-trust legislation, control of natural monopolies, — all have for their purpose the mitigation of the undue severity of industrial competition, or the struggle for industrial survival. Both protectionists and free-traders appeal to this law to support them in their contentions. The protectionists ask that the State give assistance to industries, industrially "fit" for survival, until they are able to support themselves upon their own merits. The strongest argument made by their opponents, the free-traders, is that to do so is to give an artificial assistance to industries that are "unfit" for survival, and that it is thus at the expense of society that they are enabled to maintain an ex-

[1] This is, in fact, the wider application of the law formulated by Dr. A. G. Warner, for the guidance of charity relief, which is to the following effect: "The purpose of philanthropy should be (1) to preserve those who are fit from the standpoint of race improvement from being crushed by unfortunate local and temporary conditions; and (2) to enable those who are unfit from the standpoint of race improvement to become extinct with the least possible suffering."

istence, when natural selection, if left to its normal operation, would decree their extinction.

The great evils connected with our imperfect penal methods, and with improper and indiscriminate charity relief, are simply the results of rendering possible the continued existence, and even encouraging the increase, of beings intellectually, morally and physically unfit for survival. The enormous combinations of capital in the form of trusts, that characterize recent years, are but the result of the efforts of producers to escape from that fierce competitive struggle which they see to be detrimental to their interests. So new, however, is this phase of industrial development that as yet it is a debatable question to what extent these capitalistic aggregates are properly fitted to survive from the standpoint of general interests of society, even should they prove themselves successful when considered from the point of view of their individual owners. If not socially fit to survive, the organic law of society would demand their regulation or prohibition by the State.

The Non-Essential Functions of the State. — The refutation of the individualistic doctrines, whether in their pure or utilitarian form, leads necessarily to the assumption that the State may, in certain cases, properly exercise powers other than those that are necessary for its mere existence and the maintenance of order. These other functions we term "non-essential" or "common welfare" functions. They include in general the economic, industrial and moral interests of the people. They are the activities assumed by the State, not because their exercise is a *sine qua non* of the State's existence, but because their public administration is supposed to be advantageous to the people. They are such that if left in private hands would either not be performed at all, or poorly performed.

The determination of just what powers shall be assumed by the State, is solely one of expediency, and as such lies within the field of Politics, or the Art of Government, and not within the domain of political theory. For this reason we are not here called upon to discuss the utilitarian arguments *pro* and *contra*, upon which the public control of this or that interest is to be defended or opposed. In each instance the particular circumstances of the case must determine whether or not the advantages to be derived from the public control in a particular case are more than offset by the weakening of the self-reliance of the people, by the encroaching upon their personal freedom, by the opening of the way to corrupt influences in government, or by the creating of precedents for the assumption of activities by the State that will be detrimental to the general interests. This is practically the rule followed by all modern civilized States.

In accepting this broad utilitarian basis for the State's action, as including every activity that may in any way promote the general welfare, the greatest latitude of individual opinion is permitted as to just what public functions will subserve this end. According to the weight given to the various arguments for and against State action one may differ little in practice from the limited policy dictated by the individualist, or from the extreme doctrine of the socialist or even the communist. The only point here insisted upon is that there is no *a priori* or fixed limit which can be placed to governmental activity, but that the assumption of each function must rest upon its own utilitarian basis.

The purposes of this treatise do not require us, therefore, to consider more particularly the doctrines of the socialists. That alone which distinguishes their views from the other and less radical tenets of the "General Welfare" school is the greater confidence felt in the efficiency and advisability of State action, and hence a greater readiness to use it. It is of course obvious to them that an industrial regime, in which all instruments of production are owned in common, includes inherent difficulties of organization of industry, of the establishment of a satisfactory and just method of individual remuneration, and, above all, of a necessary settlement of the Malthusian problem. But these difficulties, which to the most of us seem practically insurmountable, are not such to them. As regards, however, the principle that there is no valid objection to the use of the political power for the performance of any function that will beneficially affect the social welfare, we are in agreement with them.

By a necessary course of events the trend has been towards the assumption by the State of new functions in the control and regulation of industrial life; and the same causes that have operated in the past will continue to have their effect in the future. As industrial society develops, and increases in coherence and complexity, the social interests — those affecting the people in general — will become more numerous and important, and enlightened utilitarianism will demand the subordination of individual interests to the general weal of the community. Added to this, will be the necessity for additional power in the State for the proper maintenance of itself in its position, rendered more important and difficult by the increased complexity of the social organism. As also tending towards an extension of the State's industrial functions, is what may be termed the growing self-consciousness on the part of society of its own power potentially possessed, and hence of the possible extent to which its powers may be used for the promotion of the welfare of its individual members. Furthermore, while in the absence of popular government the administration of public affairs was largely dominated by individual and class selfishness, it was but natural that the presumption should be against State action whenever individual action was possible. As this disturbing factor is removed by the widening of political rights and the perfection of political machinery, this prejudice will be removed.

In conclusion, then, of this subject, instead of it being the duty of a State to prepare for its own decease; and instead of it being the tendency of developing civilization to render the existence of a political power less and less necessary, the reverse is the case. In a multitude of directions the force of conditions will cause the State to become increasingly important not only as a conservative but as a constructive agent. When the moral millennium shall arrive, if ever, it may be conceived that the necessity for the actual exercise of the punitive powers of the State will have diminished to a minimum, and that the increase of morality will have largely removed the necessity for the physical coercion that the State now supplies. But let it not be thought that the decrease in the exercise of force indicates in any wise the lessening of that force. The reverse is more likely to be the case. No one has made this point clearer than Stephen in his criticism upon the individualistic doctrines contained in Mill's essay *On Liberty*. As he expresses it with metaphorical vividness, in comparing the fourteenth century anarchy in Scotland with its nineteenth century order: "The first impression on comparing this spirited picture with the Scotland which we all know — the Scotland of quiet industry, farming, commerce, and amusement, — is that the fourteenth century was entirely subject to the law of force, and that Scotland in the nineteenth century has ceased to be the theatre of force at all. Look a little deeper and this impression is as false, not to say as childish, as the supposition that a clumsy rowboat, manned by a quarrelsome crew, who can neither keep time with their oars, nor resist the temptation to fight among themselves, displays force, and that an ocean steamer which will carry a townful of people to the end of the earth at the rate of three hundred miles a day, so smoothly that during the greater part of the time they are unconscious of any motion or effort whatever, displays none. The force which goes to govern the Scotland of these days is to the force employed for the same purpose in the fourteenth century what the force of a line-of-battle ship is to the force of an individual prize-fighter. The reason why it works so quietly is that no one doubts either its existence, or its direction, or its crushing superiority to any individual resistance which could be offered to it. . . . Force not only reigns, but in most matters it reigns without dispute, but it does not follow that it has ceased to exist." [1]

It is not necessary to recite here the numerous and important instances during comparatively recent years in which the State has widened her boundaries under the impelling influence of the causes which we have enumerated. If one were asked to characterize in a single sentence the development of government during the present century, it could not be better done than by describing such development as one wherein the purely political duties of the State have become progressively less important as compared with its other functions.

In the United States, the extent to which matters of public interest are economic in character is especially apparent. With arduous labor, our enterprising

[1] *Liberty, Equality, Fraternity*, ed. 1873, p. 227.

news journals are able to arouse occasional excitement on the part of the people in regard to items of our foreign relations, but as a matter of fact, public matters of purely political import seldom arise. Matters connected with the maintenance of domestic tranquillity, and defence from foreign aggression or wrong enter but slightly into our general thought. Our legislatures are mainly concerned with economic matters, such as the levying of proper import duties, with the control of trusts, with problems connected with railroads, with interstate commerce, with the assessment of taxes, with the provision of proper circulating currency, and the maintenance of sufficient banking facilities.

The extent to which this movement has already gone is evidenced by a comparison of the history of the last century with that of the latter half of the present. Then, history was little but the record of purely political events: of wars, of treaties of offence and defence, of the settlement of dynastic or territorial disputes, of struggles of factions for the possession of political power, and of the maintenance of public order. Now, the pages of our history, when they shall be written, will be largely filled with the record of industrial growth, the negotiations of commercial treaties, and of the development of this or that phase of economic life.

The Analysis of Governmental Functions. — The analysis of governmental functions, as regards their aims, discovers them to be of a threefold order.

First, those concerned with the *Power* of the State. Under this head are included, in very large measure, the essential functions, namely, those that concern the maintenance of order and the preservation of the State's political autonomy in the family of nations. In earlier times this was almost the sole conscious aim of the State. In those times when not only were its own citizens unaccustomed to order and obedience to law, but when between the States themselves there existed a pure struggle for existence unmitigated by principles of international morality, such was necessarily the case. It was therefore quite essential that the functions of the State for the maintenance of itself as a military power should dwarf, by their importance, the value of political and civic rights, and that therefore these latter should have been deemed of importance only in so far as they served to strengthen the power of the State. Thus among the Greeks, even with their high degree of intellectual development and civilization generally, no higher conception of the State was reached than that according to which it should be the all in all.

At the present day, the relative importance of this aim in the State's life varies according to conditions and circumstances. In Europe it still plays a very prominent part, as seen in the energy expended in the maintenance of navies and enormous standing armies. Geographical situation and a law-abiding spirit of its citizens make it possible for the United States government to subordinate this aim to other and higher purposes. Nevertheless, while the enormous power of our State is thus for the most part dormant, and is fully manifested only in times of imminent danger, it is none the less its most essential attribute.

The second aim of the State is, or should be, that of creating and maintaining the widest possible degree of *Liberty*. As already explained, this includes not only the perfection of its governmental machinery, whereby political liberty in the largest possible degree shall be secured, but also the guaranteeing to the individual of as wide a field as possible in which he shall have a freedom of action, protected at once from arbitrary governmental interference and private molestation. At the same time, as a corollary from this, the action of the State should be so directed as to render its citizens progressively more capable of exercising this freedom. Under this head are included, therefore, all possible efforts to improve the State's method of organization and administration, to remove selfish and class interests from the administration of public affairs, and thus to render possible not only the formulation of an intelligent public opinion, but a realization of those aims that this opinion discloses when so formulated.

Thirdly, and finally, there are those functions of the State, that, apart from any considerations of power or maintenance of individual liberty, tend by their exercise to promote the *General Welfare*, either economically, intellectually or morally.

Now we may ask ourselves, whether or not the facts and the reasoning which have preceded, point necessarily to ultimate socialism? To this a categorical answer cannot be given. They do point, undoubtedly, to an inevitable extension of the State's activities far beyond those at present exercised. But in considering the bearing of an increase in State activity upon this question, it is to be noticed that not every assumption by the State of a new function is a step towards socialism.

This is a very important point. We have already made the distinction between essential and non-essential duties of the State. The assumption by the State of a power in this latter field is ordinarily termed socialistic, but not properly so. Further consideration shows that this analysis of governmental functions may be carried one step farther. The non-essential optional duties may themselves be grouped under two distinct heads, which may be termed "socialistic" and "non-socialistic" respectively. The socialistic duties properly comprehend only activities which could be exercised by the people if left to their private initiative. Therefore, their assumption by the State, is, to that extent, a curtailment of the industrial freedom of the people. Examples of socialistic duties are the ownership and operation by the State of railroads, of canals or of telegraph lines; the ownership by the city of gas, water and electric light works, and the provision of model tenement houses for the poor by the public authorities. These, it will be seen, admit of private management, and, in fact, are, in this country, very generally attended to by private enterprise.

Under the non-socialistic duties of the government are included those which if not assumed by the State would not be exercised at all. They are duties not essential to the State's existence, and yet, from their very nature, not likely or even possible of performance by private parties. Such duties as these are therefore not socialistic, because their public assumption does not limit the field of private enterprise, nor in any way interfere with private management of any sort of industry. As a rule, they are powers educational in character rather than coercive, directive rather than controlling. Under this head come all those administrative duties that are of an investigating, statistical character, and consist not in the interference with industry, but in the study of conditions and the diffusion of the information thus obtained. Work of this kind is that performed by the United States Departments of Labor and of Agriculture, by the Bureau of Education, the Fish Commission, the Coast and Geodetic Survey, by the Decennial Censuses, etc. Public libraries and reading-rooms, boards of health, the provision of public parks, and certain branches of education also come under this head.

Likewise of this character is that large class of governmental duties, that we have before mentioned, the exercise of which results in the raising of the plane of competition, rather than destroying it. Thus, when we consider closely, we see to what a very great degree the increase of governmental activity during the present century has been in this non-socialistic field. Furthermore we discover that indications seem to point to this same field as the one to which the continued extension of the sphere of the State will probably be largely confined. The effect of the exercise of these duties is not to check or even to regulate competition. Their purpose is, not to interfere with the struggle for existence and the survival of the fittest, but to transform the environment, and, by diffusing sounder information concerning the character of the conditions and the nature of the forces by which man is surrounded, to render it possible for him either to harmonize his efforts with them, or to direct his strength and intellect to a modification of them. In fine, to increase his opportunities.

In the field of socialistic duties, the greatest extension of the State's powers will probably be seen in the ultimate ownership and operation by the State or municipalities of all those industries termed "natural monopolies"—the railroads, gas, water and electric light plants, street transit facilities, etc. Economists of the present school have generally advocated the public ownership of these "natural monopolies," and have laid stress upon the fact that, as they claim, socialistic precedents are not thereby established, basing this view upon the statement that it is only in this class of industries, which are not amenable to the healthy influence of competition, that there will ever arise the necessity for State management. This allegation served for a time as a fair argument, but the recent development of gigantic trusts, which have largely removed from competitive influences the production of a very considerable number of commodities whose production is not "naturally" monopolistic, has greatly weakened this economic distinction. As has been before said, this phase of industrial development is as yet so new, that it is not yet determined whether their influence will be ultimately for the public good or not. Should these capitalistic aggregates prosper and prove lucrative to their individual owners, but, from the extent of their power of controlling trade, tend to exert an influence detrimental to society at large, state intervention would become a necessity. Should simple legislative control be found insufficient for their regulation, the assumption of the production of these commodities by the State itself would seem to be necessary, and this would be a very long step towards socialism.

It is to be recognized, however, that together with these forces that tend to encourage and increase the activities of the State are others that will render less necessary a resort to this power. With increasing facilities for transportation and cheaper rates, and with the possible levelling of the artificial barriers to international trade now raised by excessive import duties, the maintenance of combinations of capital controlling the production, and, consequently, the price of commodities, will become increasingly difficult. More important than this, however, is the fact that the development of humanity is not along the social side alone. Together with the forces that tend to increase the social side of man, are others tending to the development of his individuality.

With increasing civilization will come higher morality, broadened altruism, and widened intellectual horizon. These are the forces which may be depended upon for the correction of imperfect conditions as they arise, without the intervention of the State. The more enlightened a people become, morally and intellectually, the more inclined and more able will they be to depend upon their own individual and voluntary powers for the regulation of their own affairs, and the less likely they will be to tolerate a regime in which a broad field of freedom of individual action is not secured. Their intellectual advancement will enable them to discover the means, in very many cases, whereby to correct abuses, without calling in the assistance of the State, and increased morality will render possible the practical operation of these means.

CHAPTER XIII

GOVERNMENTS: THEIR CLASSIFICATION

As indicated in the opening chapter, the purpose of this work does not require us to consider in any detail the organization of the State. The character of political Sovereignty is no more bound up with the manner in which its power is exercised than is man's nature determined by the form of his physical frame. When, therefore, we consider the nature of the State, we do not need to be concerned with its form. We have to do with its ontology, not its morphology. At the same time, to such an extent are governmental terms used in all political treatises and discussions, that one of the main objects of this work, which is to render political phraseology more definite, would not be performed, did we not stop to examine the nomenclature ordinarily employed in distinguishing the various forms of political organizations.

To one who has pursued the arguments of the preceding pages it need not be said that there can be no such thing as a classification of States, as States. In essence they are all alike, — each and all being distinguished by the same sovereign attributes. Hence it follows that the only manner in which States may be differentiated is according to the structural peculiarities of their governmental organizations. It is therefore the purpose of this chapter to consider briefly the various groups into which governments have been segregated, and to advert shortly to the respective merits of the principles of classification upon which these groups have been founded.

In two particulars, all governments are necessarily alike: first, their duties are of a threefold character, — legislative, executive, and judicial; and secondly, the *quantum* of their power is the same. It may be that the exercise of these three orders of functions is not entrusted to independent or distinct organs, and, indeed, their absolute separation is impossible; yet, however united or separated, they are distinguishable duties that must be performed by every State.

That the *quantum* of power exercised by all governments must be the same follows from the fact that, as has been stated, all States are necessarily completely organized within their governments. The apparent differences in the scope of powers possessed, arise from the manner in which the totality of political power is distributed among the various organs, and the character of these organs themselves. Thus, in the modern constitutional State, a very considerable amount of the State's power is denied the ordinary legislative and executive bodies, and is granted to special constitutional organs whose activity is seldom, and with difficulty, called into operation. In other countries also, where these formal legal limitations do not exist, the temper of the people and other political conditions determine the extent to which the government shall habitually extend its influence and regulative force.

Since all States are legally absolute, there can be no logical distinction between such as are free and such as are despotic. As Austin says: "Every supreme government is *free* from legal restraints: or (what is the same proposition dressed in a different phrase) every supreme government is legally *despotic.* The distinction, therefore, of governments into *free* and *despotic*, can hardly mean that some of them are freer from restraints than others; or that the subjects of the governments which are denominated free, are protected against their governments by positive law."[1] Furthermore, as Austin then explains, these terms cannot properly have reference to the amount of political liberty left to the subjects. "For the epithet 'free' importing praise, and the epithet 'despotic' importing blame, they who distinguish governments into free and despotic suppose that the first are better than the second. But inasmuch as political liberty may be generally useful or pernicious, we cannot infer that a government is better than another government, because the sum of the liberties which the former leaves to its subjects exceeds the sum of liberties which are left to its subjects by the latter. The excess in the sum of the liberties which the former leaves to its subjects may be purely

[1] *The Province of Jurisprudence Determined,* ed. 1861, p. 211.

2 A

mischievous. It may consist of freedom from restraints which are required by the common weal."[1] Continuing, he then shows that the only proper sense in which the distinction in question may be applied is as expressing a judgment whether or not a given government grants to its people all that amount of liberty which, everything considered, would best conduce to the general welfare. Thus also says Hobbes: "The difference between the kinds or forms of commonwealth consisteth not in a difference between their powers, but in a difference between their aptitudes to produce the peace and security of the people, which is their end."[2]

As has been elsewhere said in this work, the aim of written constitutions has not been to limit the

---

[1] *The Province of Jurisprudence Determined*, ed. 1861, p. 244.

[2] Quoted by Austin, *op. cit.* p. 248. "If it be objected," says Sidney, "that I am a defender of arbitrary powers, I confess I cannot comprehend how any society can be established or subsist without them. The difference between good and ill governments is not that those of one sort have an arbitrary power which the others have not, for they all have it; but that in those which are well constituted, this power is so placed as it may be beneficial to the people." To the same effect, see Paley, *Moral and Political Philosophy*, Bk.VI. Chap.VI; and Sir William Temple, *On the Original and Nature of Government*, 8th ed. Vol. II. p. 34. Cf. also G. C. Lewis, *Use and Abuse of Political Terms*, Chap. XVI. It will be observed that this last author makes a different use of these terms from that which we have accepted; *despotism* with him having reference solely to "the sovereign rule of one person," and not to be confounded with *tyranny*, which may signify the oppressive government of any number. It should be noticed here, that in the work of Lewis is contained the first serious attempt by an English writer to discriminate between the names applied to the various forms of government, and, though we have not been able to follow his judgment in the instance we have just been discussing, in other portions of this chapter we have been materially assisted by his views.

powers of the State, nor, in the aggregate, those of the government. Their purpose has been more to secure the people against their own fickleness and liability to temporary passion, and against the danger of arbitrary action on the part of their rulers. We say that this is the aim of States with *written* constitutions, for the simple adjective "constitutional" adds no additional qualification to the substantive State, for all States are necessarily such. By the constitution of a State is meant the principles that control its governmental organization and the distribution of its powers, whether these principles be reduced to definite written form or not; and in this sense the most autocratic of governments has *its* constitution, just as much as the atheist has *his* creed, as well as the most Calvinistic believer.

We have already shown in our study of the Composite State the impropriety of the division of States into sovereign and non-sovereign, and, as a consequence, the technical incorrectness of the term "Federal State," unless used simply to designate that form of political organization in which the State's territory is divided into administrative districts, to the organs of which a considerable degree of independence of action is secured.

From the standpoint of the variety of powers commonly exercised, governments have also been termed legal (*Rechtsstaat*), paternal, socialistic, or communistic. So far as these are distinguishable forms, we have considered them in the preceding chapter.

Historically viewed, governments have been classified as ancient, classic, mediæval, modern, and the like, such names obviously indicating no special peculiarities of form, except in so far as we are accustomed to connect certain types of rule with certain chronological periods. Surveying generally, however, the sequence of political forms as they have been successively manifested in history, the interesting question arises whether or not there is a natural course of governmental development under normal conditions; that is, for a State whose progress during a considerable period of time is not seriously interrupted by external interference or conquest.

The most usual form in which this alleged law of growth is stated by those who would give an affirmative answer, is that such growth is in circles, and that periodically a government returns to its original type and begins again its development, though probably each time upon a different and higher plane, much in the order of Vico's theory of the spiral progress of civilization in general. Thus it is said that in the early formative, constructive periods of a People's history, the tendency is necessarily towards a centralization of rule. Hence it was that absolute monarchy was almost universal in early times, and still exists in the less civilized countries. The evils of absolute monarchy lead in time, however, to a lessening of its individual caprice and selfishness, by a widening of the political power. This phase was represented in the abolishment of kingship in early Greece and Rome, and in the gradual curtailment of the powers of the English king. But no more than autocratic rule does the aristocratic rule that takes its place, seem qualified to endure. The increase in general enlightenment and the consequent widening of political consciousness inevitably creates in time a demand for a more general participation of the people in political rule, — a demand that is only satisfied by the establishment of democracy. Illustrations of this are seen in the constitutional history of England since the first reform act, in the republican period of Rome's history, and in Europe generally to-day. The popularization of political principles once begun, the remaining steps to complete manhood suffrage seem to follow as an inevitable result. *Nulla vestigia retrorsum* is the motto of the movement, and we have no historical instance of a people among whom popular government has proceeded to any considerable extent, that has voluntarily restricted the exercise of the suffrage, or among whom a true political aristocracy has been again established. When change does come it is rather a return to autocracy. The disorders that arise from democracy, when corrupted or pushed to its extremes, awaken the desire for a more stable and efficient public control. Thus, as in Rome under the Cæsars, and in France under Napoleon I., the State is rescued from democratic disorder by the strong hand of a military despot. Monarchy thus re-established, governmental development begins again.

Aside from the need of a firm hand to control domestic confusion, the one great factor in the creation of autocracy is war. The need of a unity of control and a full swing of power is then recognized by all as imperative; and once endowed with power, a commander with a victorious army at his back, and with a people already accustomed to autocratic rule, is easily able to retain his dominion after the necessity for its exercise is past. Thus every great danger to Holland — in 1607, 1672, 1747 — resulted in an increase in the power of the monarchical Orange party, and depressed the influence of the republican party of Grotius and De Witt. In times of foreign danger, Rome, with all her hatred of kingship, was obliged to submit to the Dictatorship.[1]

Such, in short, as above stated, is claimed by many to be the normal course of governmental development. By those who characterize the State as a "natural organism," this is viewed as a description of its "life" — its birth, growth, decay, death, and new creation.

But we scarcely need seriously consider the claim of a "natural" or irresistible law of political development. The statement of the above observations contains, however, a suggestion of a valuable truth, in that it indicates, that to each form of government is joined its peculiar weaknesses and special dangers; that autocratic power is apt to lead to selfish and cruel rule; that aristocracies cannot long maintain their power unless their privileges be founded upon ability and repaid by actual ser-

[1] Cf. Roscher, *Politik*, pp. 145 et seq.

vices; and that democracy demands widespread intelligence, active participation in political matters, and a love of liberty united with a law-abiding spirit and tolerance of proper control.

But there is no *necessary* lack of permanence in any of these forms of government. Their duration depends only upon avoidance of error and adaptation to circumstances. Given the proper conditions and a certain degree of wisdom on the part of those in power, and there is no inherent reason why any regime should not persist for all time. The Chinese Empire demonstrates the possibility of a comparatively unenlightened and inefficient form of public control existing for many centuries.

Turning now more directly to the classification of governments, irrespective of their good or bad qualities, we find it a comparatively easy task to separate them into distinct groups according to the possession or non-possession by them of some one selected feature. Thus, for example, it is entirely feasible to classify them according to whether founded on written or unwritten constitutions; whether possessed of unicameral or bicameral legislatures; whether the chief executive power be in the hands of a single individual or of a number; whether this executive, single or collegiate, be hereditary or elective, and, if the latter, whether the tenure of office be for a number of years or for life, etc., etc. At the same time it does not need to be said that groupings such as these are of an eminently unsatisfactory character. They demand a segregation of governments which, though agreeing in the possession of the feature selected as a basis of distinction, are otherwise widely dissimilar. Nevertheless, differences of structure seem to offer the only true means of distinguishing governments in kind. Our problem, therefore, necessarily narrows itself down to the discovery of that one among the several possible bases of distinction that best embodies the essential fundamental principles of civic life.

The Aristotelian Classification. — We have already used the terms "Monarchy," "Aristocracy," and "Democracy," as indicating in a general way the rule of the one, the few, or the many. Employed in this sense they constitute the most widely accepted, as well as the oldest, classification of governments known to history. Pindar, in the fifth century B.C., in his second Pythian Ode, distinguishes between the rule of a tyrant, of a democracy, and of an aristocracy composed of the wise. Herodotus too makes a substantially similar distinction in his History, where he narrates the debate that followed the death of the false Smerdis, between the Persian chiefs as to what form of government should be established; Thucydides implies the same in his report of the speech of the Syracusan Athenagoras, as does Socrates, according to his *Memorabilia* as preserved by Xenophon. The best and most classic statement, however, of this triple division is that given by Aristotle.[1] Wherefore this classification has since borne his name.

It will not be of any material service to us to show the manner in which Aristotle connected a corrupt form with each of the normal forms, — tyranny with monarchy, oligarchy with aristocracy, and ochlocracy, or the democratic rule of the worst classes, with "polity" (πολιτεία), or constitutional democracy.[2] Nor shall we be benefited by showing historically the manner in which this classification was received by succeeding philosophers. It is sufficient to say, that, if not literally copied, it was substantially

---

[1] *Politics*, Bk. III. Chap. VI.; *Ethics*, Bk. VIII. Chap. XII.

[2] Blackstone, who accepts substantially the Aristotelian trinity of governments, together with their "corrupt" types, is criticised in the following characteristic manner by Bentham: "Other species of governments, we are given to understand, there are besides these," says Bentham, "but even those others, if not 'reducible to,' are but 'corruptions of these.' Now what there is in any of these to be corrupted, is not so easy to understand. The essence of these several forms of government, we must always remember, is placed by him, solely and entirely, in the article of *number;* in the ratio of the number of the govern*ors* . . . to that of the govern*ed*. If the number of the former be, to that of the latter, as *one* to *all*, then is the form of government a Monarchy; if as *all* to *all*, then is it a Democracy; if as some number *between one and all*, then is it an Aristocracy. Now then, if we can conceive a fourth number, which, not being more than all, is neither one nor all, nor anything between one and all, we can conceive a form of government, which, upon due proof, may appear to be a corruption of some one or other of these three. If not, we must look for the corruption somewhere else. Suppose it were in our author's *reason*." And in a note, he adds: "A more suitable place to look for *corruption* in, if we may take his (Blackstone's) own word for it, there cannot be. 'Every man's reason,' he assures us, 'is corrupt'; and not only that, but 'his understanding full of ignorance and error.' With regard to others it were as well not to be too positive, but with regard to a man's self, what he tells us from experience, it would be ill manners to dispute." — *Fragment on Government*, Chap. II. § xxix.

adopted as a rule by them all until comparatively recent times. What modifications this division has received at their hands, and what substitutes have been offered for it, will appear in our inquiry as to its scientific adequacy,—an inquiry to which we now proceed.

An examination of this subject will show to us, we think, that the terms "Monarchy," "Aristocracy," and "Democracy" do not lend themselves to the description of distinct forms of government; and that, as commonly used to-day, they represent the loosest order of political thinking, being employed sometimes to describe merely formal distinctions, at other times to denote the location of legal sovereignty, and at still others, to indicate the actual extent of that diffusion of political influence which ultimately conditions, though it does not voice, the legal will of the State.

No one has pointed out this confusion more plainly than Sir G. C. Lewis in his *Use and Abuse of Political Terms*. Beginning with Monarchy, he shows that while the term is usually defined as that form of government in which the sovereign power is in the hands of one person, yet, as a matter of fact, States are to-day universally termed monarchical in which the nominal chief, as in England, possesses only a shadow of the supreme power; and, on the other hand, States denominated democratic in which the chief executive has a very considerable degree of legal power. And to this it cannot be retorted that in the one case the rule is obtained by hereditary descent, and in the other by election, and that this may therefore be the determining test; for history gives examples where the monarch is elected, as, for example, the Roman King before the expulsion of the Tarquins. As a conclusion, therefore, it appears that, according to popular usage, the term "Monarchy" is used simply in the formal sense as designating those States whose political chiefs happen to be called King or Prince, and irrespective of the actual structure of government or the distribution of political power. Thus, according to this phraseology, Austria, Russia, and England are grouped together as monarchies and opposed to the United States as a republic or democracy; while in truth the institutions of England are far more similar to those of the United States than to those of the countries with which it is classified.

In the second place, the Aristotelian classification furnishes no distinct line of demarkation between aristocracy and democracy, when it defines the one as the rule of the few, and the other as the rule of the many; or, as it has been otherwise expressed, with an attempt at greater definiteness, as the rule of the minority and the majority respectively. When democracy is spoken of as being the rule of the many or of the masses, of how many are we speaking, and who are to be held as constituting "the masses"? It is of course not meant that, in such a form, every individual participates in the conduct of the affairs of the State, for women and minors are almost universally excluded. Nor does it mean in common usage that certain classes of adults may not be excluded from political privileges by means of the imposition of an educational or property qualification. Thus, as a matter of fact, in the most popularly organized governments of to-day, the electorate includes scarcely more than a fifth of the entire population. If, then, the distinction between democracy and aristocracy is to be one of numbers, where is the line to be drawn? At what point does democracy merge into aristocracy? The boundary line is not between the minority and the majority.

But there is still another difficulty. We have been speaking as though the extension of the suffrage were synonymous with that distribution of political power upon which the Aristotelian trinity is based. But such is not the case. This point has already been indicated in our treatment of the location of Sovereignty. Voting capacity for the election of public officials is not equivalent to participation in the sovereign power, the one being merely the power of assisting in the determination of what person shall possess a share of the supreme power; and the other being a direct exercise of that power. Nor is the condition changed, when reference is had to the exercise of actual political influence as contrasted with legal power. "Legislate how you will," says Stephen, "establish universal suffrage, if you think proper, as a law which can never be broken. You are still as far as ever from political equality.

Political power has changed its shape, but not its nature. The result of cutting it up into little bits is simply that the man who can sweep the greatest number of them into a heap will govern the rest. The strongest man in some form or other will always rule the rest. If the government is a military one, the qualities which make a man a great soldier will make him a ruler. If the government is a monarchy, the qualities which kings value in counsellors, in generals, in administrators, will give power. In a pure democracy the ruling men will be the wire-pullers and their friends; but they will no more be on an equality with the voters than soldiers or ministers of state are on an equality with the subjects of a monarchy. Changes in the form of government alter the conditions of superiority more than its nature. . . . In all ages and under all circumstances the rank and file are directed by leaders of one kind or another who get the command of their collective force. . . . In short, the subdivision of political power has no more to do with equality than with liberty."[1]

The matter is not mended, when to the electoral right is joined that of eligibility to office. Such eligibility creates at most only a potential political power, which does not become realized until its possessors are actually elected or appointed to office. In all governments, however popularly organized, there is then the virtual rule of a small minority, whether we have reference to the exercise of legal power by

[1] *Liberty, Equality, Fraternity*, ed. 1873, p. 240.

those in office, or to the party leaders who are able to "sweep together" the greatest number of political bits.

It may be asked, however, whether it will not be proper to term that government an aristocracy, *in sensu strictiore*, in which the sole rule is in the hands of a minority, who hold their power by their own right; that is, independently of election or appointment. Such has been the definition sometimes given to this term, but it is to be observed that though sufficiently definite, it is futile, as being scarcely applicable to a single government now existing. Classes of citizens having special political and other privileges of their own right exist in many countries in the Old World. But in none of these do they possess the totality of the sovereign power. They therefore constitute but one of the elements of their respective governments; and, so long as their power is shared by monarchical or democratic organs, there is no sufficient reason for terming such governments aristocratic rather than monarchical or democratic.

The final conclusion that we must draw from the above somewhat long commentary is, that the only valuable use to which the three terms, which we have been considering, may be put, is as descriptive, not so much of the *forms* of governments, as to the diffusion of political consciousness and influence therein. That is to say, the adjectives monarchic, aristocratic, and democratic are to be employed as distinguishing certain characteristics of State life; and, as such, may all three coexist in the same political organization. According to this, a given government may be designated in a certain, though not very definite, sense as either democratic, aristocratic or monarchic, according to which one of these elements is respectively of predominant influence; just as a person is termed good or bad, selfish or benevolent, and the like, without meaning thereby that such person is wholly good or selfish, or the reverse. It would be a task of supererogation to cite those elements and institutions that are usually connected with one or another of these terms; how the concentration of power or dignity in the hands of a single ruler is monarchic, the existence of class privileges aristocratic, and the general diffusion of power democratic. Nor will it be necessary to show further than has been already indicated, that any government *must* contain, in varying degrees, all three of these elements. The amount of discretionary power necessarily left in the hands of the chief executive in any popular government is monarchical in character, and the result of the representative system is to combine the rule of a selected few with general democratic power.

Schleiermacher has pointed out how fundamental is the distinction based upon the degree of diffusion of the political power.[1] The State, however organized, necessarily rests upon the people and is an organization of them, and no more essential prin-

---

[1] *Ueber die Begriffe der verschiedenen Staatsformen* (*Abhandlungen der Berliner Akademie*, 1814).

ciple can therefore be discovered than that which has reference to the extent to which the political consciousness has pervaded their minds as a whole, and led to a participation in, or at least a determinative influence upon, the administration of public affairs. The only trouble is, as has been already said, that this affords a criterion of distinction that does not admit of sufficiently definite determination to serve as a means of exact classification of governments. The spirit of constitutions changes long before their names and forms, and thus in periods of transition it is frequently a matter of individual opinion whether this or that element is relatively dominant.

The impossibility of conceiving given governments as purely autocratic, aristocratic, or democratic, early led to the theory of the so-called "mixed" State, or that State in which these several features are united in varying proportions. The acceptance of this hybrid type dates from the earliest times, being accepted by Aristotle himself, by Plato, Polybius, Cicero, and Tacitus, and by mediæval and modern writers generally; some holding that all governments are necessarily mixed in character, others asserting that there may be both simple and mixed forms. To those who deny that there are any simple governments, that all are mixed, Lewis remarks that "to call this a *classification* of governments is not less an abuse of language than to call the offence of one man a conspiracy; it is, in effect, a denial of all classification, an abolition of all distinction between different classes of governments, which are thus joined together in one undistinguished heap."[1]

But, as Lewis further points out, to speak of any government as being mixed is necessarily to abandon the threefold classification based upon the number admitted to rule. "This notion," says he, "is subject to the obvious difficulty that, as the triple division of governments is strictly accurate and logical, it must be exhaustive, and its members must be opposed to one another; whence it follows, that there can be no form of government which is not one of these three, and that a combination of any two of them, much more of all three, is as inconceivable as that a number should be odd and even at the same time; inasmuch as the notion of one excludes that of any other. For example: monarchy is the government of one, aristocracy of more than one: therefore, as a State cannot be governed both by one person and by several, it cannot, at the same time, be both a monarchy and an aristocracy. Aristocracy is a government of less than half, democracy of more than half, the community; therefore, as a State cannot, at the same time, be governed by more and less than half its members, it cannot be, at the same time, a democracy and an aristocracy. Still less can it be governed by one, by a minority, and a majority of its members all at once."[2]

The idea of the mixed State has been attacked

---

[1] *Use and Abuse of Political Terms*, p. 87.
[2] *Idem*, p. 72. Compare this with Bentham's reasoning in reference to "corrupt" forms, cited in a note on p. 360.

from still another standpoint; namely, from that of the necessary unity of Sovereignty. Thus says Bluntschli: "Such a mixture as this does not create a new form of State, for the supreme governing power is still concentrated in the hands of the monarch, or of the aristocracy, or of the people."[1] The Aristotelian division depends, says he, "upon the question to whom the supreme administrative power belongs. This latter cannot be divided, not even between a king and his ministers, for this would create a dyarchy or triarchy, and would be opposed to the essential character of a State, which as a living organism requires unity. In all living beings there is a variety of powers and organs, but in this variety there is unity. Some organs are superior and others inferior, but there is always one supreme organ, in which the directing power is concentrated. The head and the body have no separate and independent life, but they are not equal. So also for the State, a supreme organ is a necessary condition of its existence, and this cannot be split into parts, if the State itself is to retain its unity. There is not, therefore, any fourth form of State as has been called a Mixed State."[2]

While agreeing fully with Bluntschli as to the essential unity of the State (without accepting the "organic" manner in which it is conceived by him), it will nevertheless be observed that his argument

---

[1] *Theory of the State*, trans. 2d ed., p. 332.
[2] *Idem*, pp. 333–4.

is not to the point, being directed rather to the nature of the State than to the character of government. The reasoning is good as against the mediæval and early modern writers who introduced an essential duality into the State itself, by the predication of a contract, and of an opposition, between the "rights" of the People and those of the Crown; but it is not valid as against those who distinguish between the State and its government, and who recognize the State's personality, and identify Sovereignty with its supreme will: — who, in other words, distinguish between the supreme power itself, which is essentially a unit; and the exercise of that power, which may be distributed among several organs. Thus, because of the failure to make this distinction, Bodin held absolute monarchy alone as possible, while Althusius maintained a like ground for democracy. Hobbes, also, though holding either monarchy, aristocracy, or democracy possible, yet denied the possibility of a union of two or more. But all were alike at fault in identifying the agent with the State itself, whose will the agent merely utters.

In conclusion of this subject, it is to be remarked, that in accepting these terms as descriptive of certain characteristics of State life, reference is had, rather to the diffusion of that ultimate influence that conditions the exercise of the sovereign power, than to the division of the actual exercise of that power. In one sense, it is correct to hold, to be sure, that in any government the democratic element must predominate, for however autocratic be the rule, physical force is necessarily with the people, and their sentiment must be in the long run the dominant factor in politics. But admitting this, it is yet to be observed, that except in those countries where some legal means are provided whereby the people may render explicit their wills, their ultimate conditioning power is almost wholly of a negative, or restraining character. It sets the limits beyond which political oppression shall not extend, but it does not positively determine, or even influence, public action in other matters. Therefore that diffusion of political power to which reference is had in distinguishing between a monarchic, aristocratic, and democratic constitution of the government, relates to the extent to which the people generally have an influence that is effective in determining positively the public policies that shall be adopted, and the functionaries who shall execute them.

Other Classifications. — The defects inherent in the Aristotelian classification have led a considerable number of writers to prefer a twofold division of governments: namely, into those in which the chief power of the State is concentrated in the hands of a single individual; and those in which this power is divided among several. Thus says Lewis: " When the whole sovereign power over a community belongs to one person, the government is called a *monarchy;* when it belongs to several it is called a *republic* or *commonwealth.*"[1] The republic he again divides into an aristocracy or democracy according to whether a minority or majority of the people rule. This is also substantially the classification accepted by Montesquieu.[2]

The advantage of this dual classification as compared with the Aristotelian triplicity obviously consists in the initial avoidance of the confusion between the rule of the few and of the many, — a confusion that is not reintroduced unless an attempt is made to subdivide republics. But, as is equally obvious, this increased definiteness is obtained only by a corresponding simplicity of division and limitation of the analysis, which carries the classification no further than the simple distinction between organic and inorganic matter would carry the chemist in a separation of the elements.

Roscher vigorously opposes the twofold division into monarchies and republics, on the ground that the distinction between aristocracy and democracy is sharper than that between monarchy and the

---

[1] *Use and Abuse of Political Terms*, p. 49.
[2] *Spirit of Laws*, Book II. Chap. 1. Montesquieu speaks of three species of government, — republican, monarchical, and despotic, — but the last two belong to one class, both referring to the rule of a single man, and distinguished only as to the manner in which his power is exercised. Thus, he says, "a republican government is that in which the body, or only a part of the people, is possessed of the supreme power; monarchy, that in which a single person governs by fixed and established laws; a despotic government, that in which a single person directs everything by his own will and caprice." "When the body of the people is possessed of the supreme power, it is called a *democracy*. When the supreme power is lodged in the hands of a part of the people, it is then an *aristocracy*." (Book II. Chap. 2.)

other forms.[1] It will be found, however, that this position is based more on the practical administrative conditions that control the conduct of public affairs, than upon *structural* peculiarities of government. This suggests the remark, that from the standpoint of the "art of government," distinctions between governmental forms may undoubtedly have a comparatively different importance from that which they have when viewed as elements in formal descriptive politics.

The classification of Gareis, as outlined in his *Allgemeines Staatsrecht,* is one of the latest attempts at a formal division of governments, and, to our mind, though not completely satisfactory, one of the best. The character of the chief executive is made the basic principle of distinction, and, in accordance therewith, governments are divided into four classes, as follows: —

(1) Those in which the chief executive organ is a *non-responsible single person* or monarch; and he may be —

    (*a*) without constitutional limitations upon his power; *i.e.* absolute or autocratic, as is the case in Russia, Turkey, Persia, etc. Or —

    (*b*) constitutionally limited; as, for examples, the other monarchies of Europe.

---

[1] *Politik,* pp. 3 *et seq.*

(2) Those in which the chief executive organ is a *responsible single person;* as, for example, the President of the United States or of France. Responsibility is here used, of course, not in the sense of parliamentary responsibility, but of amenability to law for all acts done in a private capacity, or in excess of delegated authority.

(3) Those in which there is a *non-responsible plural executive;* as, for example, the Roman collegiate, or the joint regency in Japan before 1867. This is a comparatively rare type.

(4) Those in which there is a *responsible plural executive;* as, for examples, the French Directory, the Roman consuls, and the Swiss Federal Council.[1]

A republic is defined by Gareis as that form of control in which all executive officers are personally and legally responsible for the manner in which their duties are performed.[2] And this appears to us much more nearly in accord with common usage, than that which defines it as simply the rule of a number as opposed to the rule of one, or monarchy. As a descriptive term, it may be applied to divisions (2) and (4) of the above classification. The word "Democracy," also, according to this nomenclature, is not used as defining a distinct type, but, as we have

---

[1] *Allgemeines Staatsrecht,* pp. 37 *et seq.* (Marquardsen, *Handbuch des Oeffentlichen Rechts.*)

[2] *Idem,* p. 37.

accepted it above, as indicative of all governments in which the popular element is more or less pronounced. In this sense it is largely assimilated to that of Popular Government. Representative Government, likewise, does not constitute a type of itself. All governments, monarchical or democratic, absolute or limited, are actually representative in character. The distinctions lie in the singular or plural number of the representatives, and in their amenability to popular influence and legal control.

As intimated above, the classification of Gareis is not completely satisfactory, in that it necessitates the grouping together of such dissimilar types as the governments of Prussia and England, and the French Directory of 1795 and the present Swiss Republic. But such objections are inherent in any formal classification that has to be based upon certain selected features, to the exclusion of the rest. The sole object is to select such features as will reduce the objections to a minimum, and this, it seems to us, has been done in the above system.

Another recent classification of governments, and an extremely valuable one, is that made by Professor Burgess in the work which we have several times had occasion to cite, and the value of which we here again take the opportunity of attesting. This division, however, is determined by administrative principles as well as by structural peculiarities of government. As such, it varies widely from any of the other systems which we have considered. It is based upon four canons of distinction, which are, respectively: (1) the identity or non-identity of State and Government (Professor Burgess' distinction between State and Government will be remembered); (2) the consolidation or distribution of governmental power; (3) the tenure of office of public officials; and (4) the relation of the legislative to the executive; that is, whether the government be presidential or parliamentary. According to this, the United States government is a democratic, limited, representative, federal, coördinate, elective, presidential government; that of England is immediate, at once democratic, aristocratic, and monarchic, centralized, coördinate, partly elective, partly hereditary, and parliamentary.

Without detracting at all from the extreme value of this analysis, it may be pointed out that it is a description rather than a classification of governments, and indeed this was probably its primary purpose. Based upon the distinctions therein explained, however, not only is the analysis of particular governmental forms greatly facilitated, but a great variety of cross-classifications of governments is rendered possible, by selecting in turn, as the principle of division, each of such distinctions.

We need to lengthen but little more this chapter, for there must already have been made apparent the principles that we have had in mind to formulate. We close the subject, therefore, by merely adverting to three or four of the better-known classifications of governments suggested by modern publicists.

The fourth form, "Ideocracy," with its perverted type, "Idolocracy," added by Bluntschli [1] to the Aristotelian trinity, as illustrating that type in which the supreme ruler is conceived to be God or some superhuman spirit or idea, is evidently unscientific. As Burgess says,[2] it is of no real significance, from this standpoint, from whom the actual rulers are supposed to have derived their powers. Even conceiving the State to be under the dominion of a Deity, the question yet remains to be answered, who, in the last resort, are to interpret such Deity's will? Has this power been delegated to the one, the few, or the many, and this brings us back to the three original forms.

The classification of governments by Welcker into Despotisms, Theocracies, and Legal-States, according to whether the controlling principle of rule be egoistic, theological, or rational, is equally unsatisfactory, as an attempt to apply it to modern types will sufficiently demonstrate. The principle upon which it is based is one that cannot be definitely determined, concerning which no two people can be made entirely to agree, and which is liable to continual fluctuation.

The division of governments into Patriarchal, Theocratic, Despotic, Classic, Feudal, and Constitutional, accepted by Von Mohl, is likewise hopelessly confused, based, as it is, partly upon historical forms, partly upon principles of responsibility of those in

---

[1] *Theory of the State*, trans., 2d ed., Bk. VI. Chap. I.
[2] *Political Science and Constitutional Law*, Vol. I. p. 75.

power, and partly upon questions of legitimacy of political control.[1]

The classification of Waitz[2] is into Republics, Theocracies, and Kingdoms, according to whether the people themselves retain the control of government, or consider the ultimate authority to rest in God, or whether public authority has been finally and completely given into the hands of a single individual. For a criticism of this system, further than the principles which we have above stated will at once make manifest, reference may be had to Bluntschli's work.[3] In the same book may be found a mention of the division of F. Rohmer, by which States are classified as *Idolstaaten, Individualstaaten, Rassestaaten,* or *Formenstaaten,* according to whether their political spirit be radical, liberal, conservative, or absolutist, respectively.[4]

---

[1] Cf. Burgess, *op. cit.* pp. 73–4.
[2] "Ueber die Unterscheidung der Staatsformen," contained in his *Grundzüge der Politik*, pp. 107 *et seq.*
[3] *Theory of the State*, trans., 2d ed., p. 344.
[4] *Idem*, p. 340 (note).

CHAPTER XIV

RECAPITULATION: PRESENT POLITICAL CHARACTERISTICS AND TENDENCIES

WE have now practically completed the task assigned ourselves. Before laying down the pen, however, we may perhaps be justified in summing up the main results that have been reached, and in considering briefly the characteristic features of the State as at present manifested in the civilized world.

As regards the first point; namely, the focussing of the various theoretical conclusions that we have reached, this may be best performed by recapitulating in a very general way the historical steps by which the true conception of the State has been evolved. By the contrast thus afforded of the modern view with its antecedent and less perfect types, we shall be enabled to bring the State's essential elements into the clearest light.

An intimate relation has ever existed between abstract political theories, and the particular objective conditions which have given rise to them, and which they have been called upon to explain. Thus political systems though avowedly dealing with essentials and not with particular appearances, have yet, as their history shows, ever been intimately associated with, and limited by, particular conditions of fact. Thus it is that the variety and complexity of modern conditions afford us, if not new truths (for that is impossible) at least an abundance of suggestions that lead, on the one hand, to the discovery of deficiencies in former theories, and, on the other, to the ascertainment of elements which, but for these suggestions, would in all probability never be evolved by the reason of man moving unassisted in the realms of pure speculative thought.

At the same time, this very fact intimates to us the possibility, nay the probability, that any system that we may evolve, will prove inadequate when called upon in the future to explain political conditions, the character of which our limited powers of prevision render it impossible for us to foresee. All that we may hope for, therefore, in this attempt, is that this inadequacy will arise rather from an insufficient elaboration of the principles which we have established, than from defects in our premises or errors in our reasoning; that the fundamental truths upon which our system is based, will not be seriously disturbed, and that the alterations that may be needed, will therefore be in the collateral deductions that have been made, and along the line of further elaboration, rather than of rectification.

The tracing of the evolution of the *Staatsidee*, together with the treatment of the modern State as at present manifested to us, will naturally tempt us to consider some of the tendencies of political development that appear in present life, and to a discussion of the essential problems to which they will necessarily give rise. Any treatment of these latter topics, however, that would be at all adequate from a scientific point of view would necessitate a consideration of the entire *dynamics* of State life, which in turn would need to be preceded by a descriptive account of political institutions, or its *statical* elements. It is thus seen that a complete system of Political Science includes three main divisions: first, the determination of fundamental philosophical principles; second, the description of political institutions, or governmental organizations considered as at rest; and third, the determination of the laws of political life and development, the motives that give rise to political action, the conditions that occasion particular political manifestations, the circumstances under which certain forces are applicable, either for the good or for the bad, etc., etc.

It would appear that, *logically*, these three fields should be covered in the order stated. The antecedent determination of fundamental principles and essential characteristics is demanded for a proper description of existing types, and this description is, in turn, necessary to a consideration of these types as in active operation. While this is the logical sequence, *historically* this order has been departed from, and necessarily so. Not until a sufficient number of facts have been observed, and the sequences of cause and effect in political life remarked, is the formation of adequate philosophical conceptions possible. When formed, however, these conceptions serve to explain and harmonize the facts that have before appeared confused and contradictory. This same contradiction between the *logical* and *historical* order of evolution is observable as well in fields of knowledge other than Political Science. Thus in Ethics, the practical recognition and definition of the moral attributes of man have preceded the formation of the abstract idea of his moral personality upon which such attributes are logically founded. The same is observable in the history of Jurisprudence, the establishment of legal rights and duties long antedating the conception of a legal personality which is necessarily the subject of these rights and duties. Thus also, finally, Sociology, in its strictest sense as that special differentiated branch of psychology that attempts to determine the fundamental psychic elements upon which all the special social sciences are founded, is of but recent development.[1]

Up to this point our inquiries have been strictly confined to the philosophy of our subject. In this, the last chapter, however, the boundary line will be crossed, and, in addition to its recapitulatory purpose, the aim will be to suggest, by what will be scarcely more than a bare enumeration, the more important topics that will necessarily have to be

---

[1] Cf. F. H. Giddings, Theory of Sociology, *Suppl. Annals of the Am. Acad. Pol. and Soc. Sci.*, July, 1894, and H. H. Powers, Terminology and the Sociological Conference, *Annals Am. Acad.*, Vol. V. p. 705.

treated by any one covering the last of the other two fields,—especially if such a work would be made to have a particular bearing upon present American conditions. The field of Descriptive Politics does not lend itself to a complete treatment in a single work. For its adequate cultivation the monographic method is demanded. The domain of Politics properly so called (*Politik*), however, resembles that of Political Philosophy, in adapting itself to more comprehensive treatment. There is, however, this difference. A correct system of political philosophy should be of almost equal value to all peoples, while systems of practical politics, because of their empiric character, vary according to the particular political conditions to which they are made applicable.

It is this fact that renders the political systems that have been so elaborately developed by Continental publicists of so little value to the American people. A satisfactory work on the Art of Government written from the purely American standpoint, and with special reference to the American conditions, remains yet to be written. Works such as those of De Tocqueville, Bryce, Burgess, Woodrow Wilson, and others, abound with valuable suggestions; but a single comprehensive study of Democracy as it exists among us,—its peculiar burdens, its problems, its administrative merits and defects when applied to our federal system, to our systems of local government, to our vast territorial extent, our inherited political instincts, our industrial, social, moral, and intellectual conditions, — such a work yet remains to be prepared.

It is only as indicating some of the problems that such a needed work would necessarily have to consider that we have written that portion of this chapter which has to deal with present political conditions and tendencies.

From what has been said above, it will be seen that the matters to be discussed below, fall under three heads. *First*, a summary of the steps in the evolution of the idea of the State; *secondly*, the description or rather enumeration of present political conditions; and, *thirdly*, a statement of political tendencies and of the various problems to which they are likely to give rise. We shall speak of these in this order.

The Development of the Abstract Idea of the State. — In this section we shall take up *seriatim* the chief attributes of the State as they are at present recognized, and, by noticing the historical steps by which their recognition has been obtained, contrast the present *Staatsidee* with its former types.

First to be noticed is the complete separation of temporal and spiritual, civic and ecclesiastical, powers which is characteristic of the present day. The State, while not considered as immoral, is now held to be essentially non-moral, and its activities and interests viewed as wholly independent of those matters that particularly pertain to the spiritual life of men. So long as theological beliefs have to do only with the inward state of man, the temporal power is not and cannot be directly concerned, though it may profit by the morality that it creates. Nevertheless, the religious element enters, however, and must necessarily enter as a practical element in the life and activity of the State. Upon religion is largely founded the morality upon which the existence and health of the social life depends; and, as long as religious thought remains in anything like its present form, there will be the necessity for the State to recognize its existence. In any State, also, however liberal its policy, there must arise, on occasions, the necessity to forbid the practice of religious beliefs the instant that they conflict with its own welfare, either by way of inculcating habits of civil disobedience, or by undermining those moral or social principles upon which its own stability depends. This is a necessity based upon its essential function as sustainer of positive law and preserver of autonomous existence. Thus, for instance, granting that the practice of Mormonism, so far as its polygamous features are concerned, is subversive of public morality, the rational duty of the State (its power is of course not questioned) to coercively interfere, is undoubted. In like manner no State can consistently recognize an allegiance of its subjects to an ecclesiastical head, foreign or domestic, that extends to more than a spiritual and dogmatic obedience.

The steps by which the purely secular conception of the political power has been reached, were but slowly taken. In true Comtist sequence, the evolution of the idea of the State has developed from the theological to the metaphysical, and thence to the positive stage. We have already partially traced this progress in connection with the histories of the Divine and Contract theories.

The first twilight of history discovers an almost complete identification of matters religious and civil. Law is conceived as directly embodying divine orders, and political rulers considered, if not as themselves divine beings, as exercising an authority divinely delegated to them. This is the universal condition found existing in the earliest times, wherever we look. While, however, this conception persisted among the Oriental nations, crystallized as their thoughts and instructions became, in the unleavened cake of custom, in the Greek and Roman branches of the Aryan race the next or metaphysical stage was soon reached.

In the Grecian thought, as we have seen, the divine element, though not eliminated, was pushed back to the position of a *causa remota*, and nature (*natura naturans*) erected as the proximate or efficient cause of the State and of law. This was the essential form in which political theory appears in the writings of Aristotle and Plato.[1] In the writings of the Stoics, the metaphysical conception of Nature becomes still more pronounced, and it was the stoic view that was borrowed and incorporated by the Romans in their wonderful system of jurispru-

---

[1] In so far as Plato speaks of a directly divine character of the State, he has reference to his ideally perfect, rather than the actual, State.

dence. Of the modifications of the current idea of Natural Law introduced by the rise of Christianity, and its later fate at the hands of the Schoolmen, we have already spoken.

The idea of Natural Law was not eliminated from English jurisprudence until the time of Bentham and Austin. Upon the Continent it still persists to a very considerable degree. In this respect, therefore, the political philosophy of England, and, following her, that of America, is in advance of that of the Continent. For it is only until this last metaphysical element of Natural Law is eliminated, that the completely secular and scientific conception of the State is made possible.

Intimately bound up with the conception of the State as a completely secular and positive organization, is its character as a sovereign body. With the disappearance of the ideas of natural and divine law vanished the alleged subjection of the political power to any will but that of its own.

Logically, there disappeared at the same time all possibility of legal control from within. As a matter of fact, however, the legally absolute character of the State, as regards its control over its own citizens, remained stoutly contested long after its completely autonomous position among other nations was recognized. The refusal to recognize the independent character of the State in the former respect was based upon two errors: first, the assumption of certain inalienable, imprescriptible, inherent "rights of man" which the State, whatever its power or governmental organization, might not touch; and, secondly, the allegation that law might be created directly by the people through their own customary habit, and hence independently of the political power.

In the actual development and practical application of law, the Romans of the Republican Period founded its validity upon the will of the people and defined the State as a *res publica*, and thus reduced political life to a secular basis. They distinguished law and morality and gave to the State a purely legal organization. But the philosophical principles that necessarily lay at the base of such a practice as this, they never developed, engrossed as they were in the organization and administration of their vast conquests.[1]

The rise of the Christian Church to almost complete dominance in Europe, again plunged jurisprudence into confusion, so far as concerned the reuniting of political and theological conceptions. But what made this confusion "worse confounded" was the destruction of that distinction between public and private law which the Romans had

---

[1] Thus says Bluntschli (*Gesammelte kleine Schriften: Der Rechtsbegriff*, Vol. I. p. 24): "The Romans had a wonderfully fine sense of discrimination as to what should be commanded by law, and what should be left to the free will of the individual. . . . But in spite of that, they never obtained a clear scientific conception of the principle of this distinction. Even in the later classical jurisprudence one looks in vain for a fundamental rule of division. To the question, 'What is Legality and what Morality?' they gave the correct answer in actual practice, but not in theory. Ulpian, for example, one of the

done so much to create, and the introduction of the element of customary law, as positive law *proprio vigore*, of which we have spoken above.

The bringing in of these last two elements of confusion was of course due to the Germanic tribes, the characteristic of whose political systems and juridical thought was the enhancement of private rights at the expense of public authority; and whose ideal was personal freedom, rather than universal or absolute rulership. Thus, while in the Roman Civil Law the State had been viewed as the creator of law, in Germanic thought, it was viewed as enforcing law that had been already created by the customary habit of the people.

At the time that the relation between the State and Law began to be carefully considered in the Middle Ages, this Germanic idea of the source of private law was already widespread, and was made to oppose the Roman principle that *quiquid principi placuit legis habet vigorem*. It would lead us into too great detail to attempt to show the manner in which the mediæval and early modern writers endeavored to harmonize these opposing principles; how they attempted to distinguish between positive and natural laws, and to separate these, in turn, into

clearest and keenest of Roman jurists, declared jurisprudence to be 'the knowledge of things human and divine, and the science of right and wrong,' and declared the highest rule of law to be, 'to live honestly, not to injure others, and to give to each one his own.' In truth, a Greek, who did not understand the distinction between law and morality, might speak thus, but for a Roman, this declaration was untrue."

classes according to whether objectively or subjectively considered; how they sought to determine whether the validity of law is derived from the *will* of the legislator, or from the "*reasonableness*" of the principle enunciated, *i.e.* its conformity to general doctrines of equity and nature; and how to distinguish between the applicability of laws to the ruling sovereign. In a hundred ways such questions were debated, as, whether the monarch was bound by law both *quod vim coactivam* and *quod vim directivam* or only the latter; whether kings, though not bound by ordinary laws, might be bound by their own contracts or constitutional law; what conclusions were to be drawn from the distinction between tyrants *quoad titulum* and *quoad exercitium*. These, and countless other controversies, arose, all connected with the attempt to harmonize logically contradictory propositions, and to practically realize the sovereign independence of the State, and, at the same time, to preserve inviolate and inviolable certain rights of the individual. As one writer has expressed it, it was the old insoluble problem of trying to oppose an impenetrable body to an irresistible force.

Practically, however, the logic of events gained the victory for the irresistible force. The rise of monarchies in the place of semi-independent feudatories was soon reflected in the writings of Machiavelli and Bodin. Machiavelli first took the emphatic position, that law, whether civil, natural, or divine, is not binding even upon the ruler's conscience, but is subordinated to that higher law whose principle is the good of the State, however that good is to be obtained, whether by lying or knavery or deceit of any kind; and Bodin, who, as we have seen, first stated the doctrine of Sovereignty in much its modern form. In vain did the anti-monarchists attempt to limit the royal power by distinguishing between *majestas realis* and *majestas personalis*. The distinctions between tyrants *quoad titulum* and *quoad exercitium* likewise lost ground, and in the system of Grotius we see the tendency to view *de facto* sovereigns as necessarily *de jure* as well, a tendency that was completely realized in the work of Spinoza. Hobbes touched the apex of absolutism when he declared that no natural law or rights can persist after the origin of political society. Pufendorf attacked this doctrine, but even he had to yield to the extent of admitting that such natural law could create only an *obligatio imperfecta*,—an obligation that is in fact, of course, no obligation at all.

Only in the conception of law as created by the people themselves through custom, did there persist an element to detract from the completely sovereign character of the State. This conception, as we know, is still widely held by German publicists, and, though not admitted by them, does necessarily, by the assertion of two sources of legal command,—one of them independent of the State,—logically detract from the full competence (*allseitigkeit der competenz*) of the State.

The imposition of constitutional limitations upon governments that has characterized the present century, has had for its object, not the establishment of a control over the State from without, but a division and regulation of powers from within; it is, as so often repeated, a limitation of actual governmental powers, not of the competence of the State itself. Thus at last has been assumed the only true position, — one that protects the citizen against arbitrary rule without attacking the supremacy of the State, and renders governmental agents responsible for the manner in which their authority is exercised, without denying the legally absolute character of political Sovereignty.

Finally, in addition to its secular, positive, independent, and absolute qualities, there is the attribute of Personality that especially characterizes the modern conception of the State.

The development of this idea in its completeness, was the latest attained, not only because the most abstract, but because dependent for its full recognition upon the acceptance of the State as entirely sovereign. At the same time, adumbrations and imperfect forms of this view are met with from the very earliest times. Hence, to trace its development would require that we should again traverse the entire history of political philosophy. We can therefore permit ourselves to dwell no more fully upon this than to indicate how and why it was that the correct view was not earlier developed. This we may more clearly do by observing that the idea of the personality of the body politic has been held in three forms, the third and last of which is the only true one.

First, political personality has been identified with human personality, and the State viewed, as it were, as an enormous man, subject, as is its alleged prototype, to laws of life, development, decay, and death, to sickness and health; and, like him, resting under moral obligations. This, which we may call the anthropomorphic view, is obviously connected with that theory which sees in the State a natural organism. In this connection may be mentioned that still crasser form of this view in which the conception is so purely mechanical as to render impossible the idea of a personality of any sort. Such, for example, is that presented by Hobbes when he says in the introduction to his *Leviathan:* " For by art is created that great ' Leviathan ' called a ' Commonwealth,' or ' State,' in Latin *Civitas,* which is but an artificial man; though of greater stature and strength than the natural, for whose protection and defence it was intended, and in which the ' sovereignty ' is an artificial ' soul ' as giving life and motion to the whole body; the ' magistrates ' and other ' officers ' of judicature and execution, artificial ' joints '; ' reward ' and ' punishment,' by which, fastened to the seat of the sovereignty, every joint and member is moved to perform his duty, are the ' nerves ' that do the same in the body natural; the ' wealth ' and ' riches ' of all the particular members are the ' strength '; *salus populi,* the ' people's safety,' its ' business '; ' counsellors ' by whom all things needful for it to know are suggested unto it, are the ' memory '; ' equity ' and ' laws,' an artificial ' reason' and 'will'; 'concord,' 'health'; 'sedition,' 'sickness'; and 'civil war,' 'death.' Lastly, the 'pacts' and 'covenants' by which the parts of this body politic were at first made, set together, and united, resemble that 'fiat,' or the 'let us make man,' pronounced by God in the creation."

Secondly, there is that view that properly separates the idea of personality from human individuality, but considers this former attribute ascribable to the State only in a metaphorical or fictitious sense.

Thirdly, and finally, there is the view that gives to the body politic a personality in a true and real sense, such as we have explained in Chapter VI.

The idea of the unity of State, that its essence consisted in a community of thought, life, and interests, was a familiar one to mediæval writers. Mankind was generally viewed as bound together into a single being, the two phases of whose life were realized in the Church and the Empire respectively, and whose vital principle consisted in the divine spirit — a *corpus mysticum cujus caput est Christus*. But the idea of the State's personality was conceived of as true only in a mystical or fictitious sense. Thus the body politic was spoken of as a *persona repræsentata*, or *persona ficta*, but never as a *persona vera*, that is, as a subject really capable of legal rights and duties. Such a conception they could not reach until they had obtained the idea of the State as an abstract conception, and as resting upon a psychical basis. This they could not have as long as the confusion between State and

Government remained, and the theory of the contractual origin of the State persisted, which is, as we have seen, at bottom atomistic and mechanical.

Thus it was that so far as the ruler was spoken of as exhibiting in his own person the entire State, it was rather the dignity or majesty (*würde, dignitas*) of the State that was personified, and this only for purposes of international intercourse. Hence, Althusius, who accepted the absolute Sovereignty of the State as elaborated by Bodin (though placing this power in the whole people), and who viewed the State as an organic body with an individual life, yet identifies State and Government, and speaks of the body politic as a *consociata multitudo*, and as *homines conjuncti, consociata et cohærentes.*[1]

Characteristics of the Modern State. — Thus far in this chapter we have been considering the essential points that distinguish the modern *theory* of the State from its earlier forms. We turn now to a mention of the characteristics of its modern *governmental organization* as contrasted with former types.

The political growth of the present century may be practically summed up in the one word, Democracy — the widening of political privileges. When the dominion of Rome was established, there was apparently secured for the civilized world that result which it had been the effort to obtain for so many centuries; namely, the establishment of a public

---

[1] See Gierke, *Johannes Althusius u. die Entwicklung der naturrechtlichen Staatstheorien*, p. 162.

control so organized and so endowed with power as to provide a means whereby domestic peace, and order, and freedom from external interference could be secured to the people. Deprived, however, of the administrative integration which the principles of local self-government and representation afford, the centrifugal political forces prevailed, and Europe relapsed into the disorder of the Middle Ages. A new start had to be made, and this time under the influence of the Teutonic races. Again the centralized monarchy had to be formed. Not until after an interregnum of more than a thousand years, however, was the climax of autocratic political integration again attained.

But like its Roman imperial type, this development led to the perfection of a governmental form which gave to those entrusted with the exercise of public duties not only irresponsibility, but indefiniteness of competence, and hence opportunity for arbitrary, selfish, and oppressive conduct. Between the governing and the governed an unbridged chasm existed, and an apparent as well as an actual conflict of interests. The government was considered not so much as an organ of the State, as an instrument for the advancement of the interests and ambitions of those in whose hands its administration chanced to be entrusted. Such a condition as this could obviously persist only in the absence of popular enlightenment. Dating, therefore, from the beginning of the sixteenth century, there began to grow a force that in the following centuries was to reverse this state of affairs. Favored by the revival of learning and the declaration of freedom of thought and speech, there was born and increased a political self-consciousness of the people, a self-appreciation of their own political power, a perception of their own natural and reasonable right to determine the manner in which they should be governed, and to direct their own political destiny. England protected herself from the destroying might of this power by timely concessions to its demands. Unyielding despotism precipitated upon Europe the revolutionary period that closed the eighteenth century, and later gave rise to the democratic outbreaks of 1830 and 1848, in which, in almost all the nations of the Continent, the expanding Peoples burst violently the political shells that had so long confined them, and forced the beginning of that period of constitutional development that has proceeded uninterruptedly to the present day.

One might think that when once the principle was established and put into practice, that government is but the instrument of the State, and that its powers are to be exercised directly or indirectly by the people generally and in their own behalf — that then the struggle for good government had been successfully ended. But this was not so. Inconsistent as it may seem, it soon became evident that the people needed to be protected almost as much against themselves and their own representatives as against irresponsible rulers; that though selected by and responsible to the people, it is not safe to entrust to any one official or body of officials the supreme power that must necessarily be given to the government. Finally, that the people, even when acting in their most direct manner, cannot always be trusted to act wisely and according to their own best interests; that passions and prejudices of the moment will urge an electorate or assembly to measures destructive as well to the welfare of the State as to its stability, and that at times the despotism of the multitude can far exceed in severity that possible of exercise by the most autocratic of monarchs.

To correct these tendencies there became necessary the introduction of the so-called system of "checks and balances," a system that constitutes an essential element in all modern constitutional governments. According to this principle, the several legislative, executive, and judicial functions are distributed among distinct organs, and thus the executive made a check upon the legislative, and *vice versa*, and the judiciary upon both. The people by periodical elections and by the *referendum* are made to act as a check upon the legislature, which is itself divided into two chambers, reciprocally restraining. The power of all elective officers is restricted by their limited tenure of office, and by their amenability to law in case of mal-administration of their duties.[1]

[1] In the composite State there of course exists a series of checks in addition to those mentioned above, which have for their object the maintenance of the respective competences of the general and local governments. Thus, for example, John Adams, in a letter to John

All of these reciprocal checks in modern governmental systems have, as said, for their object the securing of the people not only from the arbitrary conduct of public officials, but from hasty and unwise action upon their own part. These checks are thus, in this latter respect at least, a self-recognized indictment of popular government.

But far above all the restrictions upon the popular will that have been mentioned, are those contained in the amending clauses of many of those constitutions that have been reduced to written form. By rendering the modifications of these instruments exceptionally difficult, as compared with other law, not only is the *status quo* of the distribution of political power maintained, but the restrictions placed upon the legislative competences of the ordinary legislatures rendered practically efficient. That is to say, certain powers of government are not given to the ordinary governing organs at all, however checked and mutually balanced they may be, but reserved to special organs or constituent assemblies that, when

Taylor, gives the following description of the United States government: "First," he says, "the States are balanced against the general government. Second, the House of Representatives is balanced against the Senate, and the Senate against the House. Third, the executive authority is in some degree balanced against the legislature. Fourth, the judiciary is balanced against the legislature, the executive, and the State governments. Fifth, the Senate is balanced against the President in all appointments to office, and in all treaties. Sixth, the people hold in their hands the balance against their own representatives by periodical elections. Seventh, the legislatures of the several States are balanced against the Senate by sexennial elections. Eighth, the electors are balanced against the people in choice of President and Vice-President."

needed, require to be specially convened. Thus the amending clauses may fairly be said to be the most important clauses of any constitution. That which is sought in the adoption of written instruments of government is the means whereby legitimate national development may be secured, and at the same time radical and revolutionary changes avoided. Thus when this power of legal development is lacking or rendered too difficult (as, for example, in the old Articles of Confederation), revolution is encouraged. Where constitutional amendment is made too easy of accomplishment, stability and continuity of political life is endangered. Just how severe these restrictions should be is one of the gravest problems that the statesman has to solve, for no fixed rule can be established, the answer in every case depending upon the temperament of the people and other objective political conditions. In periods of a State's existence, when social and economic conditions are rapidly changing, more facile amendment is demanded than in more quiescent times. There are thus many who recognize the advantage that England has enjoyed in past years in the ease with which she has been able to adapt her government to changing needs, but who now, in the face of democratic ignorance and unrest, see in this feature a grave political danger, and fear that it renders the Ship of State (to use Macaulay's expression) all sail and no keel. In our own federal constitution, these restrictions are to be found in their greatest strictness. Not only this, but within comparatively recent years there has been exhibited a marked tendency on the part of the several Commonwealths to restrict still further the competences of their legislatures, already abridged by the federal instrument, and to embody in their fundamental law, constitutional prohibitions upon legislative matters other than those relating to the organization and distribution of powers in their respective governments. Thus, for example, the constitution of California, as commented upon by Bryce, enumerates more than thirty distinct classes of acts, most of them not properly embraced within the field of constitutional law, that are removed from possibility of regulation by ordinary statute.

Upon the continent of Europe, as we have indicated in another place, constitutional prohibitions have not been legally operative because of the lack of judicial tribunals competent to declare null and void legislative acts in contravention thereto. At the same time, however, these written instruments have undoubtedly operated to some extent as a practical restraint, owing to the greater sanctity given to them by being reduced to such formal statement.

In addition to the representative principle, another feature that has operated as an efficient integrating element in modern States, has been that of local self-government. Through this means, central governments of large countries have been relieved from portions of their accumulating burdens, and, at the same time, their stability increased by rendering possible a direct participation of citizens in the management of those matters that pertain to their local and personal life. The development of this feature has of course been rendered feasible by the increased facilities for rapid transit and communication afforded in modern times. At the same time the advance of intellectual enlightenment has broadened sympathies and rendered apparent the general identity of political interests, and thus afforded the basis for a political co-operation founded on something more than mere physical coercion.

Recapitulating now the chief characteristics that distinguish the modern State from its ancient or mediæval type, we find them to be the following: (1) Church and State are divided. (2) The State, while not immoral, is essentially non-moral. (3) The representative principle is applied. (4) Legal responsibility of those in power is demanded. (5) The right of suffrage is widened, until, in the most advanced countries of the world, practical manhood suffrage exists. (6) The right to hold office has been correspondingly broadened. (7) The equality of all before the law is enforced. (8) The limits of governmental action are clearly defined. (9) The separation of legislative, executive, and judicial functions largely prevails. (10) Constitutional restrictions prevent hasty and unwise changes in State life. (11) Public and private rights are distinguished. (12) Positive written law has largely supplanted unwritten law. (13) Local self-government has been substituted for completely centralized control.

III. **Present Political Tendencies and Problems.** — We turn now to the final portion of this last chapter of our work — to the consideration of some of the tendencies that are apparent in our political life, and to a mention of the problems to which it would seem these tendencies will necessarily lead.

Beginning first with the relation of States to each other, the most obvious fact is the increasing internationality of interests that attends advancing civilization. Improved means of transportation and communication hasten this movement upon the economic side; higher ideals of humanity promote it upon the ethical and intellectual side. Already these interstate relations have become both numerous and definite. The principles of international conduct that are generally accepted by all civilized peoples already constitute a very considerable body of procedure. In numberless ways States are united by treaties, not only for purposes of mutual military offence and defence, but for the regulation of common political and economic interests. In many cases common administrative organs have been established, as, for example, for the regulation of navigation of rivers, for postal, telegraph, and railway services, etc. The State protects its citizens beyond its own limits, and with the acquiescence and assistance of friendly powers apprehends and brings back from foreign lands the fleeing criminal, and through its consular and diplomatic agents exercises, especially among the less advanced peoples, many judicial and administrative functions.

The internationality of industrial interests is seen in the tendency of workingmen's unions to pass beyond State limits. Several international labor congresses have been held, and in at least one instance, States have themselves taken official part in conventions for the discussion of interests relating to the laboring man. When recently the wharfmen of London struck, they received substantial pecuniary aid from Australia and other countries. Prices of staple commodities are no longer regulated by the conditions of the home market, but depend upon the world supply and the world's market. The prosperity of each country is bound up with the financial condition of the others. Thus, so sensitive has become the money market, that a few years ago, because of the insolvency of a South American republic, all the large banking houses of Europe were disturbed, and owing to their efforts to secure themselves, the United States in turn barely escaped a serious financial panic.

In the field of international politics proper, the present century has seen the peaceful settlement by arbitration of many international difficulties that in former times would have been submitted to the arbitrament of the sword. And there is evident an increasing disposition on the part of civilized States to resort to this peaceful means of settlement.

The facts that we have thus far mentioned tend to render closer the relations between independent States, and to make less likely a future resort to arms in cases of disagreement. But it is not to be denied that there exist, in Europe at least, factors that operate in the other direction. The chief of these are the two principles of "balance of power" and "rights of nationality"; the one giving rise to the maintenance of enormous standing armies, through the effort of each State to provide a military force sufficient to secure its present *status quo* in the society of States; and the other through the demand for autonomy of nations now joined by political ties to alien races. Within the present century this latter principle has demonstrated its force by separating Belgium and Holland, grouping the Germans of the North into a powerful empire, securing in large measure the independence of Hungary, reuniting Italy, and establishing the political freedom of Greece. In Spain, France, and Russia also, the national spirit has made itself felt, and to-day is still active in Bohemia and other non-Teutonic provinces of Austria, in Belgium as a disturbing factor between the French and Walloons, in Canada among her Gallic population, and in England herself, who, in the Irish Question, is discovering the difficulty with which Celtic and Saxon ideas may be harmonized.

What will be the outcome of these conflicting conditions, it would be a rash prophet who would predict. Whether as the result of some great war a condition will be reached in which disarmament will be practically possible; whether, as suggested in the first chapter of this work, the present demand for a coincidence of nationality and political individuality will be a passing phase rather than a permanent product of civilization, we cannot foresee. We can, however, declare its possibility. To the political optimist it is a probability.

There is in the minds of some the confident expectation that the world is yet to see a time in which the danger of war shall be practically abolished, and all States united by such firm and formal international ties as to constitute of them a veritable "World-State."

Such an idea as this was in the minds of Henry IV. of France and his great minister Sully in the project to establish a confederation of Europe under the name of the "Most Christian Republic," which was to be composed of fifteen dominions. Such was the idea embodied in the *Project of Perpetual Peace* of the Abbé St. Pierre, and again revived by J. J. Rousseau and by Bentham.

The practical possibility of a World-State is strongly urged by Bluntschli.[1] He does not consider discouraging the attempts and failures of Alexander, of the Romans, and of Napoleon, the reasons for their failures, at those times, being now apparent, and being such reasons as are at the present time rapidly disappearing with increasing civilization, or already non-existent.

"Meanwhile," says Bluntschli, "unconquerable time itself works on unceasingly, bringing the nations nearer to one another, and awakening the universal consciousness of the community of mankind; and this is the natural preparation for a common organization of the world. It is no mere matter of accident that modern discoveries and numerous new means of communication altogether serve this end, that the whole science

[1] *Theory of the State*, trans. 2d ed., Bk. I. Chap. II.

of modern times follows this impulse and belongs in the first place to humanity, and only in a subordinate way to particular peoples, while a number of hindrances and barriers that lay between nations are disappearing. Even at the present day all Europe feels every disturbance in any particular State as an evil in which she has to suffer, and what happens at her extremest limits immediately awakens universal interest. The spirit of Europe already turns its regards to the circuit of the globe, and the Aryan race feels itself called to manage the world.

"We have not yet got so far; at the present day it is not so much will and power that are wanting as spiritual maturity. The members of the European family of nations know their superiority over other nations well enough, but they have not yet come to a clear understanding among themselves and about themselves. A definite result is not possible until the enlightening word of knowledge has been uttered about this and about the nature of humanity, and until the nations are ready to hear it.

"Till then, the universal empire will be an idea after which many strive, which none can fulfil. But as an idea of the future the general theory of the State cannot overlook it. Only in the universal empire will the true human State be revealed, and in it international law will attain a higher form and an assured existence. To the universal empire the particular States are related, as the nations to humanity. Particular States are members of the universal empire and attain in it their completion and their full satisfaction. The purpose of the universal State is not to break up particular States and oppress nations, but better to secure the peace of the former and the freedom of the latter. The highest conception of the State — which, however, has not yet been realized — is thus: The State is humanity organized, but humanity as masculine, not as feminine; the State is the man."

It is not our purpose to discuss here in detail the arguments that might be raised in support or refutation of these opinions, but merely to suggest the existence of such an expectation and aspiration. Bluntschli himself cites in a note the objections of Laurent to the feasibility of the World-State, the principal ones being the incompatibility of such a universal type with the Sovereignty of the individual States, and that the World-State, if really endowed with the necessary authority and force to control the individual States, would have the power to oppress them. Bluntschli, however, assumes to answer satisfactorily these questions. He admits that ethnic, lingual, geographic, historic, and economic peculiarities require the continued existence of separate and independent nationalities, but says that their political autonomy would not be destroyed when embraced within a World-State system. It is to be observed, however, that Bluntschli finds the model of this future World-State in the *Bundesstaat*, but that according to his theory the individual members of a Bundesstaat still retain a portion of the sovereign power. This theory we have shown to be incorrect, that Sovereignty is indivisible, and that if the members of a union retain their individual Sovereignty, a *State* is not created by their association.

As time goes on the association of States will undoubtedly grow closer, and the rules of international morality will increase both in force and number, but that a genuine World-State, or a State embracing the civilized nations of the world, will ever be established, does not seem possible. Such a type would require the surrender of the Sovereignty and independence of the individual nations, — a surrender to which it is not conceivable they will ever submit.

Leaving now the developments to be expected in the relations of States to each other as members of a family of nations, we have to consider the tendencies that appear to be at work in the development of the internal life of the particular States themselves.

From this standpoint, the most striking feature of the present day is, as already said, the development of popular control of government. By its own inherent nature one step in democratic progress leads to a further one. There is always present to the party in power the temptation to broaden the franchise for the sake of the popular support that it will thus obtain. The time will always come, when, wisely or unwisely, this temptation will be yielded to. "When a nation modifies the elective qualification," says De Tocqueville, "it may easily be foreseen that sooner or later that qualification will be entirely abolished. There is no more invariable rule in the history of society: the farther electoral rights are extended, the more is felt the need of extending them; for after each concession the strength of the democracy increases, and its demands increase with its strength. The ambition of those who are below the appointed rate is irritated in exact proportion to the great number of those who are above it. The exception at last becomes the rule, concession follows concession, and no stop can be had short of universal suffrage."[1]

[1] *Democracy in America*, Am. ed. 1849, p. 59.

A striking demonstration of the above rule is seen in the steady widening of the suffrage in England during the last fifteen years. The same tendency is at work in the monarchies of Europe, though not yet carried to the same extent, the last conspicuous triumph of this principle being the modification of the electoral qualification in Belgium in 1894. The history is the same in our own country, where the tendency has been so strong as to prevent even decent restrictions upon the voting power of the newly landed and ignorant aliens who yearly crowd in thousands to our shores.

A step once taken in this direction is seldom if ever retraced. The suffrage once broadened, its subsequent restriction seems almost impossible. Such a step requires a fortitude and disinterestedness on the part of the parties in power such as history has shown them seldom to possess.

Of character analogous to the above is the precipitate manner in which several of our territories have been admitted to the Union as States — their admission being secured more by the additional political influence that it was calculated would redound to the party consenting to such admission, than to the sound expediency of the step.

It is a fair prediction, then, to say that the world is to see in the future a continued advance in democracy and popular government. This being so, we are led to consider what effect this development will have, when taken in conjunction with other changing conditions, upon good government and general prosperity.

Side by side with this movement that is hurrying the civilized world towards democracy is the increasing pressure that is brought to bear by the augmenting complexity of social and industrial relations for the State constantly to widen the scope of its activities. *Will the union of these two tendencies give us good government?* A unanimously affirmative answer is by no means given to this.

"If I am in any degree right," says Sir Henry Maine, "popular government, especially as it approaches the democratic form, will tax to the utmost all the political sagacity and statesmanship of the world to keep it from misfortune." And again he says, "We may say generally that the gradual establishment of the masses in power is of the blackest omen for all legislation founded on scientific opinion, which requires tension of mind to understand it and self-devotion to submit to it." "The nations of our time," says De Tocqueville, "cannot prevent the conditions of men from becoming equal, but it depends upon themselves whether the principle of equality is to lead them to servitude or freedom, to knowledge or barbarism, to prosperity or to wretchedness."

It must be ever remembered that the decisive point in the success of a popular government lies in the quality of its voting citizens. Of what use is it to perfect governmental forms and methods if the constituency be incapable of their proper management? There are those who would go so far as to have us believe that the exercise of the suffrage is an inherent inalienable right of the free-born citizen. It does not need to be said that it is not. It is a political privilege, and is founded only on law, and a claim to its extension to all individuals has not even that moral or utilitarian basis that supports the demand for an equality in those so-called natural rights which we discussed in a former chapter. The citizen is endowed with right of suffrage, in order that by its exercise the good of society may be maintained, and it is for society to determine to what extent, and by whom, and under what conditions this power is to be used. Amiel strikes the vital point, when he says in his *Journal*, that "the pretension that every man has the necessary qualities of a citizen simply because he was born twenty-one years ago, is as much as to say that labour, merit, virtue, character, and experience are to count for nothing; and we destroy humility when we proclaim that a man becomes the equal of all other men by the mere mechanical and vegetative process of natural growth."

But leaving this point. Aside from the evils arising from an unfit constituency, there are defects inherent in the popular control of government. In the first place, democracy leads to mediocrity of statesmanship. The leaders are selected by the masses, and it is not the highest intellectual and moral endowments that satisfy their demands.

Secondly, democracy necessarily leads to the development of the party system in all its intensity, and the excess of party enthusiasm and rivalry, but too often leads to the tyranny of the majority, a tyranny which the party discipline renders possible. The strictness of the party organization leads also to the crushing out of individuality and to the suppression of liberty of opinion, a revolt against party dictation being punished by total political ostracism. Furthermore, once established and perfected, party machinery becomes a powerful engine, capable of being utilized for the accomplishment of personal and dishonest ends. It is not intimated by these reflections that party government is to be deplored. In all popular governments, whether of the monarchical or republican type, it is a necessity. It is merely suggested that as existing in the modern constitutional state, the party system affords problems of great significance to the student of political science. How may it be organized and controlled so that its beneficial results may be obtained, while its excesses and liability to corruption are avoided.

Turning now to another point we note that governmental functions may be roughly divided into two classes, — the enactment of wise laws, and their intelligent and effective execution. The one embraces the legislative functions, the other the administrative duties.

In addition to the difficulty of obtaining an efficient and honest corps of servants for the execution of laws when enacted, there arise serious problems (especially in the United States) in connection with the composition and methods of work in the chief legislative body. The first of these is presented in connection with our size. Already the ratio of apportionment has risen from one representative to every 33,000 of population to one for every 173,901, and it does not seem feasible to still further increase this ratio. Yet the lower house of our Congress is undeniably too large.

Parliamentary government is supposed to be a government by deliberation, but deliberation, in a true sense, is out of the question in our House. Committee government has become a necessity, and there are grave objections to committee legislation, where, as in our Congress, the committees wield such influence and power. Among these evils are secrecy, lack of open debate, and practical irresponsibility.

The Caucus becomes a necessity in a large legislative body, and thus party discipline (already too strict) is introduced in organized form into the very halls of the legislature itself.

Furthermore, from bulky size, arises the necessity of the " previous question " and other extraordinary powers of the presiding officer to close debate. Even in our smaller Senate the exercise of this power has become a necessity, as was made apparent in the last Extra Session.

But autocratic power of the Speaker means the power of the majority to oppress the minority. It leaves it only to the forbearance of the party in power whether the minority shall have any opportunity whatever for the expression of their views;

and this is a check that can be least relied upon when it is most needful. But if we are to have freedom in government, the rights of the minority *must* be respected. For the tyranny of the majority is one of the evils most to be feared in a democracy, — the most to be feared because of the ease with which it can be exercised and the severity with which it operates. There can be no tyranny of a monarch so intolerable as that of the multitude, for it has the power behind it that no king can sway.

In addition to these structural difficulties in the legislative body of a democratic nation such as ours, is the difficulty of obtaining legislators of that calibre of mind that will fit them to judge intelligently regarding the enormous variety of interests, economic, social, and political, that come before them for consideration. There is now demanded on the part of our law makers, not only patriotism and political sagacity of the highest order, but scientific knowledge, and strict disinterestedness far beyond that formerly required. Many of the economic interests that are now discussed in our legislative halls require, in the highest degree, scholarly research and judgment; and the necessity for disinterestedness is enhanced by the fact that, in the settlement of these material matters, the economic interests of special classes and localities are necessarily antagonized or favoured, and thus the incentive to lobbying and corruption enormously increased.

Finally comes the question whether, however constituted and however managed, our Congress is not becoming swamped by the amount of business heaped upon it; and this is an evil which will necessarily become greater as the years advance.[1]

Democracy, as Maine has pointed out, is but a form of government; namely, that in which the people have been generally admitted, either directly or indirectly through their representatives, to a participation in the administration of public affairs. If, therefore, the evils, or at least the difficulties, that appear in its practical operation are to be obviated or overcome, measures administrative in character must be largely employed. It is true that the great desideratum is the securing of good officials and a sound public sentiment, and that given these two elements any form of government will give fairly satisfactory results. But the point here made, is, that if these necessary elements are to be obtained in a democracy, the energy of the political power itself must be consciously applied.

The late Émile de Laveleye, the eminent Belgian publicist, in his work entitled *Le Gouvernement dans*

---

[1] During the Fifty-first Congress there were introduced in the Senate 5293 Senate bills and joint resolutions, and in the House of Representatives 14,330, making a total of 19,623. Of these, 611 public, and 1579 private, bills (mostly pension bills) became laws, making a total of 2190, being a little over 9 per cent of the whole number introduced. The *Congressional Record*, covering only the first session of this Congress, included over 11,000 finely printed quarto pages. As further illustrating the amount of business coming before this Congress, it may be mentioned that 30,320 printed documents were received, which number, if multiplied by size of the editions, shows that more than 30,000,000 pieces of printed matter were handled in either House. See T. H. McKee's *Manual of Congressional Practice*, p. 294.

la Démocratie (published in 1891), emphasized no one point so strongly as that of the necessity for a substantial equality of social and economic conditions among a people organized under principles of political equality. History shows that the attainment of political equality leads inevitably to the demand for social and economic equality, for it does not take long for the lower classes to discover that equality in political rights is of but little value if they are not thereby able to raise their material condition to a comparative degree of equality with that of the other members of society. "Equality in political rights," says Ritchie, "along with great inequalities in social condition, has laid bare 'the social question,' which is no longer concealed, as it formerly was, behind the struggle for equality before the law and for equality in political rights."[1]

Thus, with the abolition of artificial distinctions, such as those of birth, wealth, and official rank, there disappears at the same time the apparent justification for an inequality in economic burdens and engagements. Need any one ask whether the French people would have so long endured the monstrously unjust apportionment of wealth and privileges of the old regime, had they not had before their eyes those distinctions of ecclesiastical and noble rank that seemed to afford a color of title to exceptional advantages?

It therefore well behooves the legislator in a democratic government, that, so far as possible, the

[1] *Natural Rights*, p. 258.

measures to which he gives his assent shall, if not positively promoting an increased economic equality, at least have no tendency to prevent it. The necessity for party government and the danger of majority tyranny have been already mentioned. Such a danger is of course rendered still more serious, if there be a separation of the community into distinct classes of rich and poor. Nothing will more quickly force a minority to desperation and incite them to physical force and lawlessness than class legislation based upon property.

At the same time there are the dangers of state socialism to be guarded against. Just as there is in the democratic state the constant pressure for an extension of the suffrage, so there is always the demand on the part of the masses for any state action that offers any apparent hope of relieving their condition. "When the people is invested with the supreme authority" (to quote again the sage De Tocqueville) "the perpetual sense of their own miseries impels the rulers of society to seek for perpetual ameliorations."[1]

Whatever may be said of the position taken by Mr. Kidd in his *Social Evolution* in regard to the part played by religion and its non-rational basis, the statement cannot be gainsaid, that, for the great majority of persons in society, as at present constituted, the laws of human competition work with unjust and cruel severity, and that, apart from some ulterior sanction, there can be no reason why such

[1] *Democracy in America*, Am. ed. 1849, p. 233.

individuals should consciously sacrifice themselves for the good of others, or for the ultimate benefit of unborn generations. Whether or not all social altruism rests upon religion, or whether religion is essentially irrational and destined to disappear as intellectual enlightenment advances, is another question, and one that we need not here consider. But we may ask ourselves what will be the attitude that will be taken by the masses generally when they come to see that the favored few obtain their advantages largely by climbing upon others' shoulders, and that in the government is to be found a force,—the control of which is in their own hands,—whereby is offered at least a possibility of mitigating the evils of their lot and of equalizing the conditions that the " struggle for existence " has rendered so unequal and, as to them, so oppressive. It does not seem possible but that the fuller recognition of these facts, which must come with the wider spread of education, must greatly intensify the demand of the lower classes for greater material equality — a demand that in default of means on their part can only be met by the employment of the power of the State. At the same time, of course, this very increase of knowledge will render more rational and feasible the plans for securing the ends that will be advocated by them. The only danger is that the pressure that will come from the more unfortunate classes will result in efforts at amelioration before the spread of intelligence and morality is such as will ensure that these efforts will be directed to the real and permanent good, not to the apparent temporary advantage only.

In still another respect, the democratically governed State is placed between two dangers. Popular government, as already indicated, is not such a form of rule as naturally attracts to its service the best officials. It is therefore necessary that such a government should offer all possible inducements to draw to itself the best of its citizens. The chief of these inducements is, necessarily, ample pecuniary reward. At the same time, until its electoral system is perfected, and a healthy moral sentiment in its politics created, to augment the remuneration of office is but to increase party spoil, and to intensify the baser struggle for public position for the mere sake of its pecuniary worth.

Still another difficulty against which the popularly organized government has to contend is that, while it, more than any other political form, needs for its successful conduct an exact and rigid enforcement of the law, there is a constant timidity on the part of its officials that arises from the fear of displeasing the *demos,* their master. Thus, in cases of riots and popular disturbances generally, in which the law of the land is violated, there is always a greater difficulty in securing prompt and decisive action for the complete enforcement of the law in a democracy, than there is in obtaining similar action from a more absolutely organized political power. We are by no means disposed to assert that in the present state of society the lower classes have secured to them by the law their full share of justice, and that under present conditions the power that wealth gives is not used in securing for its owners somewhat more than their due share of public benefits, or at least in enabling them to avoid their proper proportion of public duties; but what it is earnestly maintained is, that nowhere more than in the democratic state is it essential that there should be an exact and complete enforcement of the law, whatever it may be, at any given time when its provisions are violated. If the law be anachronistic, or in any way patently unjust, nothing will more surely secure its repeal than the odium that will attach to it from its rigid enforcement. But as long as it is *law*, it should be treated as such. A tolerated violation of it will inevitably weaken the law-abiding sentiment of the community, and it is hardly possible to conceive of a case in which the immediate benefit to be derived from the disregard of a legal rule will not be far outweighed by the ultimate disadvantages that would follow. The law-abiding habit of the Anglo-Saxon race has been its greatest glory, and chiefly to that feeling is due the success that it has achieved in its various homes in the establishment and maintenance of democratic government.

In this connection arises the vital necessity in a popular government for an intelligent and, above all, independent judiciary. And by this we mean one independent not only of the legislative and executive branches, but of popular influence and control. The tendency apparent during recent years in various of the Commonwealths of the United States to render their judiciaries elective in character, whereby they have been deprived of that former independence which had been secured to them by fixed salaries and life or long tenure of office, is therefore one that cannot be too strongly deprecated.

The above considerations show us that for the successful establishment and maintenance of democratic government there is necessary a disposition on the part of the people not only to refuse submission to a restraint that is arbitrary and oppressive, but likewise a willingness to yield to self-set control. They must be able to draw and apply the distinction between public liberty and private license, between manly self-dependence and individual lawlessness.

After all that has been said, it will seem only an obvious truism to say that popular government demands a high degree of enlightenment on the part of its citizens. "Governments such as ours," says Professor Woodrow Wilson in his usual forcible manner, "are founded upon discussion, and government by discussion comes as late in political as scientific thought in intellectual development. It is a habit of state life created by long-established circumstances, and is possible for a nation only in the adult age of its political life. The people who successfully maintain such a government must have gone through a period of political training which shall have prepared them by gradual steps of acquired privilege for assuming the entire control of their affairs. They must have acquired adult self-reliance, self-knowledge, and self-control, adult soberness and deliberateness of judgment, adult sagacity in self-government, adult vigilance of thought and quickness of insight. When practised, not by small communities, but by wide nations, democracy, far from being a crude form of government, is possible only amongst peoples of the highest and steadiest political habit. It is the heritage of races purged alike of hasty barbaric passions and of patient servility to rulers, and schooled in temperate common counsel. It is an institution of political noonday, not of the half-light of political dawn. It can never be made to sit easily or safely on first generations, but strengthens through long heredity. It is poison to the infant, but tonic to the man. Monarchies may be made, but democracies must grow."[1]

Thus far we have been considering the character, or what might be called the innate dispositions, of democracy. We may now ask ourselves what probable effect the continued or intensified operation of these tendencies will have upon the future governmental organization of the State.

The pivotal point in any democratic scheme of government is the legislative body, just as, in absolute monarchy, it is the executive. Based, as the representative legislative body is, upon the direct suffrages of the people, and conscious therefore of

[1] "Character of Democracy in the United States," published in *An Old Master and Other Essays*, p. 117.

deriving its power from their mandate, the lawmaking body wields an influence that dominates the other departments. Its very size gives an additional impetus to its action. It is a psychological fact universally observed in regard to all bodies of men, that they may be moved to extremes of action, and are subject to waves of passion to which their members as individuals are not liable. "Numerous bodies," says Hallam, "are prone to excess, both from the reciprocal influences of their passions, and the consciousness of irresponsibility; for which reasons a democracy, that is, the absolute government of the majority, is the most tyrannical of any."[1] Above all other "checks," therefore, it seems necessary that those upon the legislature should be fully operative. Nowhere, fortunately, have these legislative checks been more firmly applied than in the United States. Not only is the federal Congress restricted as to its legislative competence by the constitution, but it is divided into two houses of nearly equal influence, and an executive veto superimposed that may only be overriden by a two-thirds vote. As we have already mentioned, the restrictions upon the legislatures of the individual Commonwealths have been carried to an even greater extent. In England, the popular legislative branch has slowly but surely swept away all restrictions that have hindered the free exercise of its powers, and now stands untrammelled save for the virtually extinct royal veto and the "suspending" power of the upper chamber.

[1] *Constitutional History of England*, Chap. XVI.

And there is a strong movement on foot to do away with even this last-mentioned curb upon its will, slight as it is. In the English constitution is thus exhibited the consummated tendency, apparent in all popular governments, for the legislature, unless adequately checked, to gather to itself the paramount authority.

That which it is common to regard as one of the most efficient checks upon the legislature, is the necessity for its members to return at frequent intervals to their constituents for re-election. In one sense, this principle of short tenure of office works in a beneficial manner; but in another sense, and an important one, the control thus given an electorate over its representatives is fraught with danger. It means that the independence of the legislator is lessened, that the temptation to subordinate the general to local interests is increased, and that the pressure that is brought to bear to give immediate and complete expression to a popular will that may be ignorant or misinformed, is proportionately enhanced. Half a century ago, the keenest critic of our institutions observed that "the existence of democracies is threatened by two dangers, viz., the complete subjection of the legislative body to the caprices of the electoral body, and the concentration of all the powers of the government in the legislative authority."[1]

Representative government, if it means anything, should mean the government by the best, or at least

[1] De Tocqueville, *Democracy in America*, Am. ed. 1849, p. 165.

by those better than the general run of electors, and if the advantages of this superiority are to be obtained, there must be a certain degree of independence in the rulers chosen by the people, and a freedom to direct public matters according to their own best judgment and not according to the uninformed and momentary whims of their constituents. At the same time a legal responsibility for malfeasance of office will protect the people from the abuse of public functions.

For the correction of the various evils that appear in democratic government as at present organized, various plans have been proposed, among which the introduction of the popular "Initiative" of laws, the Referendum, and Minority Representation are the more important. It will, of course, be foreign to such a chapter as this to describe in detail the nature of these remedies, much less to enter into a critical consideration of the various arguments that may be made for or against their adoption. It will be sufficient here to point out the bearing that they have upon the problems that we have above suggested.

First of all, it is to be observed that the introduction of the popular element in law-making in the form of the Initiative and Referendum will still further increase that influence of the electorate over the legislature, which, as we have seen, is attended by some disadvantages. It will furthermore, of necessity, decrease not only the importance of the law-making bodies in the eyes of the people, but, at the same time, and what is probably more serious, greatly decrease in the minds of the representatives themselves the sense of their own responsibility for the character and effect of the measures enacted.[1] Aside from these objections, there is, of course, the question whether in any given case the average elector is intellectually qualified to judge wisely regarding the measures that may be submitted to him. On the other hand, such a plan, if introduced, would, it would seem, have a great influence in checking the corruption, log-rolling, and lobbying that disgrace the halls of so many legislatures. Its ultimately educative effect upon the electorate is also to be noticed. Still another advantage, and one that seems at first surprising, is that, as experience shows in those cases where it has been tried, however vehemently the people may cry out for radical legislative action, when it comes to the point of formal action upon their part, they are conservative rather than otherwise, and often refuse their consent to liberal measures that have already secured the approval of the legislative chambers. This apparent inconsistency Sir Henry Maine explains as follows: "It is possible," says he, "by agitation and exhortation, to produce in the mind of the average citizen a vague impression that he desires a particular change. But when the agitation has settled down on the

---

[1] It has also been objected that in the case of the United States, the introduction of such a measure would tend not a little to destroy that formal distinction between constitutional and ordinary law, now so valuable and effective.

dregs, when the excitement has died away, when the subject has been threshed out, when the law is before him with all its detail, he is sure to find in it much that is likely to disturb his habits, his ideas, his prejudices, or his interests; and so, in the long run, he votes 'No' to every proposal."[1]

If we examine this reasoning, we shall find that that which saves the Referendum from being a dangerously radical instrument, is the length of time required for its operation. Opportunity is given for a careful second thought before the act is finally consummated, just as the "suspensive veto" of the English House of Lords performs the same service for the English people.

As regards "Minority Representation," it cannot but be obvious that the aims to the attainment of which it is directed are eminently proper ones; namely, the reduction of the severity of majority tyranny, the distribution of representation according to naturally formed industrial, social, and political groups rather than by artificially created territorial districts, and the consequent encouragement of individual independence in politics. Its advocates do not claim for it the power of a general solvent of political abuses, but merely that its introduction will tend to remedy the evils above indicated, and thus prepare the way for remedial action in other directions. To our mind, the main difficulty connected with the subject is the devising of a scheme sufficiently simple to be easily understood by the average voter, and

[1] *Popular Government*, p. 97.

from the operation of which machine trickery may be excluded. And these are difficulties which we are inclined to believe can be surmounted, if indeed they have not already been overcome in more than one of the several plans that its advocates have proposed.[1]

Viewing popular government in general, it will be found that its tasks are three in number. (1) To obtain a correct expression of the General Will or Public Opinion. (2) To afford some degree of certainty that such General Will shall be an intelligent one. (3) To obtain a proper execution of the General Will when so formulated.

As regards the attainment of the first aim, that is the office of the press, and of party machinery generally, with its primaries, caucuses, conventions, platforms, campaigns, etc. Regarding the second aim, the securing of an intelligent public opinion, we have already had more or less to say. The point to be noticed here is, that it is only in respect to these first two aims that popularly organized government can claim a superiority over, or even equality with, other and more autocratically organized political bodies. In the more absolute forms of government there is afforded neither encouragement nor reason for the interest of the general mass of the people in public affairs, and hence for the formation of intelligent opinions regarding public administration; nor are

---

[1] For a description of the various systems of voting proposed, together with a very complete bibliography of the subject, see *Political Reform by the Representation of Minorities*, by M. N. Forney, published by the author at New York. 1894.

there provided means for their effective expression, if formulated. Indeed, if the autocratic government be tyrannical as well, it is to the interest of the governing that the formation of an enlightened general will should be discouraged and prevented. In popular government, on the other hand, not only are the means provided for, and encouragement given to, a wide public interest in political matters, but the very enjoyment of political privileges by the people furnishes a most efficient means for their still greater education.

When, however, we come to the attainment of the third aim of a good government, of which we have spoken, the conditions are nearly reversed. It is an undeniable fact that, *cæteris paribus*, the popularly organized government is less efficient from the executive or administrative standpoint than the monarchical or aristocratic form. The aristocratic government, especially when founded upon distinctions of office, furnishes a magistracy that, so far as administrative talent is concerned, is far superior to the governing corps that is commonly selected by a democratic society. "The governments which have been remarkable in history for sustained mental ability and vigor in the conduct of affairs," says Mill, "have generally been aristocracies. But they have been without any exception aristocracies of public functionaries. The ruling bodies have been so narrow that each member, or at least each influential member, of the body was able to make, and did make, public business an active profession, and the principal occupation of his life."[1] But without going further into the advantages of such an aristocracy by reason of the skilled bureaucracy it affords, its attendant defects are sufficiently manifest. Aside from the evils ordinarily ascribed to a bureaucratic form of government as contrasted with the elective form, there is the danger — nay, almost the certainty — that the legislation that will be had will be class legislation; that is, favorable to the class in power.

Whether the monarchical form of government will produce a satisfactory administration of public affairs is obviously one of chance. If the ruling monarch be capable and disinterested, the unity of control that his supreme power gives, renders possible the initiation and vigorous prosecution of matters of public concern that it would be impossible to obtain in a government constructed with various devices mutually restrictive of the free exercise of power. Thus from the purely administrative standpoint, what is called "beneficent absolutism" furnishes the highest possibilities of excellence. On the other hand, the rulership of a weak or selfish monarch — and the chances are that he will be such — leads to equally bad results. As Bagehot says, "the benefits of a good monarch are almost invaluable, but the evils of a bad monarch are almost irreparable."[2]

But all of this is beside the question. Whatever may or may not be the merits and demerits of other forms of government, we now live in a demo-

---

[1] *Representative Government*, Chap. VI.
[2] *English Constitution*, Am. ed. (Appleton), p. 156.

cratic age, and, as already said, there is no probability that we shall speedily emerge from it. It behooves us, therefore, to study well the defects of democracy, and thus to prepare ourselves, so far as possible, for an avoidance of the dangers to which they lead. It is for this reason, that we have been calling attention to the fact that whatever may be the educative effect and the disinterestedness of democratic government, it is inherently weak upon the administrative side. It is therefore imperative if good results are to be obtained from popular government the people should be enlightened, and that especial attention should be paid to the administrative means by which the will of the people is to be made known, and when known, put into operation.

The one great defect of democracy, regarded from the standpoint from which we have now been considering it, is its lack of constructive ability. This point is especially emphasized by Professor Wilson in the essay from which we have already quoted in this chapter. Concerning the forces of democracy, he says: "There is little in them of constructive efficiency. They could not of themselves build any government at all. They are critical, analytical, questioning, quizzing forces, not architectural, not powers that devise and build."[1] And again, speaking of public opinion, he says: "It is judicial merely, not creative. It passes judgment or gives sanction, but it cannot direct or suggest. It furnishes standards, not policies. Questions of government are

[1] *Op. cit.* p. 112.

infinitely complex questions, and no multitude can of themselves form clear-cut, comprehensive, consistent conclusions touching them. Yet without such conclusions, without single and prompt purposes, government cannot be carried on. Neither legislation nor administration can be done at the ballot-box." [1]

Professor Wilson is a believer in the superiority of parliamentary or responsible government as compared with congressional or committee government, and holds that the safest, if not the only, remedy for the democratic defects which he has above enumerated is the creation of more conspicuous personal leadership, such as the former system tends to provide. He does not suggest, however, any means whereby this result, desirable as it may be admitted to be, is to be obtained save by the introduction of cabinet government in this country. In fact, so far as we ourselves can see, there is no other method by which this aim can be directly attained. But we conceive that even were it practically possible to get the consent of our people to such an innovation, such a scheme would open the way to several of the very dangers against which our whole constitutional scheme is intended to protect us, and that, therefore, the price that we would have to pay for such a benefit would be entirely too dear a one. Responsible cabinet government of the English type, if introduced here, would necessarily concentrate power in the lower branch of Congress and

[1] *An Old Master and Other Essays*, p. 130.

destroy the President's veto, and, in fact, the independence of the executive power generally, as distinct from the legislature. Furthermore, there is reason to believe that the union of these two powers, together with their concentration in a single chamber, would render the influence of that chamber so paramount as to endanger the constitutional independence of the federal judiciary, and the administrative autonomy of the several Commonwealths.[1] We would thus be led to the tyranny of the legislature, which, as has been before said, is one of the greatest evils that we have sought to avoid.[2]

To our mind, the only feasible way in which the constructive force of democracy may be enhanced by the increase of true personal leadership in politics, is indirectly along general educative lines, whereby the people will be rendered able to discern the true qualities of statesmanship, and inclined to select for their guides and representatives, persons possessing them.

[1] The arguments upon which the preceding statements are based are to be found admirably stated by A. L. Lowell in an essay entitled, "Cabinet Responsibility," published in his *Essays on Government*, 1889. See, also, on this subject, Snow, "Defence of Congressional Government" (*Papers of the Am. Hist. Assn.*, Vol. III.); "Cabinet Government in the United States" (*Annals of the Am. Acad.*, No. 57); "Shall we Americanize our Institutions" (*Nineteenth Century*, December, 1890); Sidgwick's *Elements of Politics*, Chap. XXII.; Wilson, *Congressional Government* and *Overland Rev.*, January, 1884; and Bagehot, *English Constitution*. Relative to the question of the independence of the judiciary, it might be mentioned that Professor Wilson, in the essay from which we have quoted, himself shows the weakness of our federal judiciary even as it is, and compares its position to that of the House of Lords in England.

[2] Says Jefferson: "The executive in our government is not the sole, it is scarcely the principal, object of jealousy. The tyranny of the legislature is the most formidable dread at present, and will be for years."

Finally, in conclusion of this chapter, already too long extended, it is to be said that many of the deficiencies of representative government may be largely corrected by improvements in the procedure of our legislative bodies. Aside from the character of its members, which, of course, depends upon the electorate, there are two great evils that may overtake a legislative body. In our modern complex age, it may become overburdened with business; and it may attempt the performance of other than its proper deliberative functions. As regards the first evil, from which our Congress is already suffering, despite its sixty or more sub-committees, relief is possible; first, through the reference of particular subjects, such as contested elections, etc., to outside judicial bodies for determination, reserving for itself only the final ratification of the decisions reached; and, secondly, the establishment of a special procedure for private bill legislation, as has been done in England, whereby not only is the introduction of improper and unnecessary private bills discouraged, but provision made for the determination outside of the legislative halls of the facts involved and the interests effected. The introduction of this one reform would enormously lighten the present burdens of Congress. As has been noticed in a preceding note, of the 2190 acts of the Fifty-first Congress, 1579 were of a private character.

The second danger, that of the legislature stepping beyond its proper deliberative sphere, is directly connected with the first in that its correction will necessarily lessen the seriousness of the first. As Mill so clearly pointed out in his Essay on *Representative Government*, and as history has since so abundantly demonstrated, a body of men of any considerable size is by the very fact of its size disqualified from efficient administrative action. A sufficient unity and concert of action and a definiteness and stability of policy for such work cannot be obtained. There is a radical difference between the control, and the actual performance, of the business of government. The representative legislative body should restrict its functions to those of discussion, oversight, and determination. It should see that the proper activities of government are provided for and properly distributed, and should keep sufficient watch to see that their actual performance is properly done; but it should not attempt to perform them itself, or, what is practically the same thing, strive to determine in such detail the manner of their performance as to deprive the proper administrative officers of all responsibility and powers of discretion. The one great evil from which the present French government is suffering, is the extent to which its legislature interferes and meddles with administrative measures, introducing into them thereby its own fickleness and lack of technical skill. In our own country, also, we are not free from this error.

A third means, to which Mill calls especial attention, by which the legislative efficiency of large bodies may be increased, is the establishment of a smaller inside body composed of experienced members whose duty would be the proper *framing* of laws. For this work technical legal skill and accuracy are demanded. The creation of such a body would therefore not only lighten the labors but increase the value of the product of the legislature. The larger body would of course still retain the entire power of *enacting* law. Only the formal and technical work would be given to the smaller committee. Thus in large measure this law-framing committee would bear the same relation to the whole assembly, that such assembly bears to the electorate in countries where the Referendum obtains.

Fourthly, and finally, an almost unlimited relief to overburdened national legislatures is possible through a further decentralization of functions. The extent to which this may be carried, varies in different cases, and depends upon conditions that we do not need here to consider.

In concluding these reflections upon the democratic State, it may appear that we have been able to discover only defects and difficulties, and that consequently only the most pessimistic predictions may be made regarding its future. But such is not the case. We have by no means a low opinion of the merits of popular government. On the contrary, the manly self-control which is taught and practised in this political form stamps it as the best type that developing civilization has thus far disclosed, and in the continued existence of democratic control we see the highest hopes of human progress. At the same time we are not blind to its defects, and these we have emphasized because of the very general and indiscriminate laudation that popular government has received. The intention has been to show that a democracy is by no means a simple government, nor one easily administered, but rather the reverse — that it is one which presupposes a high morality, an advanced state of education, a great degree of self-control, a considerable amount of material and social equality, and, above all, the active and disinterested participation of the wisest and best of its citizens in its political life.

INDEX

Adams, H. C., *State in Relation to Industrial Action*, cited, 328.
Adams, John, quoted, 400 n.
Aims of the State, 309 *et seq.*
Alienation of Sovereignty, theories of, 58–61.
Althusius, Johannes, *Politica methodice digesta*, cited, 62, 278, 396.
Ambrose, Saint, quoted, 45.
Amendment of Constitutions, 214–19.
Analytical Jurisprudence, 69, 160–80.
Anarchistic School, 318–20.
Aquinas, Thomas, views of, regarding natural law, 104–5; *De regimine principium*, cited, 46, 47.
Aristotle, views of, regarding natural law, 96; cited, 34.
Aristocracy, 361–72.
Austin, John, quoted, 23, 69, 171, 256, 282, 283, 353 n.; definition of law, 162–5; definition of sovereign State, 182; position in regard to constitutional law criticised, 204–9; views of, regarding location of Sovereignty criticised, 293–5.
Authority and Liberty, struggle between, 312.

Bagehot, Walter, *Physics and Politics*, quoted, 311; *English Constitution*, quoted, 432.
Baudrillart, *Jean Bodin et Son Temps*, cited, 186 n.

Bentham, Jeremy, *Fragment on Government*, quoted, 21, 69, 361 n.
Bills of Rights, character of, 87.
Blackstone, Sir William, *Commentaries on Law*, quoted, 151, 181.
Bliss, Prof. Philemon, *Of Sovereignty*, quoted, 240; cited, 282.
Bluntschli, J. K., *Theory of the State*, quoted, 3 n., 10, 13 n., 33, 370, 408; cited, 379; *Geschichte der neueren Staatswissenschaft*, quoted, 137, 158; *Staatswörterbuch*, quoted, 290 n.; *Gesammelte kleine Schriften*, quoted, 389 n.; classification of governments, 378.
Bodin, *de la République*, cited, 62, 392; definition of State and Sovereignty, 185–6.
Body Politic, distinguished from society, 2.
Borgeaud, Charles, *Adoption and Amendment of Constitution in Europe and America*, cited, 88 n., 210 n.
Bossuet, *Politique tirée*, cited, 50.
Bric, *Theorie der Staatenverbindungen*, quoted, 15; cited, 194, 234.
Brownson, *The American Republic*, quoted, 238, 242.
Buchanan, *De jure regni apud Scotus*, cited, 279.
Bundesstaat, see Federal State.
Burgess, Prof. John, *Political Science and Constitutional Law*, quoted,

4, 13 n., 16, 183, 378; art. *The American Commonwealth*, quoted, 251 n.; review of Laband's *Staatsrecht*, quoted, 245; distinction between "State" and "Government" criticised, 206 n.; classification of governments, 276-7.

CABINET GOVERNMENT, 434-5.
Cairnes, Prof., quoted, 37.
Calhoun, John C., cited, 239; quoted, 241.
Calvin, John, cited, 48.
Carpenter, Edward, *Civilization: Its Cause and Cure*, cited, 97 n.
Caucus, 415.
Checks and balances, in modern constitutional governments, 399-403.
Christianity, influence of, on political theories, 100-1.
Church and State, 45-50.
Cicero, cited, 45.
Citizenship, distinct from mere individuality, 125-6.
Civil Law, distinguished from natural law, by Hobbes, 69-71.
Clark, *Practical Jurisprudence*, quoted, 23; cited, 152 n., 282.
Cockburn, Lord Chief Justice, quoted, 202.
Commonwealth, used as designating members of a Federal State, 245 et seq.
Compact, see Contract.
Competition, province of, in the development of humanity, 327-37.
Composite State, 231 et seq.
Confederacy and Federal State distinguished, 253 et seq. See also *Staatenbund*.
Confederate States, *de facto* position of, 227-9.
Constitution, adoption of, not a creative act, 130-2; power of amendment of, by a State, 214-19.

Constitutional Government, character of, 396 et seq.
Constitutional Law, province of, 141, 208-9; not a limitation upon Sovereignty, 204-9.
Contract Theory, history of, 55-88; governmental contract, 55-61; social or political contract, 61-88; Spinoza's views concerning, 68-9; Hobbes', 64-71; Locke's, 74-9; Rousseau's, 79-84; in America and Germany, 85-8; legal and historical invalidity of, 115-18.
Contract, movement of societies from *status* to, 117; government not founded on a, 300.
Conventions of the constitution distinguished from the laws of, 207-8.
Cooley, Thomas M., *Principles of Constitutional Law*, quoted, 130 n., 214, 290 n.; *Torts*, quoted, 151.
Custom, province of, in creation of law, 144-7; character of, *per* Savigny, 167.
Cynics, views of, regarding natural law, 97.

DAHN, FELIX, quoted, 44.
Dante, *De Monarchia*, cited, 46.
Darwinianism and Politics, 328-37.
Delegation or Alienation of Sovereignty, theories of, 58-61.
Democracy, the primitive form of government *per* Hobbes, 71; character of, 361-72, 374, 396-7, 409 et seq.
Dewey, Prof. John, quoted, 175, 284 n., 297.
Dicey, *Law of the Constitution*, cited, 208 n., 292 n.; quoted, 207, 211 n., 220, 295 n.
Divine Theory, of origin and justification of the State, 42-53; history of, 42-50; criticism of, 50-3.
Donisthorpe, *The Limits of Individualism*, quoted, 320.

Equity, necessity of, in development of law, 418.
Essential Functions of the State, 310 et seq.

FAMILY, theories of evolution of, and relation of, to the State, 20-4.
Federal State, see Composite State; distinguished from Confederacy, 232 et seq.
Feudalism, contractual basis of, 57-8.
Fichte, cited, 86.
Fictions, influence of, in creation of law, 150-1.
Filmer, *Patriarcha*, cited, 50.
Fisher, Prof. G. P., cited, 88 n.
Force Theory of origin of the State, 41-2; persistence of force in the State, 341.
Forney, M. N., *Political Reform by the Representation of Minorities*, cited, 431 n.
Freedom, created by law, 110; political and individual freedom distinguished, 312.
Freeman, E. A., *Comparative Politics*, cited, 44 n.; *Federal Government*, cited, 234 n.; *Essays*, quoted, 321 n.

GAREIS, *Allgemeines Staatsrecht*, quoted, 193; his classification of governments, 374-6.
General Will, 123; Rousseau's conception of, 80-4; criticised, 288 et seq.
General Welfare, aim of the State, 339.
Giddings, T. H., *The Theory of Sociology*, quoted, 2.
Gierke, Otto, *Johannes Althusius und die Entwicklung der naturrechtlichen Staatstheorien*, cited, 48 n., 59 n., 96 n., 277 n.
Giles of Rome, cited, 46.
Government, Rousseau's definition of, 79-80; distinguished from State, 8; confounded with State by Hobbes, 73-4.
Governments, *de facto* and *de jure*, 81, 224 et seq.; per Rousseau, 81.
Governments, analysis of functions of, 343 et seq.; historical sequence of forms of, 356-60; classification of, 350 et seq.; *quantum* of power of all, the same, 352; Aristotelian classification of, 359 et seq.; constitutional, 354; corrupt, 361 n.; free and despotic, 353-5; classification of Gareis, 374-6; of Burgess, 376-8.
Governmental Contract, 55-61.
Greeks, political theories of, 33-5, 43-4; views of, regarding natural law, 96-7.
Green, T. H., *Principles of Political Obligation*, quoted, 53, 107, 123 n., 224.
Grotius, Hugo, cited, 50, 58, 59, 63, 392; views of, regarding natural law, 101; influence of, upon international law, 102-3.
Gunton, *Principles of Social Economics*, cited, 37 n.

HALLECK, *International Law*, cited, 239.
Haller, *Restauration der Staatswissenschaft*, cited, 50 n.
Hallam, *Middle Ages*, cited, 57; quoted, 424.
Hanke, E., *Eine Studie über den Begriff der Souverainetät*, cited, 186 n.
Hart, Prof. A. B., *Federal Government*, cited, 234 n.
Hearn, *Government of England*, quoted, 212 n.
Helie, Art. *Nation*, quoted, 9.
Hildebrand, cited, 46.
Hincmar, cited, 46.
Hobbes, *Leviathan*, quoted, 107, 354; cited, 50, 63, 392, 394; system of, 64-74; compared with Locke and

Rousseau, 84–5; criticised, 73–4, 125; views of, regarding natural law, 89, 101.
Holland, T. E., *Elements of Jurisprudence*, quoted, 3, 108 n., 138, 161, 172; position in regard to customary law criticised, 173–5.
Hooker, Richard, *Ecclesiastical Polity*, cited, 62.
Hotman, *Franco-Gallia*, cited, 278.
Humboldt, Wilhelm v., *Ideen zu einem Versuch die Grenzen der Wirksamkeit des Staats zu bestimmen*, quoted, 323.
Hume, *Essays*, quoted, 127, 321.
Hurd, *The Union-State*, quoted, 224; cited, 274.
Huxley, *Essays*, quoted, 92, 93, 318, 333 n., 334.

IDIOCRACY, 378.
Idolocracy, 378.
Ihering, *Der Zweck im Recht*, quoted, 4; cited, 168.
Individualism, the outcome of "natural rights," 94; postulates of, 320–36.
Initiative, and Referendum, 427–30.
Innate Rights, 181.
Instinct, identified with natural law, 92.
Instinctive Theory, of origin of State, 32–8.
Internationality, 404–10.
International law, 103; not a limitation upon Sovereignty, 198–204.

JAMESON, JUDGE J. A., *The Constitutional Convention*, cited, 282; doctrine of location of Sovereignty criticised, 290 n.
Janet, *Histoire de la Science Politique*, cited, 47 n., 96; quoted, 321.
Jefferson, Thomas, cited, 87; quoted, 435 n.
Jellinek, *Die Lehre von den Staatenverbindungen*, quoted, 119, 193,
233, 238; *Gesetz und Verordnung*, cited, 135–6; quoted, 198, 212 n.; position regarding non-sovereign States criticised, 246.
Jesuits, political theories of, 58.
Jurisprudence, historical school of, 165; analytical school of, 160–80.

KANT, cited, 86; views of, regarding natural law, 104.
Kidd, Benj., *Social Evolution*, cited, 419.

LABAND, DR. PAUL, *Das Staatsrecht des deutschen Reiches*, quoted, 210 n.; cited, 245.
Lalor, *Encyclopædia of Political Science*, quoted, 9 n., 12 n.
Languet, *Vindiciæ contra tyrannos*, cited, 278.
Lasson, *System der Rechtsphilosophie*, cited, 4, 96 n., 168.
Laveleye, Émile de, *Le Gouvernement dans la Démocratie*, quoted, 14 n.; cited, 418.
Law, Hobbes' definition of, 69–71; public and private distinguished, 138; relation of, to morality, 113–14; nature of, 142–80; classification of, 142; growth of, 144–59; influence of custom on, 144–7; of fictions on, 150–1; different kinds of, 161; Austin's definition of, 162; distinction between constitutional and ordinary, one of form only, 209–15; see also Natural Law.
Legislation, growth of, 154–59; efficiency of, 155; difficulties of, in modern State, 416 *et seq.*; legislative power, 303–8.
Lewis, G. C., *Use and Abuse of Political Terms*, cited, 354 n., 362, 368, 372.
Lex Æterna, 101.
Liberty, definition of, 126–7, 183; struggle between, and authority, 312–16.

INDEX

Life, power of State over, 128 n.
Lightwood, J. M., *The Nature of Positive Law*, cited, 166, 282.
Lincoln, Abraham, quoted, 254, 255 n.
Location of Sovereignty, 275 et seq.; Austin's views regarding, 280.
Locke, John, *Two Treatises of Government*, cited, 50, 57, 63; system of, 74-9, 298; compared with Hobbes and Rousseau, 84-5; criticism of views of, 76-9, 125; views of, regarding natural law, 89.
Lowell, A. L., *Essays on Government*, cited, 282, 435 n.
Luther, Martin, cited, 48.

MACKEY, ed., *Plea for Liberty*, cited, 320 n.
McKee, T. H., *Manual of Congressional Practice*, cited, 417 n.
Markby, Justice, *Elements of Law*, quoted, 177 n.
Machiavelli, political views of, 102, 392.
Madison, James, *The Federalist*, quoted, 260.
Maine, Sir Henry, *Ancient Law*, cited, 19, 96 n., 99 n.; quoted, 57, 117, 189; *Early History of Institutions*, cited, 24 n.; criticism of Austin criticised, 168; views regarding nature of International Law, 202; *Popular Government*, quoted, 412, 429.
Majority, tyranny of, 416, 425.
Marsilius, of Padua, cited, 46, 279 n.
Mechanism, State not a, 132-4.
Melanchthon, cited, 45, 48.
Mill, J. S., *Representative Government*, quoted, 12, 432; cited, 341, 437.
Minorities, rights of, 416.
Minority Representation, 429.
Mohl, von, classification of governments of, 378.
Monarchomachi, views of, 62, 278.
Monarchy, 361-72.

Montesquieu, *Spirit of Laws*, cited, 23; classification of governments of, 372 n.
Morley, John, *Life of Rousseau*, cited, 39.
Moral Personality, distinguished from legal, 139-40.
Moral Organism, State not a, 38.
Moral Rights, distinguished from legal, 113 n.
Morality, absence of, in "State of Nature," 109-15.
Mulford, *The Nation*, cited, 50.

NATION, definition of, and distinguished from People, 9-13.
Nationality, sentiment of, 121; demand for political unity, not a necessary consequence of, 122.
Natural Law, 48, 49; criticism of theories of, 103-18; propriety of expression, 114-15; a necessary postulate to contract theory, 89; Locke's views regarding, 89; Rousseau's, 89; Hobbes', 89; Greeks', 96-7; Cynics', 97; Sophists', 96; Aristotle's, 97; Plato's, 97; Stoics', 98; Spinoza's, 94; distinguished from civil law by Hobbes, 69-71.
Natura naturans, 91-2.
Natura naturata, 91-2.
Natural Organism, State not a, 35-8.
Natural Rights, 93; see Natural Law.
Natural Theory of origin of State, 32-8. [337 et seq.
Non-essential Functions of the State,
Non-sovereign State, a, impossible, 244 et seq.
Nullification, right of, 265.

OCCAM, *Octo questiones super potestate summi pontificis*, cited, 46, 279 n.
Origin of the State, Theories of, 18 et seq.; true origin of the State, 119 et seq.
Organism, State not an, 35-8.

PALEY, *Moral and Political Philosophy*, cited, 354 n.
Patriarchal Theory, 19-20.
People, a, the creator of the State, 129; definition of, 9-13.
Person, distinguished from thing, 31.
Personality of the State, 134-41, 393-6; legal and moral personality distinguished, 139-40.
Personal Union, 237-8.
Plato, views of, regarding natural law, 97.
Pollock, Sir F., *History of Politics*, quoted, 188.
Pomeroy, *Constitutional Law*, quoted, 262 n.
Popular Government, difficulties of, 410 et seq.
Popular Sovereignty, non-legal character of, 282 et seq.; Rousseau's conception of, criticised, 286 et seq.
Political Science, province and divisions of, 4-5.
Portalis, Count, quoted, 157.
Positive Law, see Law.
Public Law, distinguished from private, 138.
Public Opinion, non-legal character of, 285 et seq.
Pufendorf, political views of, 58, 63 n., 392.
Pulzsky, *Theory of Law and Civil Society*, quoted, 26 n., 98; cited, 105 n.

QUEEN *v.* KEYN, case of, cited, 201-2.

REALUNION, character of, 237-8.
Referendum, 427-30.
Reformation, Protestant, influence of, on political theories, 48.
Renan, Ernst, quoted, 11.
Republic, definitions of a, 372, 375.
Representative Government, condemned by Rousseau, 81.
Rights, see Natural Rights, Natural Law, Legal Rights, etc.

Ritchie, Prof. D. G., Art. *The Social Contract Theory*, cited, 56 n., 57 n.; *Natural Rights*, quoted, 91, 99, 418; cited, 96 n., 100, 324 n.; Art. *The Nature of Sovereignty*, cited, 290; *Darwinism and Politics*, cited, 330 n.; quoted, 333, 334.
Rohmer, classification of governments of, 379.
Romans, political theories of, 44-5.
Roman Law, natural law in, 99-100.
Robinson, E. V., Art. *The Nature of the Federal State*, cited, 222.
Roscher, *Politik*, cited, 358 n., 372.
Rousseau, political theories of, 41, 60, 63, 79-84, 89, 315; compared with Hobbes and Locke, 84-5; criticised, 125; conception of popular sovereignty, 287 et seq.
Ruttiman, *Das Nordamerikanische Bundesstaat*, cited, 239.

SALMOND, J. W., Art. *Natural Law*, cited, 95 n., 113 n.
Sarwey, Dr. O., *Allgemeines Verwaltungsrecht*, cited, 9 n.
Savigny, *System des heutigen römischen Rechtes*, quoted, 167.
Schleiermacher, *Ueber die Begriffe der verschiedenen Staatsformen*, cited, 367.
Scholastics and Natural Law, 101.
Schulze, *Preussisches Staatsrecht*, quoted, 212 n.
Sidgwick, Prof. Henry, *Elements of Politics*, quoted, 322, 324.
Simon, M. Jules, quoted, 322.
Small, A. W., Art. *The Beginnings of American Nationality*, quoted, 271.
Social Contract, The, 61-88. See Contract.
Socialistic and Non-socialistic Functions of the State, distinguished, 346-50.

INDEX 447

Society and body politic distinguished, 2; and animal communities, 2.
Sociology, province of, 1.
Sophists, theories of, regarding natural law, 96.
Sovereignty, nature of, *per* Hobbes, 71-3; absolute character of, *per* Rousseau, 82; nature of, 181-230; history of theories of, 185-92; Jellinek's definition of, 193; Gareis', 193; Bric's, 194; not a sum of powers, 194-5; represents the supreme will of the State, 195; is necessarily a unity, 195; denotes independence, 196; not limited by so-called international law, 198-204; not limited by constitutional law, 204-9; may not be alienated by the State, though its exercise may be transferred, 220-1; not acquired by treaty, 222-3; essential to a State, 244 *et seq.*; location of, in body politic, 275 *et seq.*; history of theories of location of, 276-9; distinguished from force, 282 *et seq.*; distinguished from public opinion, 282; located in the law-making organs of government, 302 *et seq.*; development of idea of, 388-93.
Speaker, in American Congress, power of, 415.
Spencer, Herbert, political views of, criticised, 36, 97, 321, 329 *et seq.*
Spinoza, political theories of, 68, 69, 94, 108, 203-4, 225, 392.
Staatenbund and *Bundesstaat*, distinguished, 338 *et seq.* See Confederacy.
Staatenstaat, 235.
Staatsidee, 14-17. See State.
Stahl, *Die Philosophie des Rechts*, cited, 50 n.
State, preliminary definition of, 3; definition of Holland, 3; of Ihering, 4; of Lasson, 4; of Burgess, 4; and Government distinguished, 8; abstract conception of, 14-17; theories of origin and justification of, 18 *et seq.*; natural or instinctive theory, 32-8; theories of Greeks, 33-5; number of persons required to form a, 22-4; development of, compared with living beings, 27-30; not a natural organism, 35-8; not a moral organism, 38; utilitarian justification of, 38-41; force theory of, 41-2; State and Church, 45-50; contract theory of origin of, 54 *et seq.*; *per* Hobbes, 64-71; *per* Locke, 74-9; *per* Rousseau, 79-85; legal absolutism of, *per* Hobbes, 71-3; confounded with Government by Hobbes, 73-4; true origin of, 119 *et seq.*; subjective element in, 119-21; as to particular individual, based on necessity and force, 127; utilitarian justification of, 126; not artificial, 132-4; personality of, 134-41; power of, sovereignty of, 181-230; cannot alienate its sovereignty, 220-1; all law a formal limitation upon, 209-10; *de facto* States, 224 *et seq.*; composite, 232 *et seq.*; name not applicable to a non-sovereign body, 244 *et seq.*; aims of, 309 *et seq.*; essential functions of, 310; whether a means or an end, 316-18; non-essential functions of, 336 *et seq.*; development of abstract idea of, 385 *et seq.*; personality of, 393-6; character of modern State, 395 *et seq.*; checks and balances in modern, 399-403 *et seq.*; World-State, 407-10.
State of Nature, see Natural Rights, Natural Law, etc.
Stephen, Sir J. F., *Liberty, Equality, Fraternity*, quoted, 203 n., 341, 364 n.
Stoics, views of, regarding natural law, 98.

Struggle for Existence, in "State of Nature," 93; in human society, 328–37, 420.
Suarez, political theories of, 58, 59.
Suffrage, extension of, 410–12; not a "right," 413–14.
Survival of Fittest, in human society, 328–37.

TAYLOR, F. M., *Right of the State to Be*, quoted, 39, 132; cited, 95 n., 114; views criticised, 39–41.
Temple, Sir William, *Of the Original and Nature of Government*, cited, 315 n. [seq.
Tendencies, present political, 404 *et*
Territorial Element, not necessary to conception of the State, 3 n.
Thayer, Art. *Judicial Legislation*, cited, 152 n.
Thomasius, political views of, 63 n.
Tocqueville, Alexis de, *Democracy in America*, quoted, 239, 410, 412, 419, 420.
Treumann, *Die Monarchomachen*, cited, 278 n.
Tyrants, *absque titulo*, and *ab exercitio*, 60. [238.
Twiss, *The Law of Nations*, cited,

UNIONS OF STATES, organized and unorganized, 234 *et seq.*
United States, views of publicists regarding location of Sovereignty in, 239; Confederacy or Federal State, 266 *et seq.*
Utilitarian Basis of the State, 38–41, 111–12.

VATTELL, *Law of Nations*, quoted, 103.
Volk, definition of, 9–11.

WAITZ, *Grundzüge der Politik*, cited, 234, 238; classification of governments of, 379.
Walker, Pres. F. A., Art. *Growth of American Nationality*, quoted, 271 n.
Ward, Prof. L. F., *Psychic Factors of Civilization*, cited, 37 n.; quoted, 141, 329; Art. *Political Ethics of Spencer*, cited, 324 n.
Warner, Prof. A. G., quoted, 336 n.
Welcker, classification of governments of, 378.
Westerkamp, *Staatenbund und Bundesstaat*, cited, 234, 261 n.
Wharton, *Commentaries on American Law*, quoted, 202; Austin criticised by, 169.
Wheaton, *Digest of International Law*, cited, 239.
White, A. D., Art. *A Catechism of Revolutionary Reaction*, cited, 49 n.
Will, General, Rousseau's conception of, 288 *et seq.*; of the State, see Sovereignty.
Wilson, Prof. Woodrow, views regarding non-sovereign State criticised, 249–51; *An Old Master and Other Essays*, quoted, 286, 307–8, 423, 434.
World-State, 13, 407–10.

ZWINGLI, political views of, 48.

www.ingramcontent.com/pod-product-compliance
Lightning Source LLC
Chambersburg PA
CBHW031959300426
44117CB00008B/831